The Italian Renaissance

The Italian Renaissance

The Italian Renaissance

The Origins of Intellectual and Artistic Change Before the Reformation

John Stephens

LONGMAN
London and New York

Longman Group UK Limited,
Longman House, Burnt Mill, Harlow,
Essex CM20 2JE, England
and Associated Companies throughout the world.

Published in the United States of America
by Longman Inc., New York

First published 1990

British Library Cataloguing–in–Publication Data

Stephens, John N.
   The Italian Renaissance: the origins of intellectual and artistic change before
   Reformation
   1. Italian civilization, 1300 – 1494
   I. Title
   945′.05
   ISBN 0-582-06425-2 CSD
   ISBN 0-582-49337-4 PPR

Library of Congress Cataloguing in Publication Data
Stephens, John N., 1945–
   The Italian renaissance : the origins of intellectual
   and artistic change before the Reformation / John N. Stephens.
      p.   cm.
   Includes bibliographical references.
   ISBN 0–582–06425–2
   ISBN 0–582–49337–4 (pbk)
   1. Renaissance–Italy.   2. Arts, Italian.   3. Arts, Renaissance–
   Italy.   4. Art patronage–Italy–History.   5. Artists and patrons–
   Italy–History.   6. Italy–Civilization–1268–1559.   I. Title.
   DG445.S74   1990
   945′.05—dc20   89–39867
                                                                         CIP

Set in Linotron 202 10/12pt Bembo Roman

Produced by Longman Singapore Publishers (Pte) Ltd.
Printed in Singapore

Contents

PART III: THE ACHIEVEMENT OF THE ITALIAN RENAISSANCE

List of plates
(Between pages 142 and 143)

Plate 1   Simone Martini: *Virgilian Allegory* (Milan, Biblioteca Ambrosiana).

The frontispiece to a codex of Virgil with the commentary of Servius, owned by Petrarch. Petrarch, who commissioned this miniature, was the first Italian writer to appreciate the intellectual importance of painting; he was also a pioneer in using the classical commentaries on ancient texts to shed new light on ancient literature. Here he has commissioned the Sienese painter Simone Martini to depict the commentator Servius drawing back the veil of obscurity from the poet Virgil. (On Petrarch's views of art see below, pp.44, 86, 87, 95, 106) *Reproduced by kind permission of Scala, Florence*.

Plate 2   Crucifix at S. Chiara, Assisi (formerly at San Damiano, Assisi).

A famous pre-Renaissance painting embodying a religious conception of the work of art which long endured (see p.60). *Scala, Florence*.

Plate 3   Leonardo da Vinci: *The Virgin of the Rocks* (Louvre).

Leonardo's painting shows the enlarged role of the painter as the interpreter of religious scenes, which became current amongst the great artists of the High Renaissance (see pp.60–62). *Reproduced by kind permission of Giraudon, Paris*.

List of figures

Preface

The wheel has turned round since Jacob Burckhardt published his *Civilisation of the Renaissance in Italy* in 1860. The Renaissance was then seen as the origin of our world. Few scholars today would defend the proposition that the Renaissance was modern; most would deny it a large measure of importance. This change can be attributed to the way in which its culture is now perceived. The revival of antiquity, the birth of the individual, the discovery of the world and of man – achievements which Burckhardt had traced to *Quattrocento* Italy – are now frequently attached to the twelfth and thirteenth centuries or felt to be unmodern.

Today Renaissance culture is admitted to be the product of an interesting and curious world – that of the Italian city-state. In that environment letters came to reflect civic needs. Italian men of letters, who are called humanists, employed ancient learning to current purposes as the scholars of the central Middle Ages had done. Classical ideas assumed, however, a distinctive form. P. O. Kristeller has said that he is inclined to consider

> the humanists not as philosophers with a curious lack of philo-
> sophical ideas and a curious fancy for classical studies, but rather
> as professional rhetoricians with a new classicist ideal of culture,
> who tried to assert the importance of their field of learning and to
> impose their standards upon other fields of learning and of science
> including philosophy.[1]

The humanist, in other words, was a noisy and self-important official, little

---

1. P. O. Kristeller, *Studies in Renaissance Thought and Letters* (Rome, 1956), p.563.

concerned with ideas. The importance of his work lay in drafting letters and speeches for the princes and civic governments for whom he worked. His other tasks were in writing moral treatises and histories to express the civic consciousness and local patriotism of citizens and rulers.

Compared to the grandiose claims of Burckhardt this is a small scheme of things. Certainly it is acknowledged that the humanist improved the classical scholarship of former times and in promoting a civic ideal achieved something of note. Medieval scholars had had Aristotle's *Politics* and Roman law to direct them here; the Italians took in new sources and passed on their civic consciousness to later ages. Nevertheless, taking a long view, these are modest achievements and for some they are overshadowed by the deeds of scholastic theologians in the field of dialectic.

Anyone wishing to think proudly of the Renaissance can draw little additional comfort from fine art. With commendable consistency historians connect Renaissance art to similar civic needs. The humanists justified the policies of governments and the general hopes of the citizenry. Artists expressed the indulgent tastes of princes and patricians in an epoch when Italian cities were passing from communal to despotic control and even citizens were becoming aristocratic. Art was produced because patricians and rulers wished to have nice pictures housed in magnificent buildings. In this sense artistic creativity was a response to the demands of patrons. Therefore, whilst humanism has come to be seen as rhetoric, art is interpreted as conspicuous consumption.

It is odd that Renaissance historians are not chilled by this dismal prospect which they themselves continue to fill out. Their happy acceptance makes one ask whether the view does not spring more from a materialistic disparagement of culture than from any just observation of the motives of humanists, citizens, artists and patrons. Materialism sometimes prompts the thought that social and economic changes are more important to us than cultural ones; at other times, that the latter was caused by the former. The first judgement is a matter of opinion; the second can be tested by facts. It is not a coincidence that scholars who argue that economics can account for Renaissance culture are those who assert most strongly that the Renaissance is a valueless concept.

Certainly the Renaissance is a confusing term. Since the fourteenth century it has meant both a revival of culture and a period of history characterised by that revival. If we make too much of concepts it is easy to become bogged down in a debate about what words mean. There is, however, something to be said for the traditional idea of the Renaissance in that it reflects a deep-lying perception of European history. The notion of 'medieval', 'Renaissance' and 'modern' mirror a consciousness that the West is the orphaned heir of ancient culture. These periods mark the stages by which Europe has lost or regained antiquity.

It is doubtful whether we should try to shed these terms because they reflect a truth. Those economic historians who claim that the true turning-point lay in the central Middle Ages when population, towns and trade expanded, fail to perceive this. The defenders of the notion that the true Renaissance was in the earlier epoch have, moreover, never explained the gap in time between these economic phenomena and the art and letters of the Italian Renaissance. If the latter were caused by the former, why was there a lag of centuries? Equally the changes after 1400 (and any period based upon them) cannot be considered social or economic in character – they were a cultural phenomenon.

Our purpose is to decide where the achievement of Renaissance art and letters lay. By exploring the needs for which artists and humanists catered, the pressures which excited them to create and the traditions of thought they exploited, light can be thrown upon why their work took place. Is it possible to avoid materialism without retreating into old-fashioned historical scholarship where ideas and works of art were treated in splendid isolation? Surely scholars and artists were predisposed to think in certain ways by the landscape in which they worked? The scene around them included intellectual tradition as much as the contemporary environment. The point where culture intersects with society is a middle ground which has been cultivated before to good effect.

The connecting theme of the different parts of the book is the power of ancient ideas to shape and interpret (rather than reflect) contemporary experience. It will be argued that Renaissance art and letters were not produced by economic or social causes, nor even were they 'responses' to them. The humanists were not 'reflecting' the civic consciousness of Italians; they gave moral values to which men could aspire. Artistic creativity was not a reaction to the demands of patrons or the latter's love of decoration. Things changed because artists were fired by ambition to be original. In this process it will be suggested that a large part was played by artists being captivated by new ideas about the purposes and possibilities of art.

There is a sense in which attitudes changed because ideas did. This is not to recommend a return to an intellectual history where ideas and styles are treated in their relations only to each other. It is possible to accord the leading role to ideas whilst holding their importance to lie in their power of organising experience. They justify and explain feeling, show possibilities, raise hopes. Thereby they supply needs and do not reflect them. The ideas rather than the needs come first.

This applies equally to the impact of Italian ideas beyond the Alps. The ideas were influential because they had something to offer : through them men came to think differently about themselves and the world. It was a particular world they wished to make sense of and in another age the same ideas might not have served; nevertheless, the ideas came first. Thus, for instance, attitudes towards God were transformed in the Reformation because moral ideas of the humanists had wrought an effect. The new religious ideas were not shaped by the material environment; they offered sense and so shaped it (see Chapter 15).

A similar claim could be made of the role of the historical and political ideas of the humanists in the early modern period. The notions which caught the imagination of artists and intellectuals were first and foremost ancient ones. However, in the course of interpreting experience in the fields of philosophy, fine art, historical writing and political theory, they were subtly and profoundly altered. These alterations, as much as the classical ideas themselves, constitute the importance of the Renaissance.

The humanists found in ancient literature a way of looking at moral choice. Although the badly worn word is misleading, they had discovered an ideal of wisdom. This had implications for individual and collective life as well as for the roles of the sage and artist, which were concerned professionally with imparting it. The humanists were tapping late Greek ethics which contained a distinctive method and set of assumptions. These were to be found in Cicero.

Earlier Greek ideas were bound up by the latter in the rhetorician's regard for what men actually thought and felt and did together with a Roman's pride in his city's history. The master ideas moving all these parts were *humanitas* and induction. The purpose of the chapters on Humanism will be to unravel the origins of these ideas and their ramifications, first in Cicero, and later amongst the Italian humanists.

The early Italian humanists began to recognise in Cicero the values of a lost world. Other scholars were soon led to seek and to find traces of these same ideas in other ancient moralists, rhetoricians, biographers, poets and historians. All this constituted an idea of man in society. There was in this a novel method and a point of view. The inducing of rules from experience offered a means of ordering the chaotic events of human life and opened the way to the growth of political theory and, eventually, of sociology. It also validated and elevated history by placing custom higher than abstract right.

Another great achievement of the Italian Renaissance was to bring to light this tradition of ancient ethics with its message for the intellectual and the artist. Associated with this was a great work of recovering the texts of ancient literature. The elements of this recovery will be described in Chapter 13.

The second general achievement of the humanists was historical. Besides reviving a specific ethical tradition and enhancing knowledge of antiquity, they perceived that antiquity was a lost civilisation. This insight itself produced their attainments in moral philosophy and classical scholarship. Because they saw that a lost world had spawned ancient literature, they grasped that antiquity possessed distinctive and finite forms. From this same source also sprang the greatest Italian achievements in the fields of historiography and political theory. The consciousness that they were separated from antiquity led the humanists to their invention of the periodisation of European history into ancient, medieval and modern epochs. It also engendered historical explanation, which was their greatest contribution to historical scholarship in that they wished to account for the evolution of modern Italy (see Chapter 14).

This desire to understand the growth of Italy was a patriotic one. A similar feeling spurred on Machiavelli's attempts in the field of politics to explain the strengths of France and the weaknesses of Italy. He was led to examine the social make-up of the ruling classes of the two countries. This was a point of origin for sociology. The same patriotism bred of an historical consciousness was the inspiration of much of the great Italian achievements in vernacular literature. Thus, in all these fields the discovery of certain ancient methods and perspectives combined with a novel historical awareness to give the humanists an insight into both the ancient and the modern worlds.

Certain points of contact with Italian society need, however, to be given weight. The humanists were not glorified propagandists for Italian rulers and city-states, and artists were not purveyors of decor for the rich. Renaissance art and letters did not reflect social and economic 'realities'. They were the fruits of perceived truths. This does not mean that no selfish or material considerations entered the process; but materialism does not constitute their interest or account for their appearance.

All this is true, *mutatis mutandis*, of Renaissance art. Paintings and sculptures of that time were not political statements or interior design : they were visions recorded by the artist. Whilst Renaissance art cannot be called the revival of a classical method or point of view, it was powerfully affected by them. Sculptors from Donatello (*c.* 1386–1466) onwards attempted to carve or cast life-sized and free-standing statues of the type that were being dug from the ground on Roman sites. Painters as well as sculptors were affected by the same rhetorical ideas that reached the humanists.

Perceiving action, mood and gesture as signs of the soul was an ancient technique of the biographer and also of the artist. The writers, from Socrates to Cicero, who investigated the soul placed a high value on the artist's power to depict the inner life. It will be suggested later that references to this conception in Pliny and Cicero were a primary cause of the original and 'imaginative' achievements of Renaissance art in the fifteenth century. For these classical writers portrayed the artist in flattering colours as a seer.

There are, nonetheless, certain fundamental differences between the situation of artists and humanists. Artists, more often than humanists, lacked ancient models to guide them, and painters had no such models at all. The moral treatises, histories, poetry and polemics of the humanist were rarely commissioned whilst works of art were almost always so. The way was prepared for the classicising art of the fifteenth century by a tradition of religious art – represented by Giotto (1267–1337) – which owed little to antiquity.

The problem, therefore, is to explain how certain ideas appealed to artists and patrons who had been educated in a different tradition. At this juncture we are brought back to the same general considerations which influenced the humanists. Like the latter, artists furnished religious truth. For their part patrons were commissioning such work from a sense of public and moral duty. Indeed, artists and humanists competed between themselves to produce visions of truth fitting for a class of patrons possessed of a highly developed sense of religious duty.

Two factors help to account for this. The Italian Renaissance, as there has already been occasion to say, was a patriotic phenomenon. Besides being a rebirth of antiquity it represented the birth of an Italian culture. Indeed, the former can be seen as a part of the latter since Latin and Italian literature were seen as the Italian past and present. The development of an Italian vernacular literature had been retarded for centuries by the prestige of Latin; it was accelerated by the perception that Latin was the tongue of a vanished world. Again it was the new view of history which allowed this to happen. The Italian Renaissance in its classical guise was a recovery of the lost Italian past; in its vernacular form it was a celebration of modern Italy.

The other feature was the similarity of Italian lay society to that of the ancient world. The important likeness was not that they were civic societies, but that they were educated in Latin. The leading classes of Italian cities after 1300 could have access to the culture of the Church and the literature of antiquity. It will be argued that this accounts for what was the greatest single achievement of the Renaissance, the occupation by laymen of a terrain comprising theology and classical culture which had until then been monopolised by clerics (see Chapter 12 and Postscript, p. 225f).

This advance of lay culture was the greatest single achievement of the Renaissance, and in a sense it was also its cause. Humanism and art were a 'Gestalt' therapy whereby the lay society of western Europe took into its own hands the means of interpreting and controlling its destiny. The moral sentiments conveyed by artists and humanists were expressions of a lay determination to stipulate the norms of life, without regard to priests or the philosophy of the Church. This applies equally to those writings of the humanists which were not overtly moral, and to works of art which were not religious.

The letters and poetry of the humanists and the portraits, mythologies and battle-scenes of artists were as much records of the soul as ethical treatises or devotional images. The philology or classical scholarship upon which the humanists expended so much labour was the ground-work of the achievement. It gave them – and afterwards the lay world in general – that mastery and finesse which enabled them to forego the scholarship of clerics. Viewed from one angle the cause of change was the resolve of laymen to judge their own lives with the aid of ancient philosophy. It is merely surprising that it required a thousand years for this to happen. This and not any social realities is the circumstantial context of the Renaissance.

The propositions unearthed by the humanists in ancient ethics and the sacred images of artists could not escape the reaction represented by the Reformation. This reaction, however, had the effect of maintaining the moral 'therapy' of the humanists. It was carried into the heart of Protestant theology and there disguised. The strictures of the Reformers upon the impropriety of artists diminished the artist's role in the religious landscape and enlarged the secular subject-matter of his art.

For these reasons this book is not a history of the Renaissance, but an attempt to define its value. Its compass comprises the originality of the humanists and artists, the elements of ancient thought they revived and the contemporary pressures that induced them to do so. It begins, therefore, in Italy, but the Renaissance also means the effects of the Italian revival elsewhere. Accordingly, Part III will include the impact of humanistic ideas on the eve of the Reformation. Italy furnished an ideal of the intellectual which, by 1520, was beginning to be seen beyond the Alps. With classical scholarship, historiography and views of man in society, new ideas and procedures were launched from Italy. More dramatically, Italian learning brought an important influence to bear upon the leaders and theology of the Reformation.

In reaching these conclusions I am conscious of having incurred debts in many quarters. These include names which are not cited frequently in subsequent pages where references have been confined to primary sources or contentious secondary authorities. This whole book might be regarded as exploring the relationship between humanist ideas and Ciceronian rhetoric to which J. E. Seigel first drew attention.[2] Like many others, I am indebted to the work of J. H. Whitfield on Petrarch and Machiavelli[3]; his specific studies have a general application which has stood the test of time.

---

2. J. E. Seigel, '"Civic Humanism" or Ciceronian rhetoric?, *The Culture of Petrarch and Bruni'*, *Past and Present*, **34** (1966); idem, *Rhetoric and Philosophy in Renaissance Humanism* (Princeton, 1968).

3. J. H. Whitfield, *Petrarch and the Renaissance* (Oxford, 1943); idem, *Machiavelli* (Oxford, 1947); idem *Discourses on Machiavelli* (Cambridge, 1969).

In the fields of classical studies and art history A. Momigliano and E. H. Gombrich have shown how creative work can be shaped by the formal problems inherited from tradition. Gombrich has brilliantly shown how certain Renaissance pictures represented solutions to problems posed by pictorial tradition.[4] Momigliano's work on the causes of war in ancient historians, for example, is a masterly demonstration of the power of genre in directing intellectual development.[5]

My indebtedness to other scholars – for instance, the modern works of Wilcox,[6] Kelley[7] and Grafton[8] or the classics of Voigt[9] and Wackernagel[10] will be apparent in later chapters. The contribution of Charles Trinkaus to humanistic studies[11] should also be mentioned, even though his work is not cited as it deserves. I have been stimulated too by my disagreements with the views of Skinner[12] and Pocock[13] on Italy's contribution to European thought. The works of Weinberg[14] and Frances Yates[15] offer a partial justification for excluding literary criticism and natural science from this book. These topics fall to the side of the main subject addressed here and their inclusion would have made the book unwieldy.

There are debts nearer to home. I have pleasure in acknowledging what I owe to Denys Hay, Philip Jones and Lord Dacre of Glanton who have encouraged me in the past in this field. Both Robert Bartlett and Richard Mackenney have read a draft of this book and made innumerable helpful suggestions and criticisms. Michael Bury has saved me from error by kindly reading the chapters on art and Martin McLaughlin has given me valuable advice. I am very grateful for the help of family and friends over many years, including that of my wife, Margaret, my brother-in-law Robert Merrick and my mother. Above all, my sister, Eiluned Merrick, has tirelessly typed many drafts of the book and checked references on my behalf.

---

4. E. H. Gombrich, *Symbolic Images*, 3rd edn (Oxford, 1985).

5. A. Momigliano, 'Some observations on causes of war in ancient historiography' in *Studies in Ancient Historiography* (London, 1966), Ch. 7.

6. D. Wilcox, *The Development of Florentine Humanist Historiography in the Fifteenth Century* (Harvard, 1969).

7. D. Kelley, *Foundations of Modern Historical Scholarship* (New York, 1970).

8. A. Grafton, *Joseph Scaliger* (Oxford, 1983).

9. G. Voigt, *Die Wiederbelebung des Classischen Altertums*, 3rd edn (Berlin, 1893); French tr. (Paris, 1894).

10. M. Wackernagel, *Der Lebensraum der Künstlers in Der Florentinischen Renaissance* (Leipzig, 1938); Engl. tr., *The World of the Florentine Renaissance Artist* (Princeton, 1981).

11. C. E. Trinkaus, *Adversity's Noblemen* (New York, 1940) and his *In our Image and Likeness, Humanity and Divinity in Italian Humanist Thought* (London, 1970).

12. Q. Skinner, *The Foundations of Modern Political Thought* (Cambridge, 1978).

13. J. G. Pocock, *The Machiavellian Moment* (Princeton, 1975).

14. B. Weinberg, *A History of Literary Criticism during the Italian Renaissance* (Chicago, 1961).

15. Esp. F. Yates, *The Rosicrucian Enlightenment* (London, 1972).

PART I
HUMANISM

Chapter One

Introduction

The two greatest legacies which fifteenth-century Italy bequeathed to European culture – Latin letters and the fine arts – present contrasting problems. With art the difficulty is to explain why certain changes took place which themselves are fairly easy to define. The challenge with classical learning is reversed: it is not obvious where its achievement lay. Was it in philosophy or in scholarship, and what did it owe to the past?

These achievements in letters and fine art were nevertheless the products of one Italian world. Important developments began in each field around 1300. Petrarch (1304–74), the greatest early figure in humanist studies, also signalled the importance of the Italian artists of his day. At every following stage there were intellectuals who broadcast the merits of art and patrons who befriended writers and artists.

The historical climate of Italy in 1300 fostered certain moral and artistic tastes. This disposed Italians to like specific things: the explanation, however, of cultural change lies not in the social situation but in the subtle relationship between the ideas and the individuals espousing them. Opportunities were afforded by ideas for individuals to think about their human and historical situation in novel ways. This is a powerful reason why the substance of a satisfactory account of the humanists' work must concern the origins and nature of their ideas. It is all the more necessary because historians cannot agree on what these were. Nevertheless, a sketch of the historical situation allows us to glimpse how Italian men of letters were prepared for an awakening which the ideas gave them.

1. The historical situation in 1300

Italian intellectuals and artists from the late thirteenth century enjoyed what might be called opportunities for enterprise. They occupied a social position; at the same time it is simplistic to call their niche a civic one. Despite its past, Italy did not possess a strong ancient tradition which enabled the classicising achievements of the Italian Renaissance. Had this been so, the Renaissance would have happened long before. Its scholarship, other than in the field of Roman law, was little regarded and the libraries, apart from those of Bobbio and Monte Casino, were thinly stocked with rare classical books. Even in the field of fine art Italy was more remarkable for imports from Byzantium than for its native productions.

These general considerations, and the sudden flowering of Italian culture after 1300, indicate the importance of attaching weight to thirteenth-century developments. The earliest of them in date was the spirituality evoked by St Francis (1182–1226). His own poem to the sun is the earliest Italian poem, and his burial church of San Francesco at Assisi became the first great temple of a new Italian art. His connections with literature and painting were not accidental: his teaching encouraged his followers to imagine themselves present at Biblical scenes and appreciate a life-like portrayal of creation. His friars preached a piety founded on 'self-help', the accent being on private prayer and the lay confraternities.

A second influence was the residence in Italy of Emperor Frederick II (1194–1250). The centre of gravity of his empire was Italian and his presence powerfully stimulated native culture there. The first school of native Italian poets was at his court rather as the German emperor, Charles IV, encouraged Czech culture when he made Prague his capital in the following century.

Alongside the influence of these great figures a remarkable practical culture had grown up. The first landmark in its development had been the great works of Roman legal studies at Bologna in the twelfth century. In the thirteenth century, through the work respectively of Leonardo Fibonacci (1170–1240) and Taddeo Alderotti (1223–95), Italy became the most important centre of mathematics and anatomy, as it was already in the domain of Roman law.

The Italian city-states of the eleventh and twelfth centuries had not thrown up a practical culture which, in its turn by some sort of natural evolution, had progeny in the Renaissance. This practical culture was a response to immediate social and economic needs of the commune which Renaissance culture was not. The former's existence explains the orientation of Renaissance art and thought, but not why they happened at all. The advanced practical culture of Italian cities does account for the fact that leading laymen knew Latin.

4

Nevertheless, practical culture, lay education and any mentality which lay behind them, did not bring about the cultural flowering which we call the Italian Renaissance. There is no sign of the practical disciplines developing into, or giving birth to, the new departures in the fields of moral philosophy, classical scholarship and fine art.

The missing link between communal culture and the art and letters of the Renaissance is the collapse of the old order in thirteenth-century Italy. Down to that time the Italian mental horizons had been framed by the imposing bulk of imperial and papal power. Moreover, with the rise and decline of the reformed papacy and the Hohenstaufen dynasty, these powers had become, first more inspiring, and then, after 1250, suddenly weakened.

Hohenstaufen power in Italy rapidly declined following the death of Frederick II during that year, but the papacy which had sought to effect it fared little better. The Roman See had succeeded in replacing the Hohenstaufen by the Angevin family, a cadet branch of the French royal family. This very action, and the succession of numerous weak popes, made the popes vulnerable to Angevin influence, which reached its logical conclusion with the transfer of the papacy to the Angevin territory of Avignon after 1305. The political and moral landscape of Italy was now changed. The old powers were gone and they were not followed in Italy by anything as grand or acceptable, though French cultural influences strongly increased.

It may seem strange to claim that so political an event could have far-reaching cultural effects. In fact, however, there have been other instances where literature and art have often expanded or contracted with the political horizons of the communities they have expressed. This was true of Italy where the Renaissance was itself a patriotic movement. When Italian scholars after 1300 revived classical culture they believed themselves to be bringing Italian culture back to life. In turning away from the prevailing fashions of scholastic philosophy and Gothic art, they felt they were sweeping away Gothic barbarism from beyond the Alps, and recovering their own traditions.

From the days of the pre-humanists in the later thirteenth century the new interest in the classical past was associated with a rejection of the Empire. With the demise of the Hohenstaufen, the cities of northern Italy were left in a situation similar to that which they had known two centuries before. Then the commune had emerged during a time of imperial weakness. As before, the ruling classes of northern Italy fended for themselves and this time their horizons broadened.

The difference was that in the meantime the Holy Roman emperors had breathed life into an Italian culture. The subsequent humiliation of the Empire by the papacy was reason enough for many Italians to abandon the Empire. They could not reject it without putting aside their

5

own glorious past unless first they disassociated the Empire from the old Roman Empire. Thus the pre-humanists condemned the contemporary Empire as a German institution and promoted instead the Roman Empire of old as the ideal to which Italians should return. It seems likely that from this same perception of the difference between the modern and ancient empires grew a more general sense of a division between the ancient and contemporary worlds.

This mental dislocation had a further effect. Detaching themselves from contemporary culture as a German (or Gothic) phenomenon and from Roman culture as ancient, Italians were impelled belatedly into developing a native culture of their own. For this is what the Italian Renaissance was: not so much a re-birth as the birth of an Italian culture expressed at once in the revival of its ancient culture and the discovery of a new vernacular one.

The enhanced importance of Italian cities in the thirteenth century also fostered culture. As opportunities for appointment and reward in imperial service disappeared, intellectuals and artists re-orientated themselves in the townscapes of northern Italy. Where Leonardo Fibonacci had been welcomed at the court of Frederick II, Taddeo Alderotti, two generations later, found his clientele amongst the citizenry of his native city. This required the appearance of new centres of patronage more numerous though individually poorer than the old papal and imperial courts had been. Competition between intellectuals and artists for the esteem of their fellow citizens or civic patrons followed.

To succeed in this competition writers and artists needed to promote values appropriate to their patrons. Looking about them and to the past, they exalted a new ideal of nobility as springing not from birth or wealth, but from the noble heart. They also gave currency to a notion of fame earned by the moral excellence of the individual. These were values well suited to the oligarchies which were finding their feet in northern Italy. Artists and intellectuals could supply not so much 'civic needs' or values as demonstrate the moral fitness of their patrons to have a place amongst the governors or rulers of a state.

All this was strengthened by the condition of the Church in late thirteenth-century Italy. The secular clergy was in decline along with the papacy; only mendicancy was in spate. The friars asked their congregations actively to organise their own devotions – an appeal aided by the deficiency of pastoral care. What better method was there of proving one's right to be a governor than to organise or give to confraternities, build chapels where one's private devotions could be witnessed, or have them decorated by leading masters to tell the tale of Gospel truths?

This applied to all of northern Italy, especially to those areas where the struggles of Guelph and Ghibelline had been strong. They can be observed, however, more intensely at Florence than elsewhere and it is no coincidence that Renaissance culture was most creative there. It was a city which had grown more than any other since antiquity, except for Venice, and the latter had strong Byzantine traditions. Owing to the city's industrial base and broad and long-standing popular government, membership of the ruling élite was contested unusually fiercely and persistently at Florence. The city, moreover, had a powerful merchant culture and a deserved reputation for apostolic and mendicant forms of Christianity.

For these reasons Florence threw up numerous patrons wishing to demonstrate that they had moral fitness and deserved their fellow citizens' esteem. This, artists and intellectuals then competed to supply. The Renaissance therefore reflected neither the classical traditions of Italy nor 'civic' needs. It followed from the degradation and even disintegration of the sub-Roman culture of early medieval Italy, which had been dominated by northern European and Byzantine influences. At the same time humanism and art expressed individual and even universal values rather than those expressly of civic communities. This was chiefly because of the ancient sources tapped by the humanists. As much in republics as elsewhere, alike in the field of moral philosophy and fine art, the new ideas were statements of individual virtue.

The ancient moralists supplied food to satisfy a hunger for moral improvement awoken by the friars and which churchmen failed to provide. Pagan ideas could be effortlessly amalgamated with Christian ones and used to strengthen them. In this process the humanists were the heirs of priests. They prepared moral nourishment or advised on its digestion.

The artist was in an analogous position. Art was moulded by intellectual tradition and by the religious climate. The decay of the Church and the advance of religious self-help encouraged a private devotion in which religious paintings were essential props. Inevitably this pushed forward the artist as a religious teacher. The humanists discovered that ancient authors like Cicero had highly valued art, and flatteringly compared the artist to the orator. Fine art therefore developed in tandem with letters. From being a priest, the humanist became a seer while the artist was first a teacher and by 1500 a visionary.

2. Argument

An idea of the visions glimpsed by the artists and intellectuals of Renaissance Italy can be obtained from a remark of Petrarch about the great Sienese painter Simone Martini. Petrarch declared that in order for Martini to have painted the portrait he executed of Petrarch's poetic love Laura, the painter must have visited her in Paradise (see below, p.44).

Pictures were essays in divine beauty. Similarly, the moral treatises of the humanists were visions of the moral beauty to which men could aspire. Both the artist and the intellectual began with the human condition. The artist's concern was Christ, the Virgin Mary, the Saints or human subjects under the eye of Paradise, whilst the humanist considered the moral capacities of man from the standpoint of the human condition.

As we now turn to the humanists, it is not easy to recognise this elevated description in the usual scholarly accounts of their work or in their own writings. Many, though not all, historians belittle them as rhetoricians who prepared propaganda to serve the interests of Italian states. In this the humanists employed the ancient art of rhetoric for their own needs. Medievalists sometimes think them parochial and a little shabby. For them there were humanists in the twelfth century who considered man *sub specie aeternitatis*, whereas the Italian humanists were concerned more narrowly with antiquity and personal feeling – preoccupations attractive mainly to an urbane Italian world.

The Italian humanists were so named in the *Quattrocento*. It is only in modern times that this usage has been extended to twelfth-century scholars. A distinction between the two ages at once becomes apparent: we apply to the central Middle Ages an appellation they did not employ themselves. The Italians began to do so because they believed that their scholars were studying 'humanity' (*humanitas* in Latin or *umanità* in Italian).

We have the means of entering the humanist terrain. The assumptions made about them and the pattern of their careers form a starting-point. Their own conception of their central task provides a way into their mental world. We have the name by which they were known and the name they applied to their own work. 'Humanity' was a concept which the humanists had discovered in Cicero (d. 43 B.C.).

Humanitas forms a window through which we can glimpse late Greek ethics. It will be argued that what Cicero exploited was a study of wisdom established on certain lines by Socrates (d. 399 B.C.) some four centuries before and running through all the later ethical schools. By Cicero the elements of these older views were passed to the Italian humanists. It is possible to identify the different strands funnelled through Cicero's philosophy, but Cicero conceived that there was a common or perennial philosophy running down to his own time from Socrates. Perhaps there was more truth in this than it is now customary to think, in that many of these Socratic ideas were shared by the very different philosophical schools that followed him.

Cicero made this tradition of thought available to the Italian humanists. They found in his writings an approach to philosophy as an art of living grounded in the human condition and organised by the inductive method. Cicero combined contributions of his own, such as late Stoic ideas, to present an enhanced respect for fine art and a life of public service. He brought together the contradictory strands of later Stoicism to present a provocative and puzzling idea of the workings of virtue and fortune. Above all, he combined Platonism and Roman history in his theory that the ideal state and the ideal law were the actual laws and constitution of the Roman republic.

These ideas formed the basis of the work of the humanists. This is often called Humanism, but the Ciceronian phrase 'studies of wisdom' better describes it. The scholarly habit of dividing that enterprise into phases marked by the career of Petrarch, followed by the activities of the civic humanists and Neo-Platonists, is misleading. The humanists from Petrarch to Pico employed various ancient sources, and reached different conclusions. Nevertheless, all of them were pursuing the same idea of philosophy as a wisdom to guide the art of living and they employed a similar inductive method. The humanists also saw their own roles in remarkably similar ways. For them, as for ancient intellectuals, philosophy was the property not of a professional élite but of an educated lay class. The attractiveness of these ideas to the class espousing them will be explored below.

Chapter Two

Concepts and Assumptions

F ew accounts of the Italian humanists provide a description of who they were and what they did. It is harder still to find a ready definition of their achievement. Modern scholars who are friendly call the humanists 'philosophers'. Others hold that they were rhetoricians and usually deny the name humanism to their work. The reasons for doing so are that this implies that theirs was a philosophical movement. In any case the same word has been appropriated by medievalists and applied to twelfth-century thought. In short, the humanists are commonly denied intellectual seriousness and their ground has been occupied.

It will be argued that these sallies are wide of the mark. The work of the Italian humanists had not been done before and they grasped and revived a forgotten tradition of ancient philosophy. They deserve a place in the history of ideas as well as in accounts of textual criticism and social manners. The humanists have encouraged critics to be unkind; their own occupations and literary output lend credence to the notion that they were professional scribblers. If we consider, however, why Italian scholars were accorded the name of humanist in the fifteenth century, and give close attention to their work, their intellectual substance begins to emerge.

A good point of departure is the contrasting propositions that the humanists broke or failed to break with the medieval past. Recently a great medievalist has seen a path between these often canvassed extremes.

As the residuary legatee of the scientific and systematic humanism of the twelfth and thirteenth centuries, a new kind of humanism came into existence. It was the product of disillusion with the great projects of the recent past. When the hopes of universal order faded, the cultivation of sensibility and personal virtue, and the nostalgic vision of an ancient utopia revealed in classical literature, remained as the chief supports of humane values. Instead of the confident and progressive humanism of the central Middle Ages, the new humanism retreated into the past; it saw the aristocracy rather than the clergy as the guardians of culture; it sought inspiration in literature rather than theology and science; the ideal was a group of friends rather than a universal system; and the nobility of man was expressed in his struggle with an unintelligible world rather than in his capacity to know all things.

(R.W. Southern, *Medieval Humanism* (Oxford, 1970), p.60)

Some of these sentiments betray the preferences of a medievalist for his own field of study. We may choose to call the ambitions of the scholastics grandiose rather than confident and speak of the later Italian scholars advancing into a broader world when they preferred pagan literature to theology. It is a matter of opinion whether the clerical world is preferable to the virtue of the individual, the circle of friends and a lay aristocracy.

The main implication of Southern's remark is that the humanism of the fourteenth and fifteenth centuries was a less attractive and shrunken form of the scholasticism it replaced. Some alternative tunings may be mentioned here at once. In itself the fact that the Italian humanists followed an older movement and were disillusioned with it does not mean that they turned aside towards trivial pursuits. They may have examined not the success but the premises of their forebears and found them misconceived. The Italians may have encouraged the pursuit of personal virtue and yet, like Jane Austen, have preferred sense to sensibility. Furthermore, the Italians could have rejected the claim to know all things and have believed in the intelligibility of the world.

Southern's arresting judgement raises another problem. Can the intellectual approaches and moral assumptions of twelfth- and fifteenth-century scholars both be called humanism? It is natural to wonder whether this familiar word with its confusing modern connotations can be applied to either epoch. Certainly no one employed the term before the nineteenth century. However Italian scholars of the later fifteenth century did begin to be called humanists as their medieval forebears had not.

Terminology then gives support to the concept of Renaissance humanism. Confidence in its intellectual importance, on the other hand, is undermined by the pattern of humanist careers. From the end of the fifteenth century the name humanist began to be applied to bureaucrats and teachers. Some of them combined several careers.

11

Aurispa (1376–1459) was a secretary at the papal curia and a teacher (for example, at Bologna and Florence) while he tutored the son of the duke of Ferrara. Lorenzo Valla (*c.* 1406–57), who was a priest, was also a teacher and a secretary at Naples and at Rome.

The great majority of the humanists were state servants or academics: they worked as teachers and lecturers in schools and universities or they were employed as secretaries and chancellors by courts and cities. A few were ecclesiastics, citizens (Florentine patricians, for the most part who were rentiers, merchants and office-holders) or tutors. Most of the tutors – Politian (1454–94) almost alone excepted – were men whose fame as teachers had drawn the attention of princely patrons who employed them as tutors. Of the ecclesiastics, Barbaro (1453–93), Bembo (1470–1547) and Politian pursued careers in the Church after their reputation had been made in the lay world. Only Marsili (1300/10–94), Petrarch and Traversari (1386–1439) can be called clerics in an active sense. Giovanni Pico della Mirandola (1463–94) is an exception who falls wholly outside this pattern: he was of an ancient landowning family.

Because of their work the humanists were concerned professionally with the arts of writing and speaking. In this sense they were rhetoricians. There is a small group comprising Lovato Lovati (1241–1309), Albertino Mussatto (1261–1329), Petrarch and Boccaccio (1313–75) who are set apart. They were the most important early humanists but were neither academics nor teachers. The first two were lawyers; the latter pair a cleric and a merchant. From 1375 (the year in which Boccaccio died) until *c.* 1500 the majority of humanists were, however, lecturers and professors or secretaries and officials. A greater number of famous humanists are to be found in this latter period, which suggests that Latin letters prospered when they found niches in the schools and chanceries of Italy.

Nearly all the humanists wrote poetry and translated classical texts. Almost as frequently they composed ethical treatises, histories, orations and put together letter collections. The humanists also drew up many epigrams and grammatical works or 'editions' of classical authors and commentaries upon them. They published invectives, biographies, and made contributions to classical sciences of one sort or another. Moral philosophy enjoyed an important but subsidiary position in their output. The chief place was occupied by poetry and translations. Letter collections and orations might, however, be classed together as rhetoric. A still larger group consisted of classical and classicising works in general, but this is not a very clear distinction.

There is a surprising number of works in Italian. Many of the humanists wrote Italian verse. Most translations were from Greek into Latin, but there were a few scholars, notably Decembrio (1392–1477) and Guarino (1374–1460), who rendered works from the ancient languages into Italian. There were some who translated modern Latin works into Italian:

thus Donato Acciaiuoli (1429–78) put the *History of Florence* by Bruni (1370–1444) into Tuscan; Boccaccio, Alberti (1404–72), Niccolò Niccoli (*c*. 1364–1437) and Matteo Palmieri (1405–75) wrote Italian prose.

As Acciaiuoli's example suggests, there were important works on the personalities, history and culture of modern Italy. Decembrio composed lives of Francesco Sforza and Filippo Maria Visconti of Milan, Manetti (1396–1459) wrote lives of Dante, Petrarch, Boccaccio and Pope Nicholas V. Bartolomeo Scala (1430–97) was the author of a biography of Vitaliano Borromeo and Panormita (1394–1471) wrote a study of King Alphonso of Aragon, the *De Dictis et factis Alphonsi regis Aragonum*.

The humanists sometimes wrote about what might be called modern culture: the lexicon of the Bergamesque dialect by Barzizza (*c*. 1360–1431), the defence of the Italian language by Biondo (1392–1463) or the commentary on Dante by Landino (1424–92) furnish examples. Better known are the literary works, essays and histories on contemporary subjects, such as Albertino Mussatto's tragedy the *Ecerinis* (devoted to the thirteenth-century tyrant Ezzelino da Romano), an epic, the *Sphortias*, whose subject was the Sforza family of Milan, written by Filelfo (1398–1481). The works of Traversari and Vergerio (1370–1444) on the fifteenth-century Church and the histories of Florence by Bruni, Poggio (1380–1459) and Scala, that of Venice by Bembo or of Italy by Biondo fall into the same class.

Developments in Italian should not be considered separately from Latin literature and scholarship. Both were aspects of one process, which can be called the birth of Italian culture. These writings also show us something about humanist motives and viewpoint. The dual orientation demonstrates that the humanists were not dusty antiquarians. They employed their knowledge of each culture in order to comprehend the other. Moreover, a consciousness that there were two worlds was a powerful impetus to original historical scholarship.

At the same time the occupations and intellectual orientation of the humanists seem to show that they were light-weights. Their job was to use rhetoric and their works were sometimes directed to personal or partisan ends. It helps to siphon off the venom directed at the humanists when they are labelled rhetoricians. In doing so historians are being specific and derogatory. They mean that the work of the humanists was superficial and literary, and that they were contributing to a particular genre, the art of writing and speaking well which had been practised since antiquity.

The second of these propositions may be true, but not the first. The humanists *did* work in a field which in classical times had been called rhetoric. They *were* professional men of letters and their contribution *was* a philosophical one. This is not as paradoxical as it sounds. The scholastic philosophers of the twelfth century were not philosophers by 'job description', even though Abelard (1079–1142) declared that his task was philosophy. They were theologians whom *we* call philosophers. The Italian humanists were state servants, lecturers in grammar and private tutors and they gave much to moral philosophy. The number of humanist treatises expressly devoted to it was limited; however, moral and conceptual principles were embodied in their letters, speeches, histories, poems and grammatical works.

Nomenclature reveals that Italian scholars themselves, as well as some of their contemporaries, grasped that they were embarked on a serious and moral task. Petrarch referred to his 'studies'. By 1400 the expanded phrase 'studies of humanity' (*studia humanitatis*) was beginning to be heard. Around 1500 a scholar engaged in such studies was coming to be called a humanist (*umanistà*). This shows that the humanists were conceived as launching a novel quest – the study of 'humanity'.

The earliest known uses of the word *umanistà* reveal that it was applied to teachers of grammar or rhetoric and to others expert in the classics. It has been claimed that this shows that the humanists were rhetoricians (Campana, 1946; Kristeller, 1944–5). New words, however, are not coined to describe wholly familiar things. If they were describing grammarians and rhetoricians why did Italians not call them *grammatici* or *rettori* instead of 'humanists' (*umanisti*)? It was surely because what was thought to be distinctive about them was *not* that they were teachers of grammar and rhetoric (or expert in them) but skilled in 'humanity'.

The word humanity is a puzzle. Today we mean by it little more than being 'nice'. The term is derived from Latin and had been drawn by the humanists from the classical vocabulary, notably the usage of Cicero. It was the latter's frequent references to it that gave the word currency in the *Quattrocento*. The contemporary conception of 'humanity' shows that there is a hard kernel in the modern notion of Italian humanism. No such contemporary appellation justifies the name of medieval 'humanism'. To understand the work of the humanists it is necessary to examine the idea of humanity they brought to light and its derivation in ancient literature.

Chapter Three

Humanitas

Humanitas is for us a code-word because the work of the humanists was described in terms of it. If it can be interpreted their programme can be laid open. The term was employed by a number of Roman writers including Aulus Gellius (*c.* A.D. 130–180), Varro (116–27 B.C.), the Elder Pliny (A.D. 23–79), Seneca (*c.* 4 B.C.–A.D. 65), Quintilian (A.D. *c.* 40–*c.* 100) and above all Cicero (106–43 B.C.). There is a double tracery made up of the ancient and Renaissance meanings of the word. As we shall see, they broadly correspond to one another. At their centre lies a primary sense of humanity as a virtue inspired by knowledge. By defining these intricacies precisely, it is possible to discover what traditions of thought were tapped by the humanists and what use they made of them.

To examine *humanitas* is to follow the tracks of Petrarch who unearthed the concept. What did he encounter in the pages of Cicero? The basic meaning of the word is human feeling. It was applied to pleasantness or geniality. In *De Oratore* Cicero employed it to denote that friendly quality or charm which warmed the guests at a social gathering (I, vii, 27). It was used of the mercifulness which tempered anger and self-interest. Associated with justice, *humanitas* checked a man's legitimate desire for retribution (*De Officiis*, II, v, 18), and made him value a worthless slave higher than a valuable horse (ibid., III, xxiii, 89).

The word also had connotations of urbanity and civilisation as against rusticity and barbarousness. The man lacking *humanitas* was 'rustic' (*inurbanis*) and uncultivated (*De Orat.*, II, x, 40). Elsewhere Cicero remarked of Numa Pompilius, the first king at Rome, that in establishing markets, games and religious rites he discouraged warlike

15

habits and led men to *humanitas* and gentleness. Earlier they had become brutal and inhuman by waging war (*De Re Pub.*, II, xiv, 27). In a similar vein he observed in *De Legibus* that of the many excellent and divine things which Athens had given to mankind, none was better than the religious mysteries by means of which men had been pacified and 'perfected' from a rude and 'inhuman' state to *humanitas* (II, xiv, 36).

At first sight this notion of *humanitas* as refinement does not square with its primary meaning of human feeling. In fact, Romans themselves had pondered on these complex meanings.

> Those who have spoken Latin and have used the language correctly do not give to the word *humanitas* the meaning which it is commonly thought to have, namely, what the Greeks call [philanthropia], signifying a kind of friendly spirit and good-feeling towards all men without distinction; but they gave to *humanitas* about the force of the Greek [paideia]; that is what we call *eruditionem institutionemque in bonas artes*, or 'education and training in the liberal arts'. Those who earnestly desire and seek after these are most highly humanized. For the pursuit of that kind of knowledge, and the training given by it, have been granted to man alone of all the animals, and for that reason it is termed *humanitas* or 'humanity'.
>
> That it is in this sense that our earlier writers have used the word, and in particular Marcus Varro and Marcus Tullius [Cicero] almost all the literature shows. Therefore I have thought it sufficient for the present to give one single example. I have accordingly quoted the words of Varro from the first book of his *Human Antiquities*, beginning as follows: 'Praxiteles, who, because of his surpassing art, is unknown to no one of any liberal culture (*humaniori*).' He does not use *humanior* in its usual sense of 'good-natured, amiable, and kindly', although without knowledge of letters, for this meaning does not at all suit his thought; but in that of a man of 'some cultivation and education', who knew about Praxiteles both from books and from anecdote.

(Aulus Gellius, *Noctes Atticae*, XIII, xvii:

J.C.Rolfe's translation)

If this was the whole sense of *humanitas* it would be a puzzle why human feeling should have been associated with intellectual attainment or why it was so powerful an idea in fifteenth-century Italy. The usage of the word gives us some clues: Aulus Gellius derived it from Greek terminology and Cicero also associated it with the Greeks. He remarked that Greek professors of rhetoric possessed a doctrine and technique of language 'worthy of *humanitas*' (*De Orat.*, III, xxiv, 94). He opened his treatise *De Senectute* with the statement that *humanitas* was a quality that his friend Atticus brought back to Italy from Greece.

What was this import? In *De Re Publica*, *humanitas* denoted that essential quality in which men can share and without which none should be called a man. Those only are men who are perfected in the art 'proper to *humanitas*'. A story is then told of the philosopher Plato who had reportedly been shipwrecked on a foreign shore and had rejoiced to discover learned men there (I, xvii, 28–9). In another passage Cicero remarked that no tyrant should be called a man (and less a king) for he did not seek a 'community of justice nor a *societas humanitatis* with his fellow citizens and the entire human race' (II, xxvi, 48).

These references indicate that *humanitas* had come to mean intellectual accomplishment as well as human feeling because knowledge was necessary for an understanding of the nature and community of mankind. These are the tenets of the Stoics. This Greek philosophical school believed in a universal brotherhood deriving from the human condition. Reason, which they considered the divine part of man, alone could furnish a knowledge of this. *Humanitas* therefore included both man's natural love for his fellow men and that understanding by which he was led to put aside love of pleasure or fear of pain. The latter could obstruct his feeling for mankind.

Reason, therefore, which was the element man shared with God and all his fellows, was also the instrument by which he could overcome the subservience of the mind to bodily appetites and worldly expectations. By raising up his eyes to the heavens man recognised his kinship with the gods, and by affixing them again on earth he understood more forcibly a duty to help his friends, countrymen and all mankind. This was the message of 'Scipio's Dream', the sixth book of Cicero's *De Re Publica* and the only part of that work known at first hand in the Renaissance.

These are the late Stoic teachings of Panaetius, in whose school Cicero had been educated, fortified a little by Roman patriotism and a taste for rhetoric and history. Here lies the substance of what *humanitas* had meant to Cicero. It denoted the pursuit of wisdom by which the rational soul would know itself and discover its fellowship with God above and men below. Thus civilised, man would help his fellows (especially fellow countrymen) to achieve security and fame. In the pursuit of these ends it was desirable to employ precepts, rhetoric and history. Rhetoric would convince men where logic could not, because speech was the 'promoter of human society' (*De Leg.*, I, ix, 27) and could convert them to virtue by precept or by historical example.

This vocabulary of reason and humanity is most commonly employed by Cicero, but the sentiments were shared by Seneca, Varro, Aulus Gellius and some others. In *De Constantia*, for instance, Seneca declared that the wise man was unconquerable for Fortune had no power against someone working for the commonwealth of mankind (xix, 4). A passage in his *De Ira* shows that this latter phrase was another name for *humanitas*. Since men lived in communities they must cherish their *humanitas*, and they would reach this consciousness by contemplating human mortality (III, xliii, 3; cf. II, xxviii, 2).

The 'education' *humanitas* conjured up was chiefly of the literary sort but the passage quoted above from Aulus Gellius reveals that an appreciation of fine art was also seen as the mark of 'humanity'. The point is brought home by a striking passage in Varro's *De Lingua Latina*. 'One thing', he wrote, 'is enough for man, and quite another for *humanitas*. Any cup whatever will suffice for a man parched with thirst, but any cup will not answer the demands of *humanitas* unless it is beautiful' (VIII, xvi, 3).

These conceptions passed to Renaissance Italy. When *humanitas* (or *umanità*, its Italian equivalent) is encountered there it sometimes means little more than compassion. This usage is met in Bruni's *History* (*Rerum Italicarum Scriptores*, xix, iii, 46 and 148), in Machiavelli's *The Prince* (ed. Burd, pp. 281, 292, 305) and in Alberti (*Della Famiglia*, eds Pellegrini and Spongano, pp. 14, 21, 27, 34, 35, 57, 113, 123, etc.). Even in these instances there are hints of the fuller meaning of the term: Machiavelli associated it with affability (loc. cit., p. 281) and Alberti listed piety alongside *umanità* as 'amongst the first virtues of the very noble spirit' (loc. cit., p. 178, cf. p. 21.)

As in Rome the notion also meant something more. In *Della Famiglia* Alberti defined *umanità* as a duty to love one's fellow men as life is shared with them (ed. Grayson, p. 312). In the most famous of Machiavelli's letters, in which he described the writing of *The Prince*, he told his friend Francesco Vettori that during his researches in his study the ancients had spoken to him 'in their *umanità*'. By this he perhaps referred to his gaining wisdom from the ancients and their readiness to convey it. This idea of *humanitas* as a certain sort of knowledge is what was meant by Landino when he described Alberti in *The Camaldulensian Disputations* as a man 'prominent before others seen in centuries, replete with *humanitas*'. In the same passage he said that he did not describe Alberti as a man accomplished in letters, because he not only possessed the fullest grasp of them, but exercised it 'knowledgeably and prudently' (Bk I, ed. Lohe, p. 9).

In a similar vein Filelfo, in his *Commentationes Florentinae de exilio* had Rinaldo degli Albizzi ask Leonardo Bruni to leave aside his discussion of the grammarians and turn to the philosophers. By doing so he could show his *humanitas* to the other participants in the discussion (*Prosatori Latini del Quattrocento*, ed. E. Garin, p. 504). Both Landino and Filelfo contrast *humanitas* to mere learning and grammar.

A letter of Coluccio Salutati (1331–1406) and a little known work by Alberti reveal further implications of the concept. Salutati was one of the

18

earliest of the Italians to use the term *humanitas* and his usage betrays its ~~Salutati~~ Ciceronian origins. In a letter he praised his correspondent for combining learning with virtue, which Cicero had called *humanitas*. In this he exceeded princes and scholars around him. From what he goes on to say it seems that Salutati had in mind the man's particular talent as a former pupil of Petrarch which allowed him to appreciate moral philosophy or the moral character of history and poetry (Salutati, *Epistolae*, ed. Novati, iii, 504). This letter suggests that Cicero was the chief source for this attitude and it was first to be found in Petrarch and his pupils.

Why did Salutati praise the combination of virtue and letters? In a dialogue concerning Fortune (the *Intercoenales*) Alberti described a dream in which he was carried to a high place where he surveyed a river bearing the spirits of the dead. He enquired its name and asked the spirits to speak to him 'if you know anything of *humanitas* or possess any propensity towards *humanitas*, since it pertains to *humanitas* to instruct men'. He learned that the river was mortal life which some men crossed more easily than others. The most successful were those who perceived and accepted its difficulty; the least happy being those who believed in their own security and buoyed themselves up with false hope and self-importance (*Prosatori Latini del Quattrocento*, p. 646). Virtue then belonged to the wise man of Stoic sympathies whose only security (and possessions) lay within him.

The views of Lorenzo Valla should be mentioned here. They show how important were Stoic influences in forming the idea of *humanitas* and that they were filtered to the humanists by Roman legal sources as well as by Latin orators such as Cicero. In Valla's dialogue on free will, one speaker expressed doubts concerning Boethius's notions of the fore-knowledge of God and urged his fellow speaker either to agree, or in his *humanitas* to expound Boethius's view more lucidly (L. Valla, *Opera*, ed. E. Garin, p. 1001). Here Valla seems to mean eloquence and his readiness to express it, although the willingness to impart knowledge for the benefit of one's fellow men sounds a little Ciceronian. What Valla meant is illustrated by his prefaces to the third and fourth books of his *Elegantiae*.

In the former place he exhorted the legists of his day to turn to the *studia humanitatis* (Garin, p. 610) so that they could excise the 'Gothic' elements that had crept into their discipline. He implied that this could be achieved by studying the classical legal texts. In introducing the fourth book he urged the study of Plato and Cicero because they combined eloquence and wisdom (Garin, p. 614). In other words, if *studia humanitatis* meant eloquence, the latter involved uniting the skills of the philosopher with those of the orator – a formula to which Valla himself resorts.

Why bother with these studies at all? Valla recommended the Latin tongue because Roman culture could still triumph though its empire had been lost and it could lift mankind out of barbarism (Garin, pp. 594–6).

19

This advice, as he further added, was given by him for love not only of his country but for all men. There is universalism here but it was derived not from Cicero but from the *Corpus Iuris Civilis* (to which Valla alluded in the preface to Book III) – a source which combined Roman *hauteur* with a Stoic concern for mankind, the tone in fact which Valla here was adopting.

For the most part, however, the roots of Renaissance *humanitas* were Ciceronian and reached the humanists via Petrarch. Cicero had been the latter's favourite author and heads a surviving list of his most prized books (Ullman, 1955, p. 122). Petrarch had taken up the expression *humanitas* from Cicero and occasionally employed it. He could use the term to mean what is proper to man. This was perhaps his sense when he declared that the popular idea that philosophers are without feeling because they have given up pleasure is false: they have retained *humanitas* (*Ep. Fam.*, VIII, 3; ed. V. Rossi, ii, 159).

Other texts, however, show that for Petrarch humanity had Stoic implications. In one letter he said that suffering led men to compassion and a knowledge of all that pertained to man. This involved a love of *humanitas* as well as closer ties of family and friends (ibid., VI, 3; ed. Rossi, ii, 61). There is a strikingly Ciceronian passage in the *De Vita Solitaria*. Petrarch defended the solitary life because in rural ease (*otium*) we can avoid the stupidity and blindness of the town. Amongst the woods it is possible to clothe oneself in *humanitas* and throw off the 'brutality' (*feritas*) all about. Thereby we cease to be creatures and become men. This cannot be achieved in the city where there is company and it is easy to avoid oneself (*De Vita Solitaria*, ed. G. Martellotti, in F. Petrarca, *Prose* (1955), p. 294).

Petrarch also seems to have related 'humanity' to a specific idea of knowledge or education. He often referred to his 'studies' and by this phrase he meant what the fifteenth-century humanists called 'studies of humanity'. In a famous letter to Boccaccio he urged Italians to return to their 'studies' which had been neglected for many centuries (*Seniles*, I, xvii, 2). This was imitating the phraseology of Cicero who had referred to 'our studies' transferred from Greece to the city of Rome (*Disputationes Tusculanae*, IV, i, 1). In the dedicatory letter to his *Academica*, Cicero had employed this formula and had alluded to himself and his friend Atticus being tied to Varro by their common 'studies' (I, i, 1). Cicero meant the Roman study of Greek philosophy; more particularly, the 'study of wisdom' (*sapientiae studium*), an expression he adopted elsewhere.

The classical scholars and moral philosophers of fifteenth-century Italy came to be called humanists because they studied 'humanity'. This word opens up Italian humanism. To one side of it lies classical ethics; on the other is the humanist use of them. For Aulus Gellius 'humanity' was the education befitting the free man (for which the Greeks had used

20

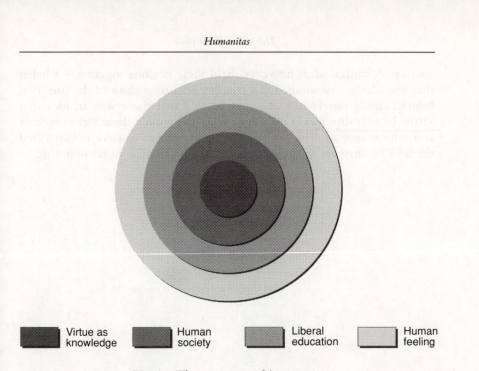

| Virtue as knowledge | Human society | Liberal education | Human feeling |

Fig.1 The concept of *humanitas*

the word *paideia*). Petrarch was responsible for passing on this general notion of the moral character of the liberal arts, besides the more specific interest in Cicero's idea of man which was deepened by the efforts of later generations after Salutati.

In Petrarch's day there was nothing new in the liberal arts themselves, for the Church had employed the principles of Roman education in its schools since antiquity. Nor was it original to teach that literary studies possessed a moral value; what was novel was the rediscovery by Petrarch of the ancient rationale of such an education. This was that it suited the free man for a life of happiness in the world. Of course, freedom did not have the same meaning in 1350 as it had necessarily possessed in the slave-societies of Greece and Rome, but the free man unthinkingly became the noble man for even in ancient sources the 'free spirit' and the 'noble spirit' were almost interchangeable phrases.

There was then a loose and a strict notion of the moral character of intellectual study, and they corresponded to two senses of the word *humanitas*. The fifteenth century received both ideas from Petrarch and employed the two senses of the word *humanitas* to describe them. 'Humanity' combined the ideas that knowledge civilised man and that it made him humane.

The subtle shadings of *humanitas* might be described by means of a diagram (see Figure 1). Human compassion merged into the civilising effects of education and a concern for men bound together in human

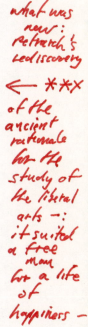

21

society. A central idea, however, held these notions together – a belief that knowledge encouraged this concern because it showed the common human condition. Hence, it could be said that there was an idea that virtue or morality *was* knowledge. Who had woven these ideas together and why was it an achievement for the humanists to have rediscovered them? The answers to these questions lie in classical moral literature.

Chapter Four

The Sources of *Humanitas*

1. The Socratic tradition

The ideas of the later Greek moralists touched every corner of ancient culture and therefore were to influence all writers since antiquity. Nevertheless, they were distinct from the scientific and logical writings of Aristotle which overshadowed medieval thought. By considering the ancient sources of *humanitas* it is possible to understand how the humanists contributed something creative to western thinking by perceiving and reviving a forgotten body of ideas.

The vocabulary of *humanitas* sets us on a road which leads back via the late Greek ethical schools to Socrates (469–399 B.C.). Both Cicero and Quintilian attributed 'humanity' to Socrates because they believed that he had inaugurated a more human approach to philosophy. What evidence is afforded by their comments of the nature of an approach which, many centuries later, was to reach the Italian Renaissance?

Cicero declared that Socrates had far surpassed other philosophers in the charm and *humanitas* which he gave to his self-mocking irony (*De Orat.*, II, lxvii, 270; cf. *Brutus*, 87, 229; *Acad.*, II, vi, 15). For Quintilian, Socrates' importance had lain in his attaching greater weight to the moral purpose of speech than to convincing men. Thus he had refused to employ sophistic arguments in his trial. This had led to his death, but his refusal had testified to *humanitas* (*Ars Oratoria*, XI, i, 9). It might be said that the *humanitas* of Socrates was either the highest form of oratory (Quintilian, loc. cit.) or it represented the detachment of philosophy from rhetoric. Cicero, who expressed the latter view, did however insist that the bonds remained close between the two disciplines (*De Orat.*, III, xvi, 60).

Humanitas was therefore Cicero's word to describe a moral approach by Socrates to questions conventionally lying within the sphere of rhetoric.

In using this approach Socrates had brought philosophy down to earth, or conversely made rhetoric a philosophical subject, but Socrates nevertheless made oratory more philosophical and philosophy more practical than it was before. It is possible to identify Socratic ideas with some confidence, but the channels by which they reached Cicero and the distortions to which they were subjected are harder to uncover. It will be argued that there are grounds for considering Greek morals as a single stream of ideas passing from Socrates through all the ethical schools which followed him.

There are notions, shared by a number of Greek and Roman writers, which Cicero (like the humanists centuries later) conceived as parts of a common philosophy. The three chief components of the latter were the belief that philosophy should be an 'art of living', the claim that virtue is knowledge (with its corollary that right is compatible with expediency) and the assumption that man enjoyed a common humanity derived from his kinship with the gods. Another important approach was the evaluation of moral questions by regard to actual belief or experience. All this encouraged an inductive technique and an emphasis upon the individual soul. A philosophical analysis of conduct and an artistic dissection of physiognomy and gesture followed because they revealed the workings of the soul. What did all this mean and how did these ideas descend from Socrates to Cicero?

Ancient moral literature was the outcrop of a philosophical tradition which had been established by Socrates. In fact, Socrates was not alone in this. The Sophists had already given a practical bent to philosophy and Isocrates (436–338 B.C.) was treating rhetoric philosophically. But the influence of Socrates was far greater and lay specifically in giving ethics a new importance within the general field of philosophy and he had lent morality a new meaning as an 'art of living'. Plato (428–347 B.C.), a pupil of Socrates, explained that this meant a search for those principles whereby man could live happily in the world (*Gorgias*, 500C). This was not the egoism which it appears to be: knowledge of the art of living came from appreciation of the human condition and in its turn this required an acknowledgement of human interdependence. It did, however, involve one convenient equation of righteousness and self-interest, which arose from the premise that virtue was knowledge.

Socrates' identification of justice with expediency may have been owed partly to his habit of deriving truth from what is actually thought and done. We have it from Aristotle's authority that this proposition, which was to challenge moral philosophers of the ancient world and the Renaissance period, had first been advanced by Socrates. For the latter, virtue was knowledge or reason; consequently, a virtuous act could not be resolved upon without regard to prudence (*Nicomachean Ethics*, 6, 13, 1144B.18–30; *Eudemian Ethics*, 7, 13, 1246B.32; cf. Cicero, *De Officiis*, III, iii, 11). These same passages record Aristotle's own acceptance of the great strength of prudence and his refusal to allow its equation with virtue. This discussion then influenced ethical controversy down to the time of Cicero. Another central tenet of Socrates was his belief in a common humanity originating in man's immaterial nature.

These were very potent ideas but the range and limits of their influence are hard to determine: his ideas were later elaborated and altered. The notion of an *ars vivendi* was not directed to immediate, material or mundane concerns. On the contrary, where the pre-Socratic philosophers had concentrated on the materiality of the world, the focus was now upon a cosmos inhabited by 'gods and men'. The Stoic definition of wisdom was *humanarum divinarumque scientia* (*Disp. Tusc.*, IV, xxvi, 57; cf. Augustine, *Contra Academicos*, I, vi, 16). This influenced individual self-perception and the idea of God. By contemplating the spirit of the gods mankind was inspired to share it: this was the origin of virtue. The conclusion followed that virtue was self-sufficient for happiness.

It is doubtful, however, whether Socrates went further and embraced any conception of God as a provident creator. Xenophon (*c.* 430–*c.* 356 B.C.) did attribute to him the view that as the soul animated the body, so the universe was governed by its own soul or God (*Memoirs of Socrates*, 1, 4, 17–19). Equally, Plato ascribed to Socrates the idea that the earth was a mother giving forth life and livelihood (*Menexenus*, 2370). These, nevertheless, probably represent Plato's elaboration of Socrates' ideas.

Whatever the exact contributions of Socrates and Plato, the notion of God's animation of the world was very attractive to later pagan and Christian thinkers. Through Plato and Zeno of Citium, the founder of Stoicism (342–270 B.C.), the ideas reached the Latin moralists. Plato favoured the notion that the world was inspired by divine ideas; the Stoics believed in God's providential shaping of the earth by fire. Thus for the later Stoic Epictetus (fl. 69–120 A.D.), God was the father of mankind and ruler of the earth (*Discourses*, 1, 3). He delivered the human race from all griefs and fears (ibid., i, 9): everything happened because of divine influence (i, 14).

For Epictetus, reason distinguished men from animals and it must be employed to observe the workings of the world of which God was the artificer (i, 6). Reason also taught a divine consolation: we have come from God and shall return to Him, therefore the injustices of the world must be accepted as merely bodily fetters whilst our spirits stay free (i, 9). In one passage Epictetus alleged that since everything in the world occurred by the rational providence of God, so also was this true of the good fortune of the unjust which may be interpreted as demonstrating the lesson that moral benefits are superior to material ones (iii, 17). These attitudes were widely diffused in the Roman world and are found in Cicero and Seneca, whose writings were some of the chief vehicles by which they were conveyed to fifteenth-century Italy.

The concern of Socrates for a world 'inhabited by gods and men' had, in short, excited later Greek philosophers to a novel view of the divine element animating and (for the Stoics) controlling the world. It encouraged the individual's spirituality. By contemplating the gods, man could discover virtue and grasp the human condition: 'the whole life of the philosopher is a preparation for death' (Plato, *Phaedo*, 67D). The leisure of the wise man was to be occupied both with self-knowledge and the needs of his fellow citizens (*Disp. Tusc.*, V, xxv, 70–2). Cicero implied that the latter view was a Socratic one in remarking that Socrates brought philosophy down into the cities of men.

The notion that knowledge derives from induction deeply affected later Greek and Roman thinkers; it may also have come from Socrates. In his *Metaphysics* Aristotle ascribed inductive reasoning to him (13, 4, 1078B.17–32):

> Two things may properly be attributed to Socrates: inductive reasoning and definition by universals. . . . But Socrates did not assign to the universal or the definitions an independent existence.

In another passage, Aristotle stated that Socrates had originated Plato's doctrine of ideas (13, 9, 1086B.2):

> but he did not separate the definitions from the particular objects, and was right in refraining from doing so.

Aristotle implied that for Socrates the universal was a general truth induced from particulars. Socrates did not merely believe in the general applicability of induction; he saw it as a method of teaching whereby the individual could learn truth from experience. This is how Xenophon interpreted the interrogatory method of Socrates. By asking questions the latter led his pupils along familiar paths of knowledge until at last the pupil accepted that he already knew strange truths (*Oeconomicus*, 19, 15). Cicero applied the name induction to this same technique (*De Inventione*, 31, 51–3; cf. *Topica*, x, 42).

Perhaps the most revolutionary of Socrates' tenets was the rejection of dialectic and science as disciplines useless to man. This idea was taken up by the Roman poets and moralists. Cicero went so far as to identify his rhetoric with the non-dialectical philosophy of Socrates, and his attitude may be compared to that of Seneca and Horace. In his *Moral Letters* Seneca criticised dialecticians who defined words rather than gave lessons in how to live (*Epist. ad Lucilium*, xlviii, 4). In poking fun at a friend, Horace likened the man's urge for material gain to the wish of the pre-Socratic philosopher Empedocles (*c.* 490–430 B.C.) to understand the motions of the seas, the stars and of nature (*Epistles*, I, xii). Later the Italian humanists would re-direct these shafts against the science of Aristotle.

Concerned as Socrates was with ethical problems, his approach addressed itself to the soul of the individual. Consequently, he influenced education and art. He wished the individual to discover truth by contemplating his soul rather than by looking at the stars. Encouragement of self-knowledge brought into use the dialogue and induction. By employing irony and a questioning technique in the course of dialogue, the participant could discover truth for himself.

This technique subtly enhanced the philosopher's role as a visionary teacher. The sage could lead men to truths which he alone could foresee whilst allowing others to discover them. Socrates similarly elevated the role of the artist as a painter of the soul. Xenophon recorded Socrates propounding a new attitude towards art which became common after this time. Xenophon has Socrates defend the proposition that the artist could portray the soul because, while the soul could not be perceived or represented directly, it might be glimpsed in posture and facial expressions (Xenophon, *Memorabilia*, 3, 10, 1–6). This conception of educating the individual by the images of the artist and the philosopher's dialogue passed via the later Greek ethical and rhetorical schools to Cicero. From him they reached Renaissance Italy.

These elements became so diffused amongst the schools which followed Socrates that it is helpful to think of them as constituting one tradition, begun by Socrates. In a famous passage in the *Tusculan Disputations*, Cicero remarked that Socrates was the first to bring philosophy down from the heavens to the cities of men and into their homes (V, iv, 110). In his *Academica* it is explained that Socrates had led philosophy from an investigation of natural mysteries to that of virtue and vice (I, iv, 15). In brief, Socrates had instituted philosophy as an art of right living (*Disp. Tusc.*, IV, iii, 6).

In fact Cicero seems to have felt that he himself was contributing to a perennial philosophy begun by Socrates and shared (for all their differences) by Plato, Zeno, Epicurus (341–270 B.C.) and the philosophers of the middle and late Academy. He observed that all the post-Socratic philosophers except Aristotle believed that happiness consisted in virtue (*Acad.*, I, v, 22). Seneca went so far as to imply that there was a single tradition from Socrates encompassing not merely the moralists but Plato and Aristotle as well (*Epist. ad Lucilium*, VI, 6). Certainly, when we come to Cicero's own writings the threads are similarly hard to disentangle. Some, which have been traced to the Stoic and Academic schools, were in fact also the property of the Epicureans. Cicero's advocacy of a life of active involvement is customarily imputed to the Stoics Panaetius and Posidonius, yet surviving fragments of the teachings of Epicurus show his own acceptance of it (*Frags.*, ed. Usener, 556–7).

Similarly, the historical treatment of society may have had both Stoic and Epicurean roots. Cicero possibly drew this idea of it from the Stoics (cf. Seneca, *Epist. ad Lucilium*, xc), but the poetry of Lucretius (*c.* 95–55 B.C.) preserves evolutionary tenets espoused by Epicurus (*De Rerum Natura*, v). The rejection of scientific knowledge, which is to be found in Cicero and whose origin was attributed to Socrates by many writers from Xenophon to Diogenes Laertius,[1] was shared by Epicurus (*Frags.*, 227) though the latter was strongly condemned for other reasons by Cicero and the Academics.

Just as Cicero drew his ideas from what amounts to the perennial ethics of the late Greek world, so this inheritance was shared by a wide Roman community. It is easiest, however, to trace in the writings of Cicero. His praise of the active life is to be found in his *Letters to Atticus*; his belief in the compatibility of utility and equity is discussed in *De Officiis*. The *De Legibus* and the *De Re Publica* are historical treatments, respectively, of law and of politics. The notion of human kinship springing from the belief that we are least ourselves when we are most ourselves is found scattered through many of his works.

Nevertheless, these Socratic attitudes were not confined to Cicero. The idea of human society as an evolution from simple beginnings was expressed by Lucretius in his great poem the *De Rerum Natura*. In *De Re Publica* Cicero had discussed the state according both to principles and to how the Roman commonwealth had evolved. In the *Ars Poetica* Horace treated poetry as a combination of ethical principle and the lessons of ordinary life.

Horace remarked there that the true source of good writing was the wisdom of Socrates. Moreover, he gave as examples an understanding of one's duties to strangers, friends and family: this was the subject-matter which the poet should treat and he should base his art upon 'life and customs' (*Ars Poetica*, II, 309–18). The 'worldliness' of Socratic ethics and the identity of virtue and happiness are commonplaces of the Latin poets and moralists, whilst the historical treatment of law lies not only in Cicero but in the Roman legists preserved in the *Corpus Iuris Civilis*.

It is possible that Cicero owed several of his ideas to the lost works of Varro. A passage was quoted earlier from Aulus Gellius in which he likened Cicero's use of the term *humanitas* to that of Varro. In the *Academica* Cicero attributed to Varro the achievement of having revealed the history of Rome. Cicero observed that while he and his fellow citizens were wandering like strangers in their own city Varro had led them back home by describing the age, evolution, topography and institutions of Rome. That this was a philosophical as well as an

1. The biographer of the Greek philosophers probably writing in the third century A.D.

historical achievement is implied by what Cicero went on to remark: he summarised Varro's achievement as being to show 'the names, kinds, moral aspect (*officia*) and causes of all divine and human institutions (*rerum*) and he had illuminated Latin language and literature and begun to describe philosophy' (I, iii, 9).

The phrase *officia et causas* (or as we might say, morality and history) could be applied to Cicero himself. This is what he had done in *De Re Publica, De Legibus* and *De Officiis*. The major works of Varro are lost but the surviving portions of his *De Lingua Latina* show that he analysed Latin with reference not to abstract principle but to its development and popular usage (loc. cit., passim, especially IX, i, 6). His whole theme might be summed up by one of his own formulae: 'we must follow custom (*consuetudo*) rather than theory (*ratio*)' (VIII, xi, 79).

Cicero, nevertheless, preserved the fullest account of these ethical doctrines and, moreover, it was in his writings that the humanists discovered them.

2. The ideas of Cicero

Cicero's writings formed a channel by which earlier ideas passed to Renaissance Italy. The most important of these was the belief that philosophy could furnish a knowledge of how to live, accompanied by a praise of induction and an hostility to speculative knowledge. Even in these instances many currents had flowed together to form Cicero's ideas. These more recent elements are conspicuous in Cicero's political ideas, his interest in virtue and works of art as mirrors of the soul, his idea of antiquity and his ideal of intellectual life.

In the fifteenth century ancient moral thinking could be understood more fully from a study of new Greek texts (for instance, those of Plato and Xenophon). It was aided as well by the discovery of forgotten Latin writers like Varro. Nevertheless, from first to last Cicero's works formed the point of departure for a new view of philosophy.

Before considering more exactly the character of the methods and beliefs which the humanists discovered in Cicero, it is important to dwell for a moment on two assumptions made about him. He is said to have been a rhetorician and a republican, when he was a thinker and a moralist.

Cicero was an orator in that his career had been made in public speaking in the law courts and political assemblies of Rome. Many of his writings were devoted to the art of oratory; all were addressed to those fellow citizens he was accustomed to persuading in the courts. His literary output can be called rhetoric because this is how he would have described it himself. He made high claims for this rhetoric as the proper vehicle for the discussion of serious topics. In his *Academica*

Cicero described as rhetoric all philosophy that was not dialectic or logical disputation (*Acad.*, I, viii, 31). In *De Legibus* he declared that someone wishing to discuss 'civil society' (*societas civilis*) – a phrase that might be rendered 'man in society' – should employ not 'subtle disputation' (dialectic) but rhetorical discourse. This, he said, was the way to understand how peoples are ruled, how the wicked should be punished, how to broadcast the names of the good, praise famous men, and issue persuasive precepts (*praecepta*) for the commendation and improvement of one's fellow citizens (I, xxiii, 62).

This was not the rhetoric of medieval Italy, or even that of Rome, narrowly understood. Cicero was not concerned about teaching how to compose a letter or a speech. In *De Oratore* he scorned writers who composed 'little books on the art of oratory and label them rhetoric' as if the discipline did not concern itself with 'justice, duties, the formation and government of city-states and the whole way of reasoning about living' (*de omni vivendi ratione*: III, xxxi, 122). In short, he meant the Socratic discourse and its subject-matter, the *ars vivendi*. This had been promoted centuries before as the proper purpose of rhetoric by Isocrates.

It has been claimed that Cicero contributed to a 'civic' or 'republican' tradition which influenced Renaissance thinking. There is, however, nothing republican in our sense about his ideas. Monarchy for him was a kind of republic (*De Re Pub.*, II, xxvi, 47), and even its best form – provided the king protected the citizenry (II, xxiii, 43). Cicero had moral and universal premises in mind rather than republican or civic ones. His political ideas were moral in that for him a healthy state (*respublica*) was uncorrupted in head and members. His ideas were universal in the sense that states were expressions of the fellowship of the human race (I, xxv, 39):

> The *respublica* is the people, but a people is not any assembly of human beings gathered together in any sort of way but the assembly of a multitude constituted as a society in agreement and fellowship in regard to justice and [mutual] advantage. The first cause of this co-operation is not so much the weakness as a certain natural fellowship between mankind (*naturalis quaedam hominum quasi congregatio*); for man is not of a solitary or savage race, but so born that even in conditions of all plenty [he seeks his fellow men].

According to Cicero the state was the people, meaning by that not a random gathering but a society brought together for the purposes of justice and mutual support and having as its basis the natural sociability of mankind (ibid., I, xxv, 39). The 'populism' which lies at the bottom of this idea is not civic but Stoic universalism, as is borne out still more clearly in other passages. Thus Cicero declared that the Roman *respublica* had its origin in the social instincts of men and that it was itself a universal *civitas*.

In *De Legibus* he quoted Cato's opinion that man has two fatherlands: his native *civitas* and that of Rome. The latter had higher claims because it was a universal *civitas* (II, ii, 5), a phrase which a little earlier he had employed of the universe itself inhabited by gods and men (I, vii, 22).

Cicero stood at the end of a long ethical tradition and many strands made up his ideas. This is evident if we consider his notion of deriving truth from the particulars of experience and action which was to constitute his greatest legacy to the humanists. The oldest of these threads was Socrates' advocacy of the principle of induction and his opposition to dialectic. In the course of time this developed into a general rejection of abstract knowledge. An example of this is Cicero's criticism of theorists who had written about states but ignored the 'popular and civil usage' proper to them (*De Leg.*, II, vi, 14).

Rhetorical, Stoic, Epicurean and Platonist elements are also discernible. In *De Oratore* Cicero observed that the knowledge of the orator consisted in understanding the thoughts, feelings, hopes and beliefs of his fellow citizens and not in describing things remote from reality as Plato had done in his *Republic* (*De Orat.*, I, lii; cf. II, ii). Here Cicero was criticising Plato not on 'Socratic' grounds but from the standpoint of the orator who acted for and persuaded citizens in the courts.

Cicero was able to give this liking for experience a more theoretical justification by reference to Stoic principles. From this source he took the notion that the 'greatest truth lies in the sense' and that every particular thing is different to every other (*Acad.*, II, vi, 19f.). It followed that sense-perceptions of particular facts were true and that general rules could be extracted from them.

Induction of this sort is the central principle of Cicero's philosophical works and the humanists were to imitate it. He defined the Orator's task as the giving of precepts (*praecepta*) for the well-being of his fellow citizens (*De Leg.*, I, xxiii, 62) and by implication *De Oratore* is itself a compilation of precepts on the orator's art. His book *De Natura Deorum* is also described as a set of precepts (I, iv, 7).

Cicero made very high claims for precept as an induction from the common experience of mankind. He said that civil customs and conventions were themselves *praecepta* (*De Officiis*, I, xii, 148). This probably owed something to the evolutionary tenets of Epicurus, which were shared by the Stoics. These same sources certainly shaped Cicero's inductive approach to politics and law, though here they were mingled with Platonist and Roman influences.

In *De Re Publica* Cicero set forth his conception of the ideal republic. He said that the purpose of his book was to describe the birth, growth, maturity and healthy state of the Roman people rather than to depict an ideal state (I, i, 3). What is remarkable is that the actual form of this particular republic is shown to *be* the ideal. The perfect republic was the

Roman republic as it had been formed and developed towards perfection. Despite Cicero's denials, there are signs of Plato's influence, because like the latter Cicero did describe an ideal republic. Cicero, however, gives Plato strange bed-fellows in Epicurus and Roman patriotism. The ideal emerged by evolution: the republic *tended* towards perfection (cf. *De Re Pub.*, II, xi, 21–2 and xviii, 33) and was the actual one of Rome.

Similar elements exist in Cicero's conceptions of rulers and of law. The former were guardians of the state, possessed of wisdom and justice and legislating for the base dispositions of men. There was a paradox here: like Plato, Cicero looked to a higher intellectual and moral power in the ruler. The founder of the state required still more elevated qualities if he was to provide those laws and institutions without which the state could not endure. Once again the ideal was the actual state of Rome which had been formed by several hands (II, i, 1–2). Cicero's *De Legibus* interprets law from the same standpoint: the best law was the actual law of the Roman people, as it had been established and perfected. When the Italian humanists met this high praise for induction they adopted it as a useful method and did not trouble themselves with its possible origin.

Cicero was therefore an ethical thinker who examined moral and social questions which fell within the very broad ambit which he allowed to the field of rhetoric. Beneath it all there was a common platform made up of the inductive method and a preoccupation with the spiritual capabilities of man. Moral concern and an implied idea of God underlay all Cicero's writing.

Everything was done by the will and authority of the gods. They benefited men, taking note of good and bad (*De Leg.*, I, vi, 15; cf. *De Divinatione*, I, xxxviii, 81). Cicero seems to have added a new note to early Stoic tradition: God was not only a rational principle but a punitive agent: the impious might fear immediate chastisement (*De Leg.*, II, x, 25). There seem to have been contradictory beliefs circulating in Stoic circles in Cicero's time. He ascribed to Chrysippus the Stoic view that God was a fate or 'necessity' which governed future human affairs (*De Nat. Deor.*, I, xv, 39; cf. I, xx, 55) but he also described as Stoic the notion that fortune or evil could not be divine because they were inconsistant, springing from desire and will (*De Nat. Deor.*, III, xxiv, 61; *Disp. Tusc.*, III, xi, 26; III, xxxiii, 81–2; IV, 7). The mainline of Stoic ethics was probably represented by the former opinion. Later it was incorporated by Seneca in his *De Providentia*. He employed there the view of Chrysippus that fate determined all by a series of interconnected causes (v, 7).

Regard for man's spirituality had its distant origin in the teachings of Socrates, but all the twists and turns of later Greek ethics were reflected in Cicero's writings. His importance partly lay in passing on the contradictory opinions of the earlier moralists. As we have seen, there are references at times in his writings to the power of God. Much more commonly, however, he accented the decisive role of individual virtue. Cicero's contribution here was to propagate a method or approach rather than a set of propositions. In it the influence of Socrates can be glimpsed still close at hand. Cicero placed man's pursuit of virtue to the forefront of his philosophical discussions. At the same time he always assumed that virtue was attainable by learning from experience and that it was compatible with prudence.

This approach to moral questions was to influence the humanists deeply, as were specific Ciceronian ideas about art, antiquity and intellectual life. Cicero's attitude towards art derived partly from his view of ethics and also from his idea of perception. He had inherited the Socratic notion that the painter educated the individual to a knowledge of his soul. From the Stoics (probably his teacher Panaetius) Cicero drew an exalted estimate of perception. A fusion produced the theory of *phantasia*. Plutarch alleged that Cicero had coined the word as the translation of a Greek concept (Plutarch, *Cicero*, xl, 2).

The idea reflected the very high opinion of perception entertained by the Stoics. The essence of the theory was that it was possible to gain a true understanding of reality by the formation of images within the soul. Cicero called such an image a *phantasia*. The doctrine of perception underlying it had probably been first advanced by Zeno (Cicero, *Acad.*, I, xi, 40; II, vi). It is not clear who had applied this to art; perhaps it was Panaetius. Cicero's writings preserved the notion and conveyed it to Renaissance Italy. The application to art required only the assumption that painters and musicians possessed this sensory power to a heightened degree. Accordingly they could penetrate to things which others failed to notice (*Acad.*, II, vii, 19; II, xxvii, 86).

The creative artist had a visionary character. Like the sage he could perceive the soul and bring fellow mortals to a knowledge of it. Both were at once seers and doctors. The analogy of artist and sage deserves to be stressed. It had been hinted at by Socrates; it was possibly discussed by Panaetius and there are numerous allusions to it in Cicero's works. The reiterated comparison of oratory and fine art dignified the work of painting and sculpture. Individual philosophers and orators such as Panaetius and Cicero himself were compared to the famous Greek artists Phidias and Apelles (*De Officiis*, III, ii, 9–10; *Paradoxa Stoicorum*, 5).

It is more important, perhaps, that the art of oratory was likened to that of painting and sculpture. Each was a discipline to which individual masters contributed whilst they varied in their talents and purposes. Cicero commented still more frequently on the similarity of their intellectual techniques. They shared in the power of portraiture and the capacity to communicate images. The orator's ability to differentiate concepts was set against the painter's distinction of objects by means of proportion.

The orator's search for variety and relief in his choice of words could be compared to the subtleties of tone in old pictures, which were less powerful and more pleasing than the brilliant colours of new ones.[2] These analogies graced painting and sculpture as an intellectual art. As we shall see, this is one reason why the Italian Renaissance witnessed supreme achievements in the fields of literary studies and of fine art; why it saw close links between them and viewed the devotees of each with enhanced respect.

Cicero was one of a group of writers of the last generation of the Roman republic who passed on a view of antiquity and of intellectual life to the humanists. Cicero and his contemporaries criticised respect for antiquity and augmented it. Varro, Cicero and the elder Pliny were all anxious to free Roman readers from dependence on Greece by furnishing them with treatises incorporating Greek philosophy and general knowledge or applying them to the history of Rome. This liberated some Romans from the necessity of reading Greek sources, but they enshrined the mental world of Greece as a distant landscape against which Latin culture must be viewed. The same Greek backdrop can be glimpsed in the poets and historians of that generation, though it is less obvious. In his characterisation of individuals the historian Sallust employed moral categories of the fourth century B.C.; Horace did the same in his poetry, with a large admixture of Stoic elements.

Whilst seeming to dispense with Greece or knock it down, such writers made a monument to it. They abhorred popular reverence for antiquity but their criticisms subtly enhanced the power of the antique. Cicero lamented the vulgar liking for antiquity but he did so in terms which reveal his own preference for it (*Orator*, 1, 169). This ambiguous attitude was shared by others. Pliny looked back wistfully to ancient times when the craftsmanship of a work of art was valued more highly than the precious materials of which it was composed; quality had declined as financial values had increased (*Natural History*, II, xxxiv). Nevertheless, we sense Pliny's admiration in the excited reports he gives of the inflated prices paid for antiques.

Had there not been this reverence for antiquity it seems unlikely that the Italian humanists would have conceived so strong a respect for the Greek and Roman past. Between the humanists and these classical writers there was an important difference in that whilst Cicero and his contemporaries had looked to Greece, the humanists took the Graeco-Roman world as a whole for their antiquity. It was, in fact, the world they glimpsed in Cicero.

The notion of a philosopher to be found in such Roman writers was

---

2. Cicero, *Brutus*, xviii, 70; *De Orat.*, I, xvi, 73, 254; II, xvi, 69; II, lxxxvii, 358; III, viii, 25–7; III, xxv, 98; III, 1, 195; III, lvii, 217; *Disp. Tusc.*, V, xxxix, 114; *Orator*, i, 5; ii, 8; x, 36; xix, 65; xxi, 73; xxii, 74; 1, 169; 1, 234.

not peculiar to them. It had originated in early Greece and was the property of most intellectuals; their writings nevertheless formed the conduit through which it passed to the Italian Renaissance. Its kernel was the casual assumption that the intellectual was rooted in the citizenry of the Greek city-states, or the ruling class of Rome. Ancient philosophers did not think themselves to be contemplatives or professionals. They were elevated socially but not above ordinary life, which they wished to inform. A sign of this is their furnishing of wisdom to the ruling classes. Socrates had given advice to the young men of Athens, Xenophon had done so to Cyrus and Seneca to the emperor, Nero.

Socrates' thoughts were recorded in the dialogues of Plato. A dialogue or discussion with friends became the characteristic form in which non-dialectical philosophy was thereafter composed. The chief of Cicero's philosophical writings (as later of the humanists) were dialogues. There were rhetorical and pedagogical benefits to be gained from this; it also reflected social life. The patricians of the Greek cities were accustomed to employing their wealth for intellectual ends. Thus one classical source recorded that Theophrastus bequeathed his estate so that his home and gardens could accommodate his friends as an 'institute for advanced studies' in which they could continue their discussions (Diogenes Laertius, *Lives of Philosophers*, v, 22). The academy, a learned circle, as well as the dialogue therefore became a typical institution of ancient intellectual life.

In Roman Italy the circle of friends naturally congregated in the villa. Literary senators could engage there in Stoic philosophy by giving vent to the class anxiety of *imagining* themselves poor. They could discover the harsh contrasts between the demands of their public duties 'in town' (*negotium*) and those of the intellectual life in the country (*otium*). The life of ancient intellectuals always encompassed both; they held public office, engaged in oratory, advised rulers. The Roman thinkers of Cicero's generation shared a preference for *otium* or cultured leisure, which was to pass to Renaissance Italy.

Two aspects of this 'leisure' were particularly important. A belief developed that the discovery of wisdom and the appreciation of culture needed solitude. This conviction probably owed something to inherited conceptions of poetry and prophecy as well as to senatorial life. Cicero remarked that some men believed their souls inspired to prophecy by contemplating groves, forests, rivers and the sea (*De Div.*, I, 1, 114). Pliny made this judgement: 'At Rome there is a multitude of works of art, but we are led away from contemplation of them by the demands of duty and business; while for their appreciation it is necessary to have leisure and great solitude' (*N.H.*, xxxv, 27). The ancient villa with its circle of friends and private art gallery was the source of an idea of civilisation in early modern times.

Even in senatorial villas no one doubted that the intellectual's task was to guide the ways of the world. Intellectuals were not quarantined then in institutions. They continued to be seen not as a professional cadre but as the purveyors of a wisdom which was available to all. For Seneca wisdom should be sought in all places, and truth belonged not to the philosopher but to all virtuous men. The latter should be taught by the genius of great men but never live in their shade or mouth their maxims. Rather men should learn from experience: truth is the property of everyone, not of earlier sages (*Epist. ad Lucilium*, xxxiii).

The twin ideas of the antique and of the philosopher possessing a common wisdom flowed together in the biographical compilations of Varro and Cornelius Nepos (*c.* 100–*c.* 25 B.C.). Varro seems to have been the first Latin writer to have imitated Greek biography. Together with Nepos he established the pattern of writing biographies of eminent men which was later followed by Plutarch (*c.* 46–after 120 A.D.). Illustrious Romans were compared to Greeks and philosophers placed alongside generals and public figures. Surviving examples are those of Atticus, Cato and the foreign generals by Cornelius Nepos. The habit of assessing achievement in relation to individual character was also preserved by Plutarch and Suetonius (*c.* 70–120 A.D.); a millennium later it was rediscovered by the humanists.

Cicero wrote no biographies, but his writings formed a window through which the Italian humanists looked at antiquity. In them they found the value-system of late Greek ethics, the potentialities of Greek philosophy for the study of history and law, an exalted view of art, a reverence for antiquity and the idea of the intellectual as a sage whose wisdom could guide his fellow citizens.

The Italian Renaissance also inherited from Cicero the concept of *humanitas*, which described the philosophic basis of his rhetoric. When the humanists undertook 'studies of humanity' they were delving in late Greek ethics as Cicero had done before them. The leitmotif of that tradition was the notion of philosophy as an 'art of living'. Cicero himself did not monopolise these terms or ideas. Indeed, the Italian *literati* discovered them in many Latin and Greek sources. Moreover, the humanists required them for different purposes. They wished to contradict Aristotle rather than Empedocles and single out their efforts from those of clerical and ultramontane scholars rather than put down the culture of rustics or slaves. Despite these differences Ciceronian rhetoric offered a powerful weapon with which Italian intellectuals could wage their paper wars and in the rediscovery of which they were profoundly to influence European culture.

Chapter Five

Petrarch and his Successors

The achievement of Petrarch and his successors was to recognise in Cicero's writings a certain approach to philosophy. Political philosophy, history and the study of moral obligation had existed during and since the ancient world. Before Petrarch they were not considered to form a distinctive vision of the world and a sort of philosophy furnishing inductive rules about life derived from experience.

The idea of philosophy as an *ars vivendi* was revived by Petrarch. The 'studies' to which he urged Italians to return were those ethical studies which Cicero had undertaken long before and to which he had applied the same name. The wisdom they conveyed was a knowledge of *humanitas*. Besides philosophy as an art of living Petrarch launched a number of specific ideas which came to form the programme of the Italian humanists down to 1500. Petrarch was the refractor of antiquity, gathering in classical notions and casting them upon the future. He was the reviver of ancient ideas rather than their inventor but it was the work of genius to have germinated seeds after so many centuries. He passed to Salutati, Poggio and Valla (and less directly to later successors) the idea of the active and contemplative lives, the Stoic idea of virtue as 'greatness of soul', a secular notion of the intellectual dispensing a rational conception of the human condition, besides a preference for induction and a hostility towards speculative knowledge. He conveyed the master ideas of the humanists.

It is customary to divide Italian humanism into phases corresponding to the work of Petrarch, and that of the 'civic' humanists of 1400 and the Neo-Platonists of the late *Quattrocento*. As the names suggest, these phases are usually thought to be stamped by markedly different philosophical ideas. But it will be suggested that the humanists contributed just as much to a perennial philosophy as Cicero had conceived himself doing. Both the humanists and the ancient moralists were searching for a common wisdom and gleaning it from many sources.

The humanists were, however, pursuing a search which Petrarch had begun and their questions had been framed by him. It will be claimed that the pursuit of a common wisdom open to all, but guided by the philosopher, was shared by all the humanists from Petrarch to Pico. The writings of Valla and Alberti in the early fifteenth century demonstrate how largely the civic humanists were examining issues raised by Petrarch or earlier still by Cicero. The approaches of these later writers were, however, influenced by the discovery of novel sources which had not been available to Petrarch. There were Latin authors amongst them like Varro and also Greek texts which were now being imported from Byzantium. In the late fifteenth century, moreover, the Neo-Platonists, who by then had gained a familiarity with the Greek sources, rediscovered an interest in abstract knowledge which the earlier humanists had expressly ignored. In this they marked a turning-point, even though the Ciceronian abhorrence of speculative thinking continued to show its effects after their day. It was to be seen, for example, in the political philosophy of Machiavelli. Nevertheless, the achievement of all the humanists from Petrarch to Pico lay in reviving one ancient ideal of philosophy and the philosopher. The ideal was of the philosopher as a contemplative who could direct the ways of the world by supplying a wisdom open to all.

Of those ideas of Petrarch that were to influence the thinking of the later humanists, the one to which it is important to turn first was his preference for a knowledge useful to man. This is the very ground on which the humanists are most commonly criticised and on which they deserve to be praised. They have been despised for ignoring the natural science of the twelfth and thirteenth centuries and for the paltriness of their moral conceptions. However, in their pursuit of humanity they were not the small heirs of a greater tradition from which they shrank through love of ease or deficiency of understanding. Petrarch was no more the residuary legatee of the scholastics than Socrates had been of Democritus or Empedocles.

In his invective *On his own Ignorance* (*De sui et multorum ignorantia*) (ed. Capelli, pp. 24–5) Petrarch ridiculed a scholastic opponent in this way:

> he has much to say about animals, birds and fishes: how many hairs there are in the lion's mane; how many tail feathers there are; with how many arms the squid (*polypus*) binds a shipwrecked sailor, that elephants copulate from behind and grow for two years in the womb . . . that the phoenix is consumed by aromatic fire and is reborn after burning. . . . All these things or the greater

part of it is wrong. . . . And even if they were true, they would not contribute anything to the blessed life. What is the use, I pray you, of knowing the nature of beasts, birds, fishes and serpents, and not knowing, or spurning the nature of man, to what end we are born, and from where and whither we pilgrimage?

This was a rejection of knowledge that was irrelevant to man. The attitude can already be found in Cicero where it is attributed to Socrates. Petrarch himself could have read in Cicero that Socrates had excelled others in claiming to know nothing because wisdom for him consisted in holding to the necessary limits of knowledge. It would be less accurate to describe this as a belief in the unintelligibility of the world than to say it was a recognition of the proper use and of the frontiers of knowledge. In the same passage Cicero remarked that Socrates addressed himself to the 'common life' because by contrast celestial matters were remote from human understanding or 'of no use to a knowledge of how to live well' (*Acad.*, I, iv, 15–16). This is close to Petrarch's formula that the facts of science are either false or do not contribute to a happy life. Petrarch was surely adopting a Socratic pose.

Petrarch's expression of scorn for knowing the abstract may be compared to a famous passage in one of his letters. Here he described his ascent of Mont Ventoux in Provence. Having reached the summit and turned his gaze towards the Pyrenees and the Alps he opened a copy of Augustine's *Confessions*. He hit upon these words: 'men go to admire the high mountains, the vast floods of the sea, the huge streams of the rivers, the circumference of the ocean and the revolutions of the stars – and desert themselves.' He remarked that he was stunned for having failed to have learnt already from pagan philosophers (he meant Seneca) that 'nothing is admirable besides the mind; compared to its greatness nothing is great' (Seneca, *Epist. ad Lucilium*, VIII, 5).

In both passages Petrarch was subscribing to the anti-scientific tendency of Greek ethics with two additions of his own. The target was not the pre-Socratic philosophers who had been lampooned by Socrates but Aristotle and his school. Aristotle was later in date than Socrates and some of his ethical writing was influenced by him. However, in his massive contributions to science, metaphysics and dialectic Aristotle represented a continuation of the pre-Socratic movement. In fact, even his ethical views (and approach) differed distinctly from those of post-Socratic moralists. It was an easy matter therefore to turn the shafts of Socrates and Cicero from the one target to the other. In attacking Aristotelian philosophy Petrarch and later Italians were setting themselves against the dominant method followed in the Schools.

Both passages also show that Petrarch was assimilating pagan morals to Christian thinking. His identification of pagan sentiments stressing man's moral greatness and immortality with Christianity is complete, but there is a reminder that he was Christian in his reference to Seneca as a pagan philosopher. Petrarch was not so much amending ancient ethics in the light of his Christian beliefs as simply equating the two. The letter on the ascent of Mont Ventoux was an allegory of the rise of the soul in which the summit represented at once the finding of virtue through self-knowledge and the discovery of the Christian God.

Petrarch was a genius. That worn word accurately denotes his achievement and his own estimate of it. He believed in his *ingenium* and he opened up paths which his successors were to follow. An idea of induction later employed by Valla, Machiavelli and others was given currency by him. This idea, which he had found in Cicero, consisted in generalising from experience and rejecting the abstract for the humane. Petrarch also revived from Cicero's writings a notion of virtue and a role for the intellectual as well as distinctive views on human progress and art which were deeply to influence European thought.

In a famous letter to his friend Laelius of 1355, Petrarch described a meeting with the Emperor Charles IV (*Fam.*, xix, 3). The Emperor had asked for a copy of Petrarch's collection of lives of famous men, the *De Viris Illustribus*. Petrarch complied on the conditions that he himself survived to finish it and that the Emperor continued a life of virtue. On being asked to explain himself the humanist retorted that the Emperor would be worthy of the gift if he proved himself deserving to be included in it. This was to be judged by the Emperor's deeds and 'nobility of soul'.

An illustrious life then was marked by nobility of soul. What did this fine-sounding phrase mean? Cicero was almost certainly Petrarch's source: the equation of virtue with nobility of soul is a Ciceronian one. In *De Officiis* 'greatness of soul' (a formula interchangeable with 'nobility of soul' in the Renaissance) was used to describe a search for truth by the independent spirit. The latter would be guided by the wise man or the wise ruler (I, iv, 13). The quality was displayed in the 'active' life of public service (ibid., I, xxi, 72; cf. I, xxvi, 93).

The concept of greatness of soul was imbued with a Stoic flavour. For Cicero it was shown in indifference to external fortune and in carrying out useful and dangerous deeds. Meanness of soul meant love of riches (ibid., I, xx, 66–9; cf. *Paradoxa Stoicorum*, 3 and 16). In *De Oratore* Cicero declared that a man's greatness lay not in gifts of fortune but the virtuous use of them. Furthermore, he associated greatness of soul with genius and wisdom as types of virtue and defined it as counting human affairs for nought (II, lxxxiv, 342–4).

Viewed from one angle, virtue was a course for the wise man to pursue. It was also a way of avoiding the snares of fortune. Accordingly, discussions by moralists in antiquity, and again after Petrarch, focussed sometimes on virtue and at other times on fortune. Since antiquity, writers had continued to acknowledge fortune's influence upon human affairs. Had other reminders been lacking, Boethius's *Consolation of Philosophy* would have conveyed the point. Such Christian sources depicted fortune as seeming chance, which, however, operated by God's design. Basing himself upon Senecan Stoicism, Petrarch set forth what amounted to a pagan view. Several scholars have commented upon the contradictions in Petrarch's views. Probably he assumed that pagan necessity and Christian providence were compatible and certainly he fused Christian and pagan elements.

Is it Christian or Stoic to have declared that it is God rather than the wise man who sets the limits of human life, and that the beauty of the soul is greater than that of the body or again to urge mankind to avoid fleeting joys and temptations? These sentiments are expressed in Petrarch's Senecan *De Remediis utriusque Fortunae* and can be squared with either point of view. When he was pressed on the issue Petrarch retreated, and in a letter some years later expressed the orthodox scholastic opinion that chance does not exist, being merely the impenetrable will of God (*Seniles*, viii, 3). Yet the drift of *De Remediis* shows that this *was* a retreat.

De Remediis tends to convey to the reader the idea of a world around whose hard rocks it is only possible to navigate by charting our own passions. The choice is not presented as trusting in the Christian God or Church or even human conscience, but in the Stoic principle of reason. A personified Reason disputes with human hope and feeling. This is spirituality but it is a Platonist and Stoic one. Moreover, it is inculcated by philosophers rather than by priests. Thus Petrarch declared that the wise man should penetrate behind visible things such as beauty to a love of spiritual things – friends, family, one's country or the divine. Philosophers should be our guides in life and Petrarch quotes the names of Plato, Cicero and the Stoics.

Weight needs to be given to both parts of the 'contradiction'. Petrarch assumed that pagan ideas were compatible with Christian morals and even that paganism could be squared with a scheme of Christian metaphysics based upon Aristotelian principles. Had Petrarch not done so would he ever have felt able to enunciate so forthrightly the 'worldly' perspective of the ancient sages? A view was nonetheless set forth which implied that the world was to be understood only by the control of our irrational expectations. This is little akin to any Christianity except the 'natural' theology of the seventeenth and eighteenth centuries which derived from it by a distant route.

The pursuit of grandeur and nobility of soul (or virtue) guided by wisdom lies at the heart of Petrarch's *De Viris Illustribus*. Ancient worthies were shown who served family, friends or country, ignoring the blandishments of fortune for this more lasting glory. Here was the inspiration of the later works in this genre from Filippo Villani (d. 1405), Benedetto Accolti (1415–1464) and others. Advice on how to govern one's life by rationally controlling appetites that disturb human tranquillity form the theme of ethical treatises by the humanists down to Pontano (1426–1505). It has been observed that these writings are few amongst the bulk of humanist compositions. The same master–ideas can be found, however, breathing life into their histories, orations, letters and poems.

The achievements of civic humanists and Neo-Platonists in the fifteenth century are sharply divided from those of Petrarch. Petrarch had extolled the contemplative life whilst the civic humanists glorified public service. The Neo-Platonists in their turn restored the idea of contemplation and strengthened it by reference to divine immanence. In the sixteenth century this spiritualism, so to call it, was buttressed by magic and astrology.

In fact, the seeds of this later development lay in Petrarch and his sources. The Platonic strand in Cicero prepared the way before the fifteenth-century translations of Plato. When Petrarch urged his readers in *De Remediis* to pierce behind visible things to the greater beauties of the divine world he was almost certainly basing his sentiment upon passages in Cicero. Equally fertile were Petrarch's opinions on the active and contemplative lives. Even though Cicero could provide the source for both choices (cf. Seigel, 1966), many scholars continue to assert that civic humanists like Salutati and Bruni promoted the active life and so reversed the priorities of Petrarch.

Yet Petrarch urged the Emperor Charles IV to undertake great deeds for the good of others whilst disregarding the benefits of fortune. Was not Petrarch at heart a believer in that contemplative virtue which he had found expressed in Cicero's *Tusculan Disputations*? It is often said that this was the reason that, having been shocked on reading Cicero's *Letters to Atticus* which he found at Verona in 1345, he composed a protesting epistle to the dead Cicero.

In one letter to Cicero, Petrarch castigated him for abandoning an *otium* proper to his mature years, his fortune and his position as a philosopher (*Fam.*, xxiv, 3). Two somewhat contradictory points were being made by Petrarch. He felt that withdrawal from active life became the philosopher, but he was not advocating this at all times and for all men. Cicero deserved criticism for surrendering *otium* in order to engage in political strife. At one moment defending the republic, at another supporting Augustus, Cicero had laid himself open to the charge that he was an inconstant friend of liberty. This is spelt out in a second letter to Cicero (*Fam.*, xxiv, 4).

Petrarch did not praise the contemplative life and deride the active one. He thought cultured leisure befitting to the philosopher and suited to himself. The active life was for the statesman and the ruler: they must plot their worldly course with nobleness of spirit and fixity of purpose. In these tasks they would be guided by the contemplative philosopher. Petrarch was not in favour of one way of life at the expense of another, but he did place the 'quiet' philosopher in a powerful and flattering position. Historians, as Seigel has observed, sometimes concentrate too closely on the Italian environments in which these ideas were revived and neglect the 'logic' of intellectual development.

In giving currency to the variously Stoic and Platonising elements in Cicero's writings, Petrarch prepared the way both for the civic humanists and the Neo-Platonists. The civic humanists themselves were as vaguely distinguished from the 'Neo-Platonists' who followed them as they had been from Petrarch himself. Alongside their obvious praise of the active virtues they did recognise the spiritual and divine element in man. This is hardly surprising: apart from Ciceronian tradition, a knowledge of Plato's untranslated writings was already being spread in their circles.

Petrarch rendered one further service to classical tradition when he renewed the ancient idea of the wise man as the adviser to the governing class. In his letter to Charles IV he had boldly remarked that the Emperor would only deserve to receive a copy of his book *De Viris Illustribus* if he merited inclusion in it. Later in the letter Petrarch likened his treatment by the Emperor to the welcome given to Plato by a ruler of ancient Sicily. In reading this passage it is necessary to allow for Petrarch's vanity. In a sense this vice should be applauded for it seems doubtful whether a less egocentric thinker could have conceived the notion – so essential to Petrarch's whole idea of antiquity – that the ancients were his particular friends who spoke personally to him.

There is something else to be noticed in Petrarch's likening of himself to Plato. Consciously he wished to revive the ancient idea of the philosopher as a sage possessed of the wisdom whereby the world could be governed. The idea had survived the ancient world in ecclesiastical guise: churchmen had donned the philosopher's garb and written 'mirrors for princes' urging the ruler to govern according to Christian values. The ideas of the older tradition had influenced Augustine and Isidore of Seville when they forged the Christian idea of the ruler, but the new ideal was not the old.

Petrarch took up Cicero's idea that it was the task of the wise man to counsel the ruler and the citizen in their duties to friends, family and the state. In this he was re-activating an ancient secular ideal. The writers of 'mirrors for princes' in the early Middle Ages had cast the ruler in the role of adjunct to the bishop: he was to be a good shepherd caring for his flock. In the 'Aristotelianised' teaching of the thirteenth century the prince was encouraged to rule wisely and well, looking for guidance to natural experience as well as to divine or clerical guidance.

This is different to the sage advising the statesmen of an earthly commonwealth how reason might guide them to attain 'greatness of soul' in public service. We are on the edge of a lay world. Like his forebears in the immediately preceding age Petrarch addressed laymen. Unlike them he possessed a 'secular' viewpoint in its deep-lying meaning that he was addressing the human condition. The direct Italian heirs of Petrarch were to be laymen. In short, Petrarch created a new role for the intellectual based upon the ancient idea of wisdom.

Besides all this Petrarch's regard for art marked a new beginning. The artists of his own day were the target rather than ancient masters. He commissioned the great Sienese painter Simone Martini (*c.* 1284–1344) to make a likeness of his poetic love Laura and to paint a frontispiece to his copy of Virgil. Giotto and Simone Martini were singled out as the greatest masters of the day (*Ep. Fam.*, v, 17). Petrarch reserved his highest praise for Giotto whom he called the prince of painters and whose works were the fruit of genius (*Itinerarium Syriacum*, ed. G. Lumbroso, *Memorie italiane del buon tempo antico* (Turin, 1889), p. 37). In the poem in which he informs us of Simone Martini's portrait of Laura he remarked that the painter must have visited Paradise for him to have rendered so good a likeness from beyond the grave (*Canzoniere*, no. 77). Petrarch owned a Madonna by Giotto which he bequeathed to the lord of Padua. In his will Petrarch declared that whilst the ignorant did not like the picture it was appreciated by masters of painting. He added that he owned nothing so worthy to leave to a lord (see below, p. 86, *cf.* p. 106).

Petrarch's attitude was unconventional. He did not employ the ancient vocabulary of aesthetic judgement, but his whole conception of art was remarkable. Laura's picture has claims to be considered the first discrete secular portrait since antiquity; the concept of genius was applied by Petrarch to Giotto as well as to the ancient masters Praxiteles and Phidias. Petrarch was using judgements, epithets and expectations of contemporary artists which he had read in accounts of classical art. Ancient ideas, however, were, as we shall see later, finely tuned to contemporary sentiment.

The notion that Simone Martini must have entered Paradise to paint Laura reflected the visionary nature of *Trecento* religious art as well as the ancient idea that an artist could see into the soul and penetrate the heavens. Certainly in his copy of Pliny's *Natural History* Petrarch inscribed a note comparing Simone's fame to that enjoyed by Apelles in ancient Greece (Baxandall, 1971, pp. 62–3). The reference to masters of art who understood his Giotto may be a reference to an ancient idea. Petrarch could have found examples in Pliny of the artist as the judge of art and of great artists who had written treatises about it.

He used Pliny's account of ancient art to produce another curious weave of ancient and modern. In the *De Remediis* there is a passage in which Petrarch criticised the veneration accorded to works of art. He referred to the fabulous sums spent in ancient Rome for paintings and statues to be carried across the seas and set up in temples, public places and the imperial palaces. He wrote nostalgically of the Greeks who had devoted themselves to philosophy rather than art and called for his contemporaries to turn their attention to God who was the greatest artist for he painted man with the senses (*Opera*, 1581, pp. 39–41). Here Petrarch was combining the ancient abhorrence of 'luxury' with an up-to-date aversion to un-Christian vanities in art. His sentiments here, however, do not agree with his general mood, which was to exalt modern art on the lines of classical painting and sculpture.

Petrarch's ideas on culture, morality and of the intellectual's role in them formed the intellectual diet amongst humanists for a century and a half after his death. Instead of the work of fifteenth-century humanists being contrasted stages of humanism, they are expansions of elements in Petrarch's thinking. A striking example of this is Lorenzo Valla's theory of language, which represented an extension of the attack on speculative knowledge by Petrarch. Similarly, the ideas of virtue as knowledge and as a certain sort of wisdom were exploited by the civic humanists and by the Neo-Platonists. In each case they had the benefit of sources not available to Petrarch.

Valla's dialectic is one of the most important monuments of fifteenth-century humanism. In it he attacked the philosophers of his own day who had abandoned the *usus humanitatis* and the common sense of words (*Dialectica disputationes*, I, 12; in *Opera*, ed. E. Garin, i, 673). The philosopher must concern himself with the language of the people (as the lawyer studied the people's law). The object of Valla's attack was the abstractions of the schoolmen and it sprang from his approach to concepts. He deflated great abstractions by concentrating upon their meaning and judged this by conventional usage. Thus Being and Truth were reduced to things that 'are' and things that 'are true'. Valla entitled his chief work on these questions 'Dialectical Disputations' which (by an irony) did not employ the common meaning of dialectic. Instead of using the term to mean the logical interpretation of language, he denoted thereby the conventional and historical senses of words.

Where had Valla encountered these ideas: was it from scholastic philosophy or from ancient sources? Valla's hostility to scholasticism and liking for Epicurean philosophy make it much more likely that he had tapped an ancient tradition at whose fountain-head stood Socrates. In Plato's *Apology* Socrates had defended himself against the charge of denying the gods by saying that he believed in divine things. He would not say that he believed in gods, but he did observe that if he taught a knowledge of divine things he must believe in them. Socrates' irony allows his remark to be variously understood. Plato and his followers might have interpreted it to mean that divine things in the world are emanations of divinity. Indeed, Plato puts his theory of divine forms into the mouth of Socrates, but the early sources repeatedly record the insistence of Socrates on limiting himself to what could be known.

Nearer to hand, in the fifteenth century, lay the doctrines of Epicurus and the writings of Varro. Valla professed himself an Epicurean and it is very likely therefore that he was influenced by him. According to Cicero, Epicurus rejected logic for 'natural philosophy' as a guide to life or thought. By natural philosophy Epicurus had meant the posing and classifying of problems (Cicero, *De Finibus*, ch. xix). Elsewhere in the same work Cicero asserted that Epicurus and his followers depended upon Socratic definitions as the essential method for posing problems and advancing arguments, though they denied this (ibid., II, i, 3–4). It is therefore likely that Valla consciously looked back to Epicurus's rejection of logic and to his stress upon the meaning of words.

Valla also seems to have been influenced by the *De Lingua Latina* of Varro which he could have read at first hand following its discovery at Monte Cassino in the late fourteenth century. Varro's book interpreted language as the vocabulary of the people. It was historically engendered and to be understood by the test of popular, instead of academic, usage. A proof that this was the root of Valla's idea lies in the latter's insistence that custom rather than reason is the yardstick by which to judge language. In one of his tracts Valla remarked that the 'propriety, force, meaning and interpretation of Latin words consists not in reason but in the authority of the ancient writers' (*Antidoti in Poggium* II, in *Opera*, i, 288). By this he meant the faithful testimony of such writers to popular usage. This is the very theme of Varro's *De Lingua Latina* and in one instance Varro expressly warned against following reason (*ratio*) rather than usage (*consuetudo*) (VIII, xli, 79).

This same hostility to speculative knowledge is to be found in the writings of later humanists and in the political theory of Machiavelli. The much vaunted method of Machiavelli's *The Prince* is best understood in these terms. When Machiavelli described his purpose as being to depict the 'effectual truth' of things rather than the imaginary republics and principalities outlined by earlier writers, he was echoing the words of Cicero. The latter claimed to have described the actual hopes and fears of citizens rather than the remote things imagined by Plato (cf. Stephens, 1988, pp. 258–67).

In its anti-speculative tendency Petrarch's Ciceronianism was handed on to Valla and his successors. Did the fifteenth-century humanists also inherit his stress on induction, the Ciceronian approach to virtue and to the intellectual's role? Alberti and Pico furnish telling instances: they represent phases of humanist thought which are usually contrasted to Petrarch's. The former was a key figure in civic humanism, the latter a leading Neo-Platonist.

Sixty years from Petrarch's death in 1374 brings us to the most famous moral tract of the fifteenth century, Alberti's *Della Famiglia*. The work affords an opportunity to identify the master ideas in *Quattrocento* thought and at the same time to focus on certain dilemmas which were beginning to emerge from the tradition. In *Della Famiglia* there is an inductive conception of knowledge as a set of rules which can be drawn from experience. Another theme is the interpretation of virtue as a knowledge of the human condition. This idea of virtue was self-evidently Socratic. Its chief importance did not lie in offering a support on which to hang accounts of the 'art of living' but for conveying a half-formed idea of God. In itself the Socratic idea of virtue implied a view of God, which the Italian humanists combined with Roman and Christian ideas.

It is emphasised throughout *Della Famiglia* that a knowledge derived from experience (*pruova*) and use (*uso*) is preferable to 'judgement' or book learning (eds Pellegrini, Spongano, pp. 207–8, cf. p. 388). The knowledge of how to make yourself liked and how to judge others' fitness can be gained only in the *piazza* and the theatre, from activity and experience (ibid., p. 287, cf. p. 299). These injunctions were in a Ciceronian mould, for Cicero had written of the orator learning from 'use' (*usum*) and in the forum. Alberti's insistence that experience taught hard truths about human nature is also Ciceronian. The definitions and descriptions of the scholar are useful, but it is necessary to struggle 'in the public domain amongst the actual ways and dispositions of men' and employ constant vigilance and care (p. 285).

Experience is useful and necessary; it is, however, less good as a teacher than the collective experience of mankind. History knows still more of human disposition and the nature of things than can be learnt from individual experience (ed. Grayson, p. 288f.). From this, individual and collective learning precepts or rules can be induced. There are many examples of these in *Della Famiglia*, and in Books III and IV it becomes evident that the general argument of the work is conceived by Alberti as a set of precepts.

In Book III Giannozzo's counsels for family government are described as 'precepts' and his advice for not wasting time is called a 'rule' (*regola*) (Pellegrini, pp. 261, 267). In Book IV, which is devoted to friendship, the word precept is used to describe the argument as a whole. Blended somewhat incongruously with this was an assumption of how things have come to be. Men live together and only mutual need can explain why this is so. Thus for Alberti, as for Cicero, the beginning of republics and all civic concord was mutual inter-dependence: what one man needs, another can supply (p. 199, cf. p. 325). At the beginning of the next century Machiavelli would base his political theory upon similar rules which could be derived from experience (see Chapter 11, Section 3).

Alberti's *Della Famiglia* also reveals that the Stoic idea of virtue as a knowledge 'of human and divine affairs' was revived in the fifteenth century in its Ciceronian guise. The Stoics had preached that God is Destiny: a necessary and reasonable force which could not be evaded or controlled, but which could be understood. Human lives, therefore, could be rationally ordered according to divine principles. This knowledge of right living was virtue, whereby human lives could be made conformable to necessity.

Cicero had preserved this doctrine mixed with a dash of Platonism and of Roman notions of God as a personal force intervening in human lives. Cicero's ideas here were ambiguous. God was both a rational principle and (though uncommonly) a supernatural force. Virtue constituted a knowledge of right living with the aim at once of happiness and success. The implication was that virtue was not merely its own reward, but that it would bring divine and worldly blessings. There are echoes of these ambiguities in Alberti.

In certain passages in the book Alberti laid overwhelming emphasis upon the power of *virtù*. Virtue and vice brought their own rewards and penalties: he implied that good and ill fortune are conferred upon ourselves. At the start of Book I the triumphs of ancient Rome and the later decline of Italy, as well as the fate of individuals in general, are attributed to the existence or want of *virtù*. Both individuals and states attain great things by industry, art, wisdom, good customs, honesty and reasonable expectations. This insistence on the prevailing power of virtue is summed up in Alberti's phrase: 'as is your *virtù*, so is your *fortuna*'.

Yet this position is not consistently maintained in *Della Famiglia*. Riches, beauty and power are called the temporary gifts of fortune (Bk IV, ed. Grayson, p. 306). It is implied that the ill fortune suffered by the Alberti family was owing to no just cause. It is explicitly declared that even good men suffer misfortune whether due to their own defects, to enmity or to an act of heaven (p. 323). In another passage the noblest pursuits are said to be those not depending on fortune, but since all success *does* partly require good fortune it is essential to employ judgement and discretion (pp. 218–19).

Further confusion is introduced by references to circumstances controlled by God. Alberti's God is not, however, a remote principle or original creator. He is angered by vice (pp. 197–8) and rewards *onestà* (p. 215). The providence of God is so great that anything can be accomplished with His help (p. 171). The impression that the 'temporary gifts of fortune' are divine blessings is fortified by Alberti's comments on the evil fortune of his own family. In one passage God is described as the judge of those Alberti enemies who had been the agents of misfortune (p. 369). It would seem therefore that God is Fortune and the casual equation of the two conceptions is to be found throughout the work.

God can be equated with Fortune, but how can these two notions be related to virtue? How could it be that 'as is your *virtù*, so is your *fortuna*' if Fortune is God? An interlocutor in the dialogue declares that the Alberti had prospered because God had shown them *gratia* as a reward for their *onestà* (p. 215). Shortly after it is said that *onestà* will bring a man *favore, gratia, lode* and *onore* which are more important than fortune (p. 226). It is evident, however, that these benefits *are* good fortune. Giannozzo declares that Fortune depends upon others, especially one's family. Earlier he had said that no man is deserving of good fortune unless he in his turn helps his kinsmen, and that no one gains help who does not enjoy the favour of his own family (p. 325).

The proposition that virtue brings good fortune may be considered part of an attempt by Alberti to square a circle. There are contradictions in *Della Famiglia* that cannot be reconciled. God rewards the just (for instance, the good works of the Alberti: pp. 214–15) but the latter also suffer from an ill-fortune which afflicts the good (p. 323) even though fortune represents the workings of God. Similarly, virtue (*onestà*) is a consolation for the misfortunes suffered by the just (p. 226) and a ground on which they can hope for a good fortune delivered by an equitable God. In short, Alberti does not seem able to decide whether God is equity or fortune. Alberti is equally uncertain if virtue is the Stoic principle of rational self-sufficiency and a procedure to secure worldly success or a divine principle deserving of reward by the gods.

At the root of this idea lies the God of the Greek philosophers who was the creator and provider and also the power of Reason. The humanists met this view first in the Roman moralists, where it was marbled with late Stoic and Roman beliefs in man's moral greatness and of the reward he enjoyed for nobility of soul. Once these ideas gained currency again they affected deeply the outlook of religious thinkers. Whilst these ideas did not necessarily contradict prevailing Augustinian and Thomist ideas, they did pass by the concerns of the scholastics.

They offered a more rational and mundane conception of life in which reason could guide the search for a happy life. At the same time they contained thought-provoking ambiguities. Could man at one and the same time seek glory by actions in this life and conceive the latter as but a preparation for death? Was God both a beneficent provider and dismal necessity? Could not an ethical viewpoint that shifted from rational perception of the human condition to planning for earthly rewards be seen as a human canniness ill-deserving of blessings by God?

In his application of the inductive method and discussions of virtue as a knowledge of human and divine affairs, Alberti was exploiting that Stoic tradition which Petrarch had revived. He went directly back to the Ciceronian sources of it. Humanists of Alberti's generation in Florence were, however, influenced by a wider range of ancient sources, including the Greek originals of Plato's dialogues which were beginning to be known. He found there not only a method but an *idea* of intellectual life. This induced an elevated conception of art which he expressed in his formative writings on painting, sculpture and architecture. In addition, Alberti helped to create a model for the intellectual to follow. Along with other Florentines of his generation, like Niccolò Niccoli, Palla Strozzi and Cosimo de' Medici, he was responsible for launching the ancient ideal of wisdom as a pattern for patricians and princes to imitate (see further, Chapter 12). Alberti was nevertheless singularly important in transmitting this ideal to leading Italians of a later generation.

Alberti's life and works bear witness to the fact that the humanists of the early *Quattrocento* were not reversing the tenets of Petrarch. On the contrary, Alberti's ideas demonstrate the continuing force of Seigel's contention that Bruni and his circle (the observation could be extended to include Valla) were mainly exploring different elements of Ciceronian thought which Petrarch had resurrected. Some scholars since Seigel have failed to absorb the implications of his insight. When they stress the 'civic' character of early fifteenth-century thought they neglect its spiritual dimension. At the same time they exaggerate its difference from Petrarch beforehand and the Neo-Platonists afterwards.

The Neo-Platonists of the late fifteenth-century, notably Ficino and Pico, seem to lie well beyond Petrarchan traditions. Ficino and Pico overtly professed the Christian faith and they preferred Platonist to Stoic and Epicurean tenets. Thus they appear to belong in the company of the scholastics. Are *humanitas* and those preoccupations that had concerned Italian men of letters since Petrarch any longer to be found? We appear to meet an altered tradition which Pico and his ilk were to pass on to alien heirs in the realms of sixteenth-century magic and theology.

The tradition of Petrarch had become attenuated by the late fifteenth century but Ficino and Pico had not moved beyond it. There is evidence for this in the most celebrated work of these scholars, Pico's *Oration on the Dignity of Man*. On the surface the work seems quite foreign to the writings of the earlier humanists like Poggio, Bruni, Alberti or Petrarch. It contains few references to the ancient moralists and instead is dotted with biblical, hebraic, arabic, scholastic and earlier quotations. The tone is metaphysical and the work devoted to such topics as free will and the mysteries of God, which had been typical concerns of the schoolmen.

The *Oration* sounds a different note to the orations and treatises of the early *Quattrocento*. It begins with Pico disassociating himself from the arguments which others had advanced to explain the dignity of man. For Pico human excellence lay not in the acuity of the senses, reason or intelligence but in free will. Alone of the creatures God had made man an indeterminate being, neither celestial nor earthly. God's design meant that man himself could choose his nature: he might be reborn either amongst the brutes or with the higher divine beings (paras 1–3).

Pico would appear to be separating himself from the Stoic moralists for whom reason alone set man on the path to heaven. Was he not siding with the Christian theologians for whom free will was God's essential gift to man? Pico's distinction, however, between free will and reason is not so clear. For the ancient moralists man could rise above the beasts by employing reason; the inference is that he might also fail to do so. For Pico, as for the ancients, it was 'right reason' which allowed the philosopher to rise above the earth (para. 5). In emphasising the importance of free will Pico was perhaps influenced by the ancient ethical teaching that good and evil are things we *will*.

The appearance of Pico's idea of the philosopher is also revealing. The wise man guided by right reason ascends by Jacob's ladder to heavenly peace (paras 9–13). Closer inspection shows, however, that the ideas are familiar ones.

> By what means is one able either to judge or to love things unknown? Moses loved a God whom he saw and as judge administered among the people what he had first beheld in contemplation upon the mountain . . . [the chief order of contemplative philosophy] is the one for us first to emulate . . . the one from whence we may be rapt to the heights of love, and descend, well taught and well prepared, to the functions of active life.
>
> (Chap. 9; *Ren. Phil. of Man*, p. 228)

Pico employs biblical language: he speaks of cherubs, seraphs and of Moses; his vocabulary of love implies a Platonist point of view. But the sentiments are those of the late Stoics recorded by such as Cicero, Seneca and Horace. For them the sage, inspired by an elevated wisdom he had secured by contemplation, descended to guide the world. The peace discovered by Pico's philosopher is not so much a Christian peace as the Stoic mastery of passions like wrath and violence (para. 13).

One of the most important passages in the *Oration* contains Pico's assertion of the unity of truth. When he wrote that he was 'pledged to the doctrines of no man' (para. 26) we seem to be reaching the grand eclectic philosophy of the sixteenth century. In fact, when Pico used the phrase he was echoing the words of Horace's first epistle. In that letter Horace had explained that he had abandoned poetry for philosophy, entrusting himself to no one school (*Epist.*, I, i, 1–14). At the end of this epistle, however, Horace declared his preference for the Stoic idea of the sage who alone could be perfect in the search for wisdom (I, i, 106–8). In short, Pico's unitary truth is the notion of one wisdom pervading all schools which, as we have seen, was a commonplace of the ancient moralists.

The work of Pico therefore attenuated the Ciceronian tradition which

Petrarch had revived: Neo-Platonism represented a development of earlier thinking without which it would not have come to pass. Nevertheless, Neo-Platonism self-evidently combined new elements with the old. Pico was not content with occupying the old ground of moral philosophy: he proceeded from it via dialectic and magic to theology. Moreover, the stated purposes of the *Oration* – and the statement could define the programme of the Neo-Platonists – was to penetrate the plan of the universe and the mysteries of Christian theology (para. 23).

This Christian and metaphysical bent separated Pico and his school from the more inductive and 'terrestrial' concerns of earlier humanists. Indeed, the importance of the Neo-Platonists lay precisely in this spiritual adaptation of the older preoccupations. The change affected sixteenth-century thought deeply. The adaptations formed the beginning of a demonic approach to controlling nature by magic or by a magical science. At the traditional level of Christian revelation, they altered and strengthened theology in ways, unexpected by Pico, which were to fashion the thinking of the Reformation.

There was not an abandonment of the old interests or a simple resurrection of scholasticism. It was that theology was interpreted in terms of the moral concerns of Cicero, Plato and his earlier followers. How was it possible to employ right reason to rise above a brutal level towards divine truth? Might it not be possible to learn from all branches of philosophy and from all philosophers? How, having grasped truth by contemplation, could humanity return earthwards to govern the affairs of the world? These were the questions addressed by Pico and they represent the subjection of humanist concerns to the needs of theology.

Instead of this being a move away from humanism or one back to scholastic theology, it was a development of humanist concerns: the 'Ciceronian' approach to theological questions, and the very interest in them had grown from the work of Valla two generations earlier. The latter had applied philology to the text of scripture; he had written on free will and he had launched a more eclectic procedure by employing Epicurean arguments in his *De Voluptate*. The development of humanism was not the successive resurrection of ancient philosophical schools, nor yet a move away from theology or back towards it. Rather it meant the continuing exploitation of the common (and hence enduringly eclectic) tradition of ancient ethics. The importance as well as the limitations of the work of the humanists was that none of them from Petrarch to Pico cut their ethics free from that theology which it was sometimes their purpose to attack or make it an academic exercise in the recovery of ancient knowledge. It is this that explains a tremendous impact which humanist ideas were to make on religious thinking in the sixteenth century.

Through the intellectual vicissitudes of the fifteenth century the idea of the intellectual remained intact. The intellectual, as a layman, who on the basis of ancient sources proffered advice to his fellows on how to live, was inherited by Pico and passed to the northern humanists like Erasmus (*c.* 1469–1536), Thomas More (1478–1535) and their later successors. This was all the more novel and potent in that intellectuals like Pico were beginning to master traditional theology, which had previously been monopolised by the Church. As we have seen, Pico had been foreshadowed in this role by Valla but the Neo-Platonists' influence was in some ways greater because their ideas were expressed in a garb which scholastic theologians found more familiar.

The Italian Neo-Platonists formed a watershed from which several streams fell away to the sixteenth century. A considerable current ran north to humanists like Erasmus and from them a tributary connected to the Reformers, notably Bucer (1491–1551), Melanchthon (1497–1560) and Calvin (1509–64); even Luther and the German princes were affected. The main stream in Italy flowed via the sixteenth-century Neo-Platonists like Francesco da Diacceto (b. 1466) to Campanella (1568–1639). Italian thinkers of 1500 including many of the great Latin scholars such as Bembo (1470–1547) and the writers in Italian, like Castiglione (1478–1529), were influenced. Within the peninsula the Neo-Platonists were important also in carrying forward older concerns. The circle of Lorenzo de' Medici is usually associated with Neo-Platonist tastes, but from Landino's *Camaldulensian Disputations* it is evident that Ciceronian interests were equally fashionable there. Subsequently, they were borne via the aristocratic circle of the Rucellai Gardens to Machiavelli.

The humanist had begun in Petrarch as a sage and ended in Pico as a visionary magician, uncovering the workings of the universe. This story cannot be understood unless note is taken of the social position of the Italian intellectual as well as of tradition. Both, however, were more important than the narrow political environments surrounding them. The ethical philosophy recognised by Petrarch in Cicero's writings was a threshold over which the humanists passed to find truths which inspired them to perceive and think differently. What they discovered was not an ideology which 'reflected' their social or political circumstances, but truths which their circumstances allowed them to welcome.

The ancient ethics revived by Petrarch gave the Italians first a novel sense of their identity. They discovered the means to rid themselves of their intellectual dependence on 'barbarian' learning – the philosophy of the French and German schools. They were delighted to find that there was an ancient philosophy sharply different from the logical writings of Aristotle which formed the backbone of scholasticism. A better knowledge of antiquity thus furnished the humanists with texts and techniques to belabour northern scholars.

The humanists did not encounter in Cicero, and later in ancient ethical writing generally, a civic philosophy and a rhetoric to aid them in the propaganda issued by city-states, or a cult of personal sensibility grounded in a personal belief that the world was unknowable. From Petrarch onwards the humanists ridiculed the scholastics for seeking truths that were beyond their reach, or which were unavailing to mankind. The starting-point was a conviction that the human condition was a mystery whose implications could only be perceived by accepting that there are some values in which we do believe and some circumstances we cannot control. On this basis the humanists, like the ancient moralists before them, constructed a more rational morality which each individual could discover.

Here was the material for a moral re-armament of the laity. The re-armament was not undertaken by a broadly based social group. There have been few attempts by scholars to determine the dissemination of the new learning in Italy. One statistical study of the composition of the private Florentine libraries in the fifteenth century suggests, despite the conclusions of its author, that a knowledge of humanist texts did not expand in the *Quattrocento* (C. Bec, 1968). It was a small élite which took possession of the new classical scholarship and the idea of 'humanity'. It was only after 1500 that changes in education and the effects of printing slowly spread this knowledge. From the first, however, interest in the work of the humanists extended to leading members of the governing classes of the peninsula. Its social significance lay in their endorsement and their belief that a knowledge of antiquity fitted them for office.

From a cultural angle the important novelty was that from the fifteenth century onwards the laity was equipped with the philosophy of antiquity which until then had been reserved to the Church. This point will be explored further in a later chapter, but it is important to stress here that this was an occupation of *moral* ground previously held by clerical scholars.

The humanists were to have their most enduring effect in arrogating to laymen the moral authority of the priest. First, they themselves took on the task of advising others how morally to govern their lives; then educated laymen began to interpret the ancient sources for themselves. The dramatic consequences of this became visible in the Reformation (see Chapters 12 and 15). The artist was similarly invading moral ground unfamiliar to him: like the humanist he came to depict the human soul. It could be said that both of them – to reverse the scholastic adage – showed divinity *sub specie humanitatis*. Both looked to heaven from the human condition. In this they were inspired by the same classical sources and were providing a service to Italians ill served by a decadent and conservative Church. The theme of the ensuing chapters on art will be this change.

Part II
THE ARTIST, THE PATRON AND THE SOURCES OF ARTISTIC CHANGE

Chapter Six

Introduction

1. The nature of the problem

The great works of Renaissance art, like Leonardo's *Virgin of the Rocks* and his portraits, or the sculptures of Michelangelo, can be readily conjured up. Immediately we have some impression of artistic achievements. The humanists offer the challenge of endeavouring to define the novelty of their work. It is relatively easy to comprehend why they turned to the ancient sources and how they found there something which complemented existing intellectual traditions. The problem with art is less what artists attempted than why they did so.

Renaissance sculpture and architecture were heavily influenced by newly appreciated classical models, but this was not true of painting where antique examples had failed to survive. Why did artists (above all painters) come to produce original works and why did patrons commission them? Answers to these questions commonly assume banal forms: wealth led to the patronage of art and patrons sought fame. Rich communities and individuals, however, did not need to invest their money in art or could have chosen to buy *old* masters. Fame is a vague word begging further questions: why was the commissioning of pictures and buildings thought to confer fame?

A few social and economic historians have produced general theories to explain Italian art. These attempts have related art to superficial features of Italian life and failed to concentrate closely on the agents commissioning works of art or the artists producing them. Recent scholars have perceived that it is necessary to focus on patronage. All important paintings, sculptures and buildings during the fifteenth and sixteenth centuries were produced for a patron; the latter's wishes were therefore crucial.

In the ensuing chapter, an aspect of the culminating phase of Renaissance art, the painting of the High Renaissance, will form a point of departure. How did a picture of Leonardo differ from one produced two centuries before and what does this show about the changing role of the artist and the subject-matter of his work? It will be argued that what changed was less the subject than the role of the artist. Works of art came to be seen as expressions peculiarly of his hand. The difficulty is to relate this expanded contribution of the artist to the scholarly emphasis upon patronage. The stereotype of the romantic artist producing his works of genius isolated from the world used to be found in accounts of Renaissance art. It has been replaced by that of the painter and sculptor working in response to the demands of the patron.

The original pictures and sculptures of the Renaissance period were the outcome of a relationship between artist and patron. To understand this we need to attach as much weight to human as to the contractual and commercial side of their relationship. The thesis that patrons determined artistic output deserves to be questioned. Isabella d'Este's relations with the painter Perugino are sometimes used to show this. It will be suggested that even so 'authoritarian' a patron as she, looked to her artist to supply the essential features of skill and style. It is possible to say this and not resort to the old-fashioned proposition that the artist created solely for his own aesthetic satisfaction. He did so in order to please the patron.

Important novelties in Renaissance art were conceived expressly by their creators in order to satisfy patrons. The patron's needs were met by allowing the artist freedom to exercise his imaginative talents. The numerous originalities thrown forth in Renaissance Italy beg further questions. This creative ferment implies that there was competition between artists to secure the approval of patrons, for otherwise there would have been no pressure to please. Equally, there must have been competition between patrons or they would have lacked the incentive to treat an artist well. The case of Florence demonstrates how such a competition could generate change.

Competition itself is not the end of the story. It is necessary to know what it was that *impelled* patrons to compete. Moreover there are anecdotes in the early sources which indicate that it was not enough for artists to be allowed licence. The encouragement needed by them to produce great work was a positive, and even an intellectual, understanding. This (like the competition between patrons) could not have happened without patrons holding art and the act of creation in high esteem. A principal reason for this was the ancient regard for art and the artist which Petrarch had been the first to revive. A second cause was the prevailing religious purposes of art, especially in respect of painting. These influences combined to stimulate an elevated and even visionary art. Patrons therefore were supporting a certain sort of art, to which they were attaching themselves. Commissioning great works of art required understanding and interest on the part of the patron; it also needed his money.

Why did patrons use their resources to encourage both sacred and profane art? Was the raising of buildings and commissioning of paintings a sort of 'display' ritual whereby patrons sought to impress fellow citizens, courtiers or subjects? Conversely, were they attempting to arrogate to themselves certain high purposes of art? An examination of the contemporary vocabulary by which such commissions were described suggests that patrons were seeking to demonstrate their moral worth rather than 'show off'. When they were described as being magnificent, this meant that they wished high-mindedly to rise above their wealth and use it for lofty and public purposes rather than display it.

Ancient pagan ideas and current religious needs explain why art came to be held in high regard. It was the way in which the commissioning of art became the magistrate or prince's badge of office that accounts for the eagerness of the governing classes to cultivate artists. A coincidence of factors brought this about. The religious traditions of thirteenth-century Italy had encouraged a spirituality directed towards imaginative visions of the Gospels and the next world. This spirituality reflected itself in the visions of the Franciscan Spirituals and mystic poets, and also in the religious paintings of the time which were themselves visions.

The friars had sought to inspire this spirituality in laymen, and there was no resistance from an Italian regular clergy which was singularly poor or corrupt. The upper-class families of Italy therefore built their own chapels in which to practice their devotions. They had the further incentive to commission eye-catching paintings for such locations, in that their claim to belong to the governing class was justified by little else than their intellectual and moral worth, since most of them had come there neither by military prowess nor very ancient birth. Two other circumstances influenced this process. It was a patriotic duty amongst the *literati* of the peninsula to revive antiquity, since it represented the national past when Italy had last been great.

This aspiration was not reserved to a professional corps of intellectuals, but was shared by the leading classes who were themselves educated in Latin. In Italy, as nowhere else in Europe, the governing class from 1300 had access to ancient culture and conceived it as their duty to revive it. The Italian Church had suffered a double inroad into that monopoly of culture and religion which, in northern Europe, it preserved until the sixteenth century. It lost the sole hold at once of classical culture and of devotion. Religious visions came to be supplied not by the clergy but by lay poets and artists whilst their patrons became connoisseurs of religious life. Thus the visual arts joined classical literary culture as a vehicle for the Italian ruling class to show its intellectual and moral cultivation.

2.   The character of artistic change in fourteenth and fifteenth-century Italy

The distance travelled by Italian artists from 1200 to 1500 can be gauged by comparing a *Dugento* Italian painting with one by Leonardo da Vinci (1455–1519). The church of Santa Chiara in Assisi preserves a crucifix claiming to be the one before which St Francis had prayed at the church of San Damiano in the first decade of the thirteenth century. Certainly it belongs to that period and is characteristic of it. In keeping with spiritual values which St Bernard had helped to forge a century before, Christ is portrayed as a man suffering in death. The painter's conventions, however, invoke the Byzantine East rather than the Romanesque art of Burgundy. The painting is a gilded object, and in portraying Christ the artist was evidently more concerned with the surface effects of line and colour than with depicting a living body suspended in space.

Leonardo da Vinci's *Virgin of the Rocks* from the Louvre, executed around 1480, displays an opposite tendency as far as the design is concerned. Whereas the Crucifix of 1200 might be called an opening into heaven, Leonardo's painting is a window into nature. In the former work the eye does not seem to penetrate the surface on which the forms lie. The mind's eye, however, impressed by the subject and the work's hieratic qualities, is carried up. In this the Romanesque altarpieces of Italy resembled icons which indeed had influenced them. Conversely, the surface of the *Virgin of the Rocks* is like a window through which the observer peers into a natural world. The persons, animals and rocks appear to be real objects suspended in air.

The artist also intrudes in Leonardo's painting. History does not record the authorship of the Assisi painting, whilst the *Virgin of the Rocks* was already associated with Leonardo in the sixteenth century. In fact, the design of the work is obviously his. Pictorial and religious tradition did not determine the arrangement and setting of the figures. Certainly by 1500 the importance of design had been well established as well as conventions concerning the proper portrayal of religious scenes.

Leonardo's *Virgin of the Rocks* contains the figures of the Virgin, an angel, the infant Christ and infant John the Baptist against a rocky background. Fra Filippo Lippi (*c.* 1406–69) had already painted a Virgin and Child which included rocks and John the Baptist as a child. Behind both pictures may have lain an apocryphal story telling how the Holy Family had rested in a cave on their flight into Egypt. Nevertheless, Leonardo's painting bears small resemblance to Lippi's.

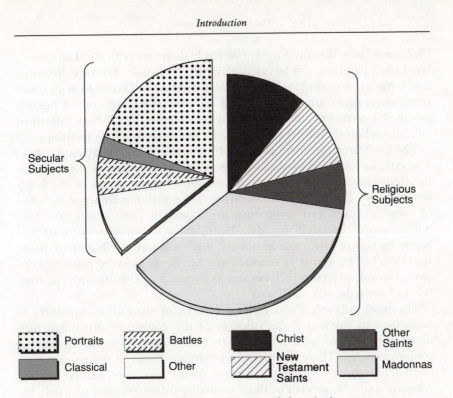

Fig.2 The subjects of Leonardo's paintings

The disposition of Leonardo's figures (and the symbolism thus conveyed), the emphasis placed on the rocks and the distinctive style were new. The viewer was invited to participate in a mystery which was of Leonardo's devising. The angel looks out of the picture, directing attention by a commanding gesture to the frail Baptist. The whole work signifies perhaps mankind dwarfed by the mighty forms of nature and blessed by Christ.

Nearly three centuries separate Leonardo from the San Damiano panel. In this time painting had altered. Style, composition, a painting's purpose and the role of the artist had all changed. As a result, a painting had come to be seen as a work of art in that it was perceived to derive from the painter's 'art'. Had the subject-matter also been altered? The theme of the *Virgin of the Rocks* was religious. It was a devotional painting and its sister-work, the nearly identical *Virgin of the Rocks* from the National Gallery in London, seems to have been commissioned by a Milanese confraternity. We are still recognisably in the religious world of 1200. Individuals and groups commissioned paintings before which they prayed in the church, chapel and confraternity, and had those prayers informed by meditation upon the humanity of Christ.

However, Leonardo also painted the *Mona Lisa*, the portrait of a

Florentine lady. Was the *Virgin of the Rocks* therefore typical of Leonardo's work? His paintings can be easily classified (Figure 2). Of the thirty-nine surviving or lost works which can be attributed to Leonardo with some confidence, eight are portraits, and this comprises the second biggest group. Nevertheless the first place is occupied by Madonnas (fifteen in all), and religious subjects make up the majority of all his paintings.

The San Damiano crucifix and the *Virgin of the Rocks* are extreme points. The crucifix long preceded any development customarily associated with the Renaissance and Leonardo was an idiosyncratic genius of the High Renaissance. There is a case, therefore, for remaining amongst the class of creative artists and comparing the works of Giotto (*c.* 1266–1337) with those of Botticelli (*c.* 1445–1510). New developments in art had begun by Giotto's time and he himself made a great contribution to them. Botticelli had his painterly eccentricities but he was a noted painter of the new classical subjects which became fashionable in the fifteenth century, where Leonardo was not.

The work of both artists raises problems of attribution, but there is no reason to think that the subjects of the doubtfully attributed pictures were unrepresentative of work being done by them or leading contemporaries. There is a significant change between the paintings of Giotto and those of Botticelli. No secular work survives by Giotto, whereas some 34 per cent of those probably painted wholly or partly by Botticelli fall into this category. Including lost works of Giotto recorded in the early sources, some 6 per cent of his works were of secular subjects (see Figures 3 and 4).

For all this, the large majority of Botticelli's paintings were religious, like those of Leonardo after him. This is striking, considering that Botticelli was a painter famous for his portraiture and classical themes. Changes in the subject-matter of art were evidently less marked than those in the technique, role and stature of the artist. Does this also suggest that novelties were initiated in the sphere of religious art and later introduced elsewhere?

As the art historian, Giorgio Vasari (1511–74), noticed, Italian art developed in the period between Giotto and Michelangelo (1475–1564), with an intervening spurt of creative activity around 1400. The beginnings can be detected in Giotto of those achievements in composition and in conveying a sense of space which are to be observed in the *Virgin of the Rocks*. Giotto concentrated on depicting a few essential figures so as to convey a story more powerfully. In this, and in giving a greater solidity to his figures, Giotto began the process by which the painting became a 'window into nature'.

A century later came the ground-breaking discovery by Brunelleschi (1377–1446) of the mathematical laws of perspective. This discovery was applied to painting by Masaccio (1401–28). The first picture in

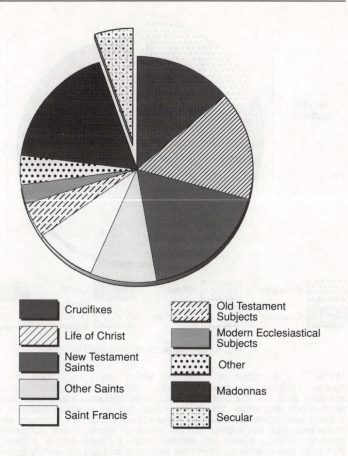

Fig.3   The subjects of Giotto's paintings

■ Crucifixes	▨ Old Testament Subjects
▨ Life of Christ	▨ Modern Ecclesiastical Subjects
■ New Testament Saints	⠿ Other
▤ Other Saints	■ Madonnas
▭ Saint Francis	▨ Secular

which Masaccio achieved this, his *Holy Trinity* in Santa Maria Novella in Florence, still survives. Masaccio also lay in Giotto's tradition in that he depicted his figures as living bodies. Leonardo and the painters of his time were the heirs of these developments. With these painters the attempt to portray 'nature' (as Vasari and many later art historians have termed it) was not a mechanical attempt to depict some loosely conceived 'reality', but rather to convey the *vital* element of an individual, group or scene.

These changes in the field of painting followed a parallel course to those of the other arts. Nevertheless, in one sense, developments in sculpture and architecture around 1400 stood out more starkly against their background. The sculpting by Donatello (*c.* 1386–1466) of life-sized figures in full relief

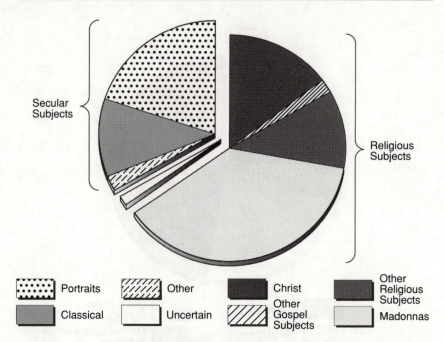

Fig. 4 : The subjects of Botticelli's paintings

NOTE: It is a matter of judgement which works to include in compiling these figures. *Included* are those paintings attributed to Botticelli by several leading scholars. *Excluded* are probably unauthentic attributions and also probable workshop productions and other copies. Workshop copies in which Botticelli may have had a hand are, however, included. Where the opinions of scholars are very divided, preference has been given to the views of more recent authorities. *Fragmented paintings*: Fresco cycles are entered singly by their central subject, but Frescoes that have been removed from their locations and are separately preserved are listed as individual works, as are panels which only uncertainly belonged together. Excluded also are literary references to works by Botticelli unless these have certainly failed to survive and cannot be confused with an extant painting. Late literary references are ignored.

and Brunelleschi's building of the great dome for the cathedral of Florence were not evidently foreshadowed around 1300. However, much of their work was designed to complete or decorate buildings which themselves had been begun at that earlier date. It is also true that the advances of 1400 were consummated in the great sculptures and buildings of the early sixteenth century, notably that of Michelangelo. In that sense, sculpture and architecture did follow the pattern of painting.

Chapter Seven

Theories

1. Older social interpretations: Antal

A rt was once treated as the expression of patrons' values; more recently it has been seen as a token of their sufferance or power. The German historian Antal represented the older school in claiming that art reflected a dominant class. In a famous book (*Florentine Painting and its Social Background* (English trans., 1947)) Antal argued that industry and international trade gave Florence an unusually developed bourgeoisie. Renaissance art mirrored the vicissitudes of this élite. Its triumph in the late thirteenth century produced the art of Giotto which was spatial, rational and humane. The retreat of the same class in the mid-fourteenth century before an advancing petty bourgeoisie gave birth to a new art that was popular, emotional and hieratic. The upper bourgeoisie and Giotto's art revived again after 1380. This revival reached its peak in the 1420s with the sculpture of Donatello and the painting of Masaccio.

Antal wrote of the bourgeoisie; if he had made patrons his target he might have avoided the unhelpful vagueness with which he employed the concept of social class, and have demonstrated a closer link between the artistic novelties and the class whose values he believed them to reflect. The plain facts of who commissioned what artist to execute which picture or sculpture would have made it easier to grasp whose values these artists embodied in their work. The creative artists mentioned by Antal were Giotto, Donatello and Masaccio – too few for them to represent the bourgeoisie. If class values had existed to be reflected, why had not more mirrors appeared to catch the gleam? The humbler possibility that the artists responded to the values of their patrons would have been easier to prove.

Had Antal correctly posed the problem? Sir Ernst Gombrich has suggested that the social interpretations of art have tended to begin with a view of the world and then looked to see reflections of this in artistic style (cf. Gombrich, 1963, p.86). Antal's approach fails to give priority to artistic change; it pays even less attention to the acceptance of innovation. Doubtless there have been many changes in the history of art, which are not 'innovations' because they have not been accepted as such.

This general point has a particular force in application to Renaissance art since the innovations were few in number and their influence was slowly felt. The significant changes were not the spontaneous work of many hands: the processes of appearance and acceptance can be separated. Recently this problem has been avoided by concentrating on patrons and the part played in a commission by their feelings.

2. Baxandall

An important example of this concentration upon patronage is Michael Baxandall's book on fifteenth-century Italian painting (1972). Its thesis is that a painting was the 'deposit of a social relationship' between patron and artist in which the former played the determining role controlling the painting's subject, materials and delivery date (pp.1–5). The style of pictures was determined by the method of payment, whether it was by the area painted or as a recompense for the painter's skill. The patron commonly stipulated the subject-matter by means of an agreed drawing. The artist's freedom was restricted further by the limitations of his patron's ability to appreciate his work – and this in turn by the visual skills of the patron. Thus, for the artist 'his public's visual skills must be his medium'. Baxandall's book contains a brilliant account of how contemporary aesthetic judgement was shaped by prevailing customs. The approach in general brings the artist into focus with the patron and solves the problem of how artistic innovations were accepted by reference to the taste of the latter.

These conclusions are not dissimilar to those which Wackernagel had advanced in a famous work on the Florentine artist (first German edition, 1938). For him the patron exercised the decisive role in producing a work of art. Wackernagel attributed the original achievements of Florentine art to the co-operation and sufferance of great families. The building and decoration of public monuments, for example the mendicant churches of Santa Croce and Santa Maria Novella with their private chapels, sprang from the readiness of leading citizens to act together and accept schemes of decoration which were in advance of their tastes.

3. The theory of patronage

These views have been rightly influential and the relationship of artist and patron has come to be placed in the foreground. All major works of

Renaissance art were produced for a client and the artist often contracted to portray a particular subject and agreed to a delivery date. Sometimes the patron laid down details of its composition and materials.

It is important to give weight to the patron's role. The revaluation of it has nonetheless been carried too far and measured in misleading terms. Observations made recently by students of iconology suggest this. A generation ago Panofsky (1939 and 1969) felt free to interpret the meaning of a painting largely by reference to the programme that could be deciphered within it. This programme would have been given to the artist by the patron or by a humanist advising the latter. Since then a call has been made for more attention to be given to the intentions of the artist (Gombrich, 1972, pp.1–23). It has even been claimed that purely aesthetic considerations were paramount and that the artist was not guided by any instructions of an adviser (C.Hope, 1981). Does this suggest that the general stress upon patronage should be challenged? Is there a middle path which will acknowledge that artists wished to please patrons whilst denying that they were controlled by them?

One reason to be suspicious of current ideas is the determinism which is evident in them. For Wackernagel art was production in response to demand. Baxandall believes in physiological and social determinism. According to this view, a painting is a 'response' to the visual skills of the patron or public, which were honed by the brain's interpretation of the data presented to it by eye and optic nerve. The brain is in turn influenced by knowledge, assumption, mental categories and habits. In fifteenth–century Italy discrimination was fashioned by such daily habits as devotional practice, dance and practical surveying. A social determinism is also implied: paintings were deposits of a 'social relationship' and 'more or less conscious responses by the painter to the conditions of the picture trade' (p. 27).

Are market forces and psychological conditioning the right way to understand the actions of artists and patrons? Renaissance paintings were executed for patrons and artists were paid. Thus far there was demand, but does it explain the achievements of Renaissance art? Demand may account for the volume of production, but it cannot be the reason for quality and form. There was demand for art during the Roman Empire but the response this evoked was the imitation of Hellenistic works. There were too few innovators in *Quattrocento* Italy for market forces to be an appropriate concept to explain their appearance. It may be doubted whether innovators were influenced by a market or trade at all. There was no trade for which artists supplied pictures; they competed between themselves to gain the employment of patrons, whilst the latter vied to obtain their services.

The work of art was the 'deposit' of this relationship but the relationship is one better described as human than social. It was certainly contractual, financial and conventional. It was also one between two individuals or, less commonly, between an artist and a small group of patrons, whether the brothers of a confraternity, the officers of a guild or presiding magistrates. What explains why one artist achieved greater things than another is rather human skills. We should think less of responses to conditions and more of imagination and intellect. Similarly, the artist was disposed to provide a certain sort of painting not by way of a more or less conscious response, but by the exercise of his intellect and imagination in order to create a work satisfying the wishes of his patron. This is not to credit artists and patrons with high motivation; merely with free will.

An understanding of how innovations came about is best approached by considering specific cases. Isabella d'Este's purchase of the painting of the *Battle of Chastity and Lasciviousness* by Perugino highlights the detail of such an operation. The picture of patronage in a great city is provided by Florence where many of the most important developments took place. Between them these examples enable us to clarify the respective roles of artist and patron.

4.   The case of Isabella d'Este and Perugino's
Battle of Chastity and Lasciviousness

The relations between Isabella d'Este, duchess of Mantua (1474–1539), and Perugino (1445/50–1522) are unusually well documented. There is extant a series of letters between the two concerning a painting depicting a battle of Chastity and Lasciviousness, which make this one of the best recorded commissions in Renaissance art. Between 1502 and 1505 the painting was ordered for Isabella's salon, known as the Grotta or *camerino* in the Gonzaga Palace at Mantua. Since 1496 she had commissioned various works for this room, including one by Mantegna (*c.* 1431–1506) to hang beside the Perugino. The letter survives in which Isabella wrote to an agent requesting him to discover the readiness of Perugino to work for her, as well as the one she wrote some three years later thanking the artist for the completed painting. The detailed instructions given by Isabella to Perugino are also available to us, together with the picture itself. The documents afford a unique insight into the patron's role.

Isabella's letter to her agent Malatesta of 15 September 1502 reveals that she expected to stipulate the measurements of the painting and its story or 'invention'. She also referred to her *fantasia* by which she either meant the theme or its imaginative conception. Malatesta's reply (24 October 1502) shows that Perugino was to be notified of the measurements, subject and figures of the picture. The contract signed with the artist on Isabella's behalf in January 1503 shows that Isabella laid down the detail of the work. This included not merely the size but the canvas on which it was to be painted. She carefully instructed Perugino how he was to execute the subject of the work or her 'poetic invention'. He was allowed no licence in the choice of the major figures of Venus, Diana, Pallas and Cupid (*Amore*), or the minor ones, such as Polyphemus, various nymphs, fauns and cupids or a river in the background. The figures were described and their actions specified. Isabella's written instructions were accompanied by a drawing in which her scheme was depicted.

Perugino was allowed to decide the attitude of the minor figures and reduce their number if he considered the painting to be too crowded. In December 1503 he wrote asking Isabella for the size of the figures in the paintings beside which the new commission would be hung. It seemed to him that the figures in the drawing he had been sent were too small in proportion to the size of the proposed painting. Isabella duly sent him the measurements of the figures in Mantegna's adjoining painting in her Grotta.

Isabella had to wait more than two years for the picture and her correspondence in 1505 shows that she was discontented with certain aspects of it. In a letter to Agostino Strozzi (February 1505) she complained that in order 'to display the excellence of his art' Perugino had departed from the drawing by portraying a nude Venus. Strozzi was to prevent further unwelcome licence because 'by altering one figure [Perugino] will pervert the whole sentiment of the fable'. The correspondence closes with a letter dated 30 June 1505 in which Isabella acknowledged receiving the picture, but complained that Perugino had finished it carelessly and that she would have preferred him to have used oils rather than tempera. This complaint had been prompted by a report to her that Perugino, having been slow to complete the painting was doing so finally in a hurry.

The leading part which the patron could take in producing a painting comes across forcibly in these documents. Isabella d'Este laid down the subject, figures, actions and background of her painting. In the event, Perugino did not satisfy her wishes in every particular. He only erred, however, where these wishes had not been put in writing. Venus may have been given clothing in the drawing but neither this nor the paints to be used nor the date of delivery had been specified in the contract. Perugino was either ignorant of Isabella's wishes in these instances or could claim that he was.

In other respects he seems to have been pliant. We have today not only Isabella's letters but the painting which is in the Louvre. An examination of this reveals that Perugino deviated only where he was expressly allowed to do so, by omitting certain minor figures: there is no Polyphemus in the finished work. Perugino appears to have conceded the point about Venus's nudity: she is dressed in a diaphanous gown.

It may seem evident that the patron played the determining role in the production of the *Battle of Chastity and Lasciviousness*. But before agreeing to this conclusion it is necessary to consider the nature of

Perugino's contribution and whence the patron may have derived her own ideas. The letters of Isabella reveal that she contributed the scheme; Perugino provided his skills and style. She had chosen him (and other artists) to execute pictures for her Grotta because they were famous: 'we desire to have in our *camerino* pictures by the excellent painters now in Italy, among whom Perugino is famous'. (Letter to F. Malatesta, 15 September 1502.)

Naturally, she wished for paintings displaying those qualities which had made the artists famous and which were to be seen in their works elsewhere. Isabella's correspondence impresses us with the smallness of the artist's contribution because it takes for granted his skill and style. The latter is presumed, however, in the clause of Isabella's contract with Perugino where the latter 'is obliged to complete the said work himself'.

Isabella had conveyed to Perugino not merely a description of the subject but a drawing. Does this not suggest that the patron helped to shape the very style of the painting? We do not know what was in the drawing, which fails to survive, but there would have been no point in indicating more than the disposition of the main figures, since Isabella had expressly allowed Perugino to decide upon the attitude and number of the minor ones. The drawing probably placed the main figures and showed their clothing and aspect. It is not likely that it was supposed to suggest the style in which they were to be painted for this was precisely what the patron would have expected the artist himself to supply. Moreover, whatever precise role such a drawing was supposed to play, it leads us back to artistic imitation.

It would not have been Isabella who drew the sketch, but some court painter, perhaps that Lorenzo of Mantua whom she tells us had inadvisedly informed Perugino that the Mantegna beside which his painting was to hang had been done in tempera (letter to Perugino, 30 June 1505). The drawing shows not a patron controlling an artist, but one artist influencing another through the medium of the patron. It is possible that the sketcher had devised his drawing in a manner which he knew would be pleasing to Isabella, for instance, by imitating the disposition of the figures in the paintings she possessed by Mantegna. In any case an artist came first.

The classicising turn of Italian art in the fifteenth century did not simply depend upon the tastes of patrons and men of letters. It owed much to artists, who themselves had been influenced by literary fashion, independently pursuing studies of classical art. In fact, it seems likely that Isabella's wish to have painters like Perugino and the Venetian Giovanni Bellini (*c.* 1430–1516) execute pictures on classical subjects sprang from her liking for the classicising paintings of Mantegna at Mantua. The latter seems to have developed his skill in this field independently. According to Vasari, he pursued his own studies of ancient statuary as

Masaccio and Brunelleschi had done before. What we may be observing in the case of Isabella and Perugino is the influence of a great originating artist being passed on to the next generation of artists via the patron. Certainly artists like Mantegna would have 'pursued' their classicising art confident of the classical tastes of their patrons and even intending to please them. Sometimes the efforts of an artist to satisfy his patron were crowned with such success that the patron sought to perpetuate his approach in later commissions. Even then, however, a painter like Perugino would contrive to please the patron by the exercise of his own talents, supplying his style and imaginative conceptions.

What, then, can be concluded from the commissioning of the *Battle of Chastity and Lasciviousness*? The patron planned the work, contracted the artist to paint it and sought to control its execution through her agents. She did not, however, determine the work's final form in that she did not control its most important elements, the skill and style of the artist, which it was her very purpose to possess. Moreover, her own conception of the scheme would in its turn have been fashioned by that court painter who made the sketch for Perugino, and above all from the great example of Mantegna.

So far as famous artists are concerned the case of Perugino and Isabella represents an extreme example of the patron's power. The lives and letters of Giovanni Bellini, Michelangelo and Leonardo all furnish instances of patrons failing to secure their employment or determine the subject of a painting being executed for them, or at least failing to have it finished according to their wishes. If the case of Isabella and Perugino does not demonstrate that the patron determined artistic change, the examples of other famous masters will do so less easily.

The argument advanced here bears some resemblance to the interpretation of Charles Hope (1981). He has suggested that the Perugino commission does not allow us to assume that the patron performed the crucial role. His argument is nevertheless somewhat different to the present one. For Hope, Isabella d'Este 'gave [Perugino] no opportunity to display his talents' (p.308) and to this cause he has attributed the poor quality of the finished painting. His main concern was to show that the relations of Isabella and Perugino were untypical of those of sixteenth-century artists with their patrons. The composition of a work of art was normally determined by purely formal or aesthetic considerations: how to create a good design or achieve mastery of some problem of composition such as in depicting landscape or the human body.

It is surely right to stress that we cannot conclude from the Isabella d'Este and Perugino episode that artistic change or originality were controlled by patrons. According to the view put forward here, even so extreme a case as this commission demonstrates that the artist enjoyed one vital freedom. He supplied his skill and the style in which the picture was to be painted. In short, Perugino did possess an opportunity to display his talent. Given the same constrictions, a very different picture of a battle of Love and Chastity could have been produced by, say, Mantegna, Piero di Cosimo (*c.* 1462–?1521) or Raphael (1483–1520). The corollary of this is that the artist and not the patron must be blamed for any deficiency in the completed work. There will, furthermore, be occasion later to question the proposition that the form of a painting (and the aesthetic concern of the artist) can be separated from its content. Equally, while the humanist may have rarely played a decisive role in artistic production as the adviser to a prince, he or his ideas may have done so more often as an influence on an artist.

The suggestion that Isabella was impressed by Mantegna's work leads us to consider how creative artists were able to persuade their patrons to accept their novelties. Does this not introduce the power of patrons by a different route: were they not the determining agents in that the great achievements of Renaissance art could never have happened without their say-so? The greatest number of original artistic achievements happened in Florence and it was precisely in explanation of them that Wackernagel argued that the crucial factor was the readiness of patrons to co-operate in an artistic project and to tolerate the avant-garde. The case of Florence and the thesis of Wackernagel therefore deserve close scrutiny for the light which they can cast upon the processes of creation in fifteenth-century art.

5. Wackernagel and Florence's contribution to art

Isabella d'Este was commissioning paintings as the wife of a ruler. During the *Quattrocento* there was no one resembling her in Florence in status or power. Nor could court artists be found there of Mantegna's type. Until Cosimo de' Medici (1389–1464) began to commission whole buildings, the great artistic monuments of the city contrasted with princely commissions.

The former were collective undertakings of individual citizens under the aegis of the government (as at the cathedral), or of guilds (in the decoration of Orsanmichele, the communal grain store). Sometimes particular families combined – for instance, in the adornment of the individual chapels within the great mendicant churches of Santa Croce and Santa Maria Novella. Such schemes led Wackernagel to write of Florentine art being produced in response to civic demand, and of the collaboration and tolerance of leading citizens.

However, the buildings of Florence do not entirely show art being brought forth in response to the pressures of demand. Nor does Florentine art suggest that original paintings contravened the wishes of patrons. There must have been demand or no altarpieces or frescoes would have been worked at all. However, even in Florence few great Renaissance buildings and (its cathedral apart) a small number of great architectural monuments were raised. Its achievements, like those of most cities other than Rome, were small-scale and often fragmentary or incomplete. Demand in Florence was not such as to transform the townscape or the interiors of most buildings.

The cathedral took two hundred years to be finished and the façade remained in undressed brickwork down to the nineteenth century. The exterior marble-work around the drum of the cupola, having been criticised by Michelangelo, has remained unfinished. The fronts of Santa Croce, San Lorenzo and Santo Spirito similarly stayed in unclad brick. The marble façade of Santa Maria Novella, on the other hand, was an outstanding achievement of private patronage in the fifteenth century.

It was only in the *Quattrocento* that buildings began to be influenced by the new antique styles, and even then, with very few exceptions, the changes were limited to courtyards, façades, or decorative details such as capitals or a dome. Other than with paintings (mostly altarpieces), there is little evidence of a high *volume* of demand. There are even instances of uncompleted paintings, notably the great battle scenes planned by Leonardo and Michelangelo for the Palazzo Vecchio. Here the Florentine incapacity to undertake, or in this latter case complete, large-scale commissions might suggest an insufficiently strong demand.

Florentine citizens co-operated to embellish certain churches with decorated chapels and façades. Equally, the rivalry between citizens frustrated important commissions. A dispute between Castello Quaratesi and the Calimala Guild over the display of coats of arms ruined the former's plan to finance the construction of a façade for Santa Croce. The failure of citizens to agree wrecked successive schemes for the front of the cathedral. Here was certainly no civic harmony in the services of art.

Political decisions could be damaging. Monies were diverted which had been put aside to carry forward Niccolò da Uzzano's bequest in his will to create a university building. Changes of government in Florence led to the exile of patrons and the destruction of works of art. Palla Strozzi (1372–1462) and Felice Brancacci (*c*. 1382–1449), two leading patrons of their time (respectively of Gentile da Fabriano and Masaccio), were exiled on the coming to power of Cosimo de' Medici in 1434.

Later turmoil produced similar effects. After the Medici had been banished in 1494 some of their art treasures were dispersed and soon Savonarola made a bonfire of profane artistic objects. When the Medici had returned and their own regime experienced difficulties in the 1520s, the Florentine government melted down the silver treasures of the churches and the guilds. Florence even demolished the buildings of the suburbs in a vain attempt to resist the siege of 1529–30. This was not the happy exploitation of a private readiness to give in pursuit of a greater artistic good.

Do such failures, rivalries, exiles, dispersions and conflagrations show that it was rather the limitations of demand which explain the Florentine achievements? There were many small-scale commissions and a paucity of large ones, whilst, in terms of artistic achievements, few great monuments and many innovations. Can all this in its turn be accounted for by the political character of Florence?

Until 1530 no family dominated the state completely enough to have deployed its resources for artistic purposes in the way that happened in the princely states. No buildings or schemes of decoration were completed in Florence on the scale of those of Viscontean Milan or of the principalities like Urbino, Mantua and Rome after 1400. Nevertheless, small proved to be best. The control of resources in the courts enabled the commissioning of larger schemes. It allowed the better exploitation of the talents of a single court artist and the fruition of ideas. However, the courts did not prove equally fertile.

The two great paintings depicting the Florentine battles of Cascina and Anghiari illustrate the frustrated creativity of Florence. They were commissioned in 1503–4 from Michelangelo and Leonardo for the walls of the great hall of the Palazzo Vecchio. Only the cartoons for them (and one scene of the *Battle of Anghiari*) were finished, but their influence was enormous. Michelangelo left his work in order to paint the Sistine Chapel, a more ambitious work than anything he had completed in Florence. Leonardo left for Milan and there he finished works like the *Last Supper*. Yet even those great projects cannot match the originality and influence of the fragmentary Florentine battle scenes, whose remains provided stimulation for later artists. Indeed, Kenneth Clark has claimed that the whole evolution of the classical and romantic traditions in European art derive from this source (K. Clark, 1939, p.126).

The multiplicity of Florentine commissions generated originality whilst the limited size of the commissions produced competition between artists. Vasari recorded that Michelangelo's *Battle of Cascina* was done 'in competition' with Leonardo's *Battle of Anghiari*. He gave other telling examples of this tendency. Brunelleschi had urged that he and Lorenzo Ghiberti (1378–1455) should be given joint charge of the building of the dome of the Florentine cathedral so that each would be encouraged to demonstrate his art in competition for honour and profit (Vasari, ed. Milanesi, ii, 356). On another occasion Donatello wished to return to Florence from Padua, despite the greater praise he was receiving there, because he needed the more critical atmosphere of Florence to inspire his art (ed. Milanesi, ii, 413).

Michelangelo and Leonardo's work in the Palazzo Vecchio suggests that the key feature of the competition may have been the reserving of two walls of the same room to different artists, a fact to be attributed in its turn to the number of the commissioning agents and their relative poverty or modesty. Perhaps a similar competition applied to the 'collaborative' frescoes (*c.* 1484/85) on themes from Greek mythology by Ghirlandaio, Perugino, Botticelli and Filippino Lippi at the lost villa of Lorenzo de' Medici at Spedaletto, near Volterra. No less competitive were the many figure sculptures commissioned by the guilds for external niches on Orsanmichele in the early fifteenth century or the family chapels of Santa Croce and Santa Maria Novella.

The sculptures of Orsanmichele may have been designed for comparison. In the mendicant churches several artists worked alongside one another, or one artist's work could be compared to that of another in an adjoining chapel, or to murals in the nave. Very telling here is the remark of Vasari on Botticelli's portrait of St Augustine for the gallery (*tramezzo*) of the church of Ognissanti. The artist expended great efforts on this painting, 'seeking to surpass . . . Domenico Ghirlandaio who had executed a St Jerome on the other side' (ed. Milanesi, iii, 311).

The special circumstances of 'demand' in Florence therefore influenced its art. The limitation of demand was more important than its extent. But there were other influences at work, including the instability of Florence's ruling class and the slow growth there of an artistic tradition. As everywhere else in northern Italy after 1300, the leading families of Florence displayed a strong desire to legitimatise themselves. However, the strength of the Guelph and Ghibelline polemics in the city throughout the fourteenth century suggests that this wish to be right-thinking as well as lawful was especially strong there (see further below, p. 105).

Florence lacked tradition before 1300, but once a Florentine artistic school had been established in the days of Giotto it took on a life of its own. The stories in the early sources of the famous *Quattrocento* artists who studied Masaccio's frescoes in Santa Maria del Carmine, or of Michelangelo who learnt from Giotto's paintings in Santa Maria Novella, show that this tradition incited creative effort. If these were apocryphal stories they are ones testifying to a belief in a Florentine tradition.

The names supplied by Vasari of masters under whose guidance successive generations of Florentine painters worked reveals the same powerful belief. We can reconstruct from some of these names a family tree extending from Giotto to the High Renaissance; (see Figure 5) but some of this is legend and much of it we cannot corroborate. For all that, it records a truth. There was a peculiar consciousness in Florence of the tradition of studios within which the painters worked. By 1400 this had given a momentum to the development of Florentine art.

Tradition, by definition, cannot account for innovation and attention needs to be paid to the Florentine preparedness to accept it. Wackernagel

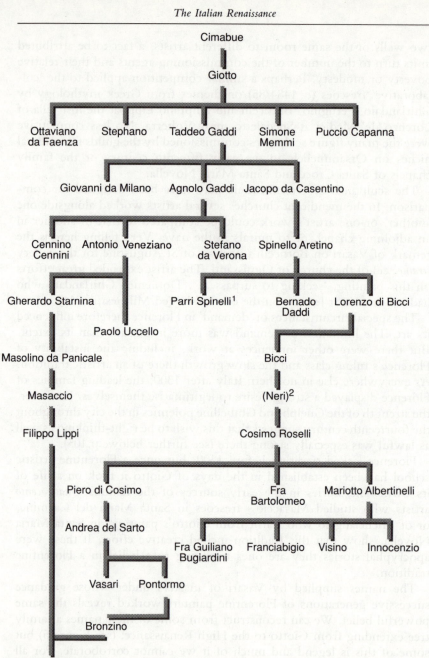

Cimabue

Giotto

Ottaviano da Faenza   Stephano   Taddeo Gaddi   Simone Memmi   Puccio Capanna

Giovanni da Milano   Agnolo Gaddi   Jacopo da Casentino

Cennino Cennini   Antonio Veneziano   Stefano da Verona   Spinello Aretino

Gherardo Starnina   Parri Spinelli[1]   Bernado Daddi   Lorenzo di Bicci

Paolo Uccello

Masolino da Panicale   Bicci

Masaccio   (Neri)[2]

Filippo Lippi   Cosimo Roselli

Piero di Cosimo   Fra Bartolomeo   Mariotto Albertinelli

Andrea del Sarto   Fra Guiliano Bugiardini   Franciabigio   Visino   Innocenzio

Vasari   Pontormo

Bronzino

Raffaellino del Garbo

1 According to Vasari also studied under Ghiberti
2 According to Vasari the brother of Bicci

Fig.5   Florentine painters and their masters (after Vasari)

was surely right to perceive that the novel achievements of Florentine art depended upon their acceptance by patrons and ecclesiastical authorities. It requires, however, to be explained why this happened, and whether Wackernagel was correct in his further observation that innovation was something that patrons (and presumably the authorities also) suffered to allow, since it went against their wishes.

It is possible at once to detect something quite unlikely in this thesis. There was no law compelling a patron to accept a commission against his wishes. One patron might fail to stipulate what he desired, but a second could learn from his mistake. Viewed from the other angle, there would be no incentive to be original (however competitive the situation) if an original work would have gone unappreciated. The artist might have his ears pricked for applause from other hands than those of his patron, but that situation could not have persisted had patrons not valued novelty. There is, besides, little evidence of an opposition of taste between artist and patron. The sources rather emphasise the high status enjoyed by the great artists and the eagerness of patrons to employ their services. In other words, whilst the great innovators may have been in 'advance' of taste, they must have been able to persuade their patrons that the new styles were not merely solutions to artistic problems, but answered to patrons' needs.

Common sense suggests the necessity of this hypothesis, but documents are unhelpful in proving it. Too often they record pious platitudes or generalities. When Giovanni Ruccellai (1403–81), the patron of Alberti, recorded in his family memorial (the *Zibaldone*) that he had enjoyed spending money as a monument to himself and for the honour of God and of the city (*Zibaldone*, ed. Perosa, p. 121) we are left wondering why he felt that unusual buildings and works of art would fulfil this wish better than conventional ones.

Chapter Eight

Artistic Innovation and the Artist's Relations with his Patron

How did the most original artists around 1420 – like Brunelleschi, Donatello and Masaccio – present their innovations to the patron? The early fifteenth century is most revealing, for too little is known of the age of Giotto, and by 1500 so many novelties had been introduced that their acceptance is hardly a problem to be explained. Broadly speaking, there were three different sorts of innovation in this period: changes in technique (as in the use and preparation of materials), in style and in subject-matter.

Around 1400 only the first two changes were to be found. It was not until the later part of the century that iconographical novelties in the form of pagan subjects were being produced by artists like Piero di Cosimo, Mantegna and Filippino Lippi for the villas at Florence or the court at Mantua. Classicism accounts for architectural and sculptural innovations. Knowledge that great domed buildings and free-standing or life-sized sculptures had existed in antiquity explains why Florentine citizens accepted them in the work of Brunelleschi and Donatello. The problem then is to explain why Florentines (whether the patron, public or authorities) welcomed the original painting of Masaccio for which no surviving antique work had prepared them.

Masaccio was original in his technique and also in his style. In respect of the latter, his 'classicising' treatment of architectural backgrounds and details, his use of perspective and his painting of figures were all novel. Masaccio's new technique in mural painting was to abandon the practice of painting on the dry surface for the less usual one of painting directly onto the wet plaster. Some of these changes are easier to explain than others. 'Classicising' details were the fruit of intellectual fashion. The advantages of painting on wet plaster could be readily grasped by patron and artist:

the method enhanced the durability of the painting itself and the speed of its completion.

Perspectival painting, on the other hand, was a dramatic change. To a limited extent Italians were already accustomed to 'illusionism' in art. Ever since the work of Giotto and his contemporaries, visitors to churches had been presented with paintings and mosaics that tried to convey a sense of 'space' through fore-shortening and modelling. To some degree, therefore, Florentines would have been disposed to accept Masaccio's novelties for the same reasons that they would have allowed the more modest sense of space achieved by earlier masters. Nevertheless, the change was very marked and all the more so since there had been something of a retreat from 'illusionism' in the previous three generations.

All the same, Masaccio's *Holy Trinity*, which was the first painting in which mathematical perspective was used, must have been self-evidently appealing to the patron. It formed a part of one of the two types of important family memorials in the great mendicant churches of Florence. There were the chapels of the transepts and the aisles and the family altars in the nave, often bearing family altarpieces or superimposed memorials. Masaccio's *Holy Trinity* is a wall painting above the Cardoni altar in Santa Maria Novella. Such an altar was less prized than a chapel, and it would naturally be very pleasing to a patron if an artist could in any way remedy this deficiency. By his use of perspective, Masaccio offered the illusion that it *was* a chapel: his painted crucifix above the altar was made to seem a real crucifix, suspended in air, with the chapel recessed behind by means of perspective.

What were the attractions of Masaccio's figure painting? He extended 'illusionism' to the central figures of his pictures – to give them a monumental and sculptured quality. Thereby he conveyed the impression that they were living and they were sometimes modelled upon individual Florentines of his day. Would Felice Brancacci, the patron of the frescoes in Santa Maria del Carmine where these novel qualities were strongly set forth, not have been startled to see the apostles bear the countenances of contemporaries and appear mundane? The life of Masaccio is ill recorded, but there is a passage in Vasari's *Life* of the artist (ed. Milanesi, ii, 295) which perhaps records the traditional Florentine reaction to his frescoes. Vasari declared that

> Anyone who does not know St Paul, looking at that [face] will apprehend all they should of Roman civic virtues (*civiltà Romana*) along with the unconquered fortitude of that most devout spirit wholly intent on the nurture of the faith.

Two points emerge from this observation. Masaccio's paintings had a value even for the ignorant and they furnished a better understanding of the

Gospels. Nothing could be more traditional. Paintings were customarily conceived as books of the unlearned conveying a religious message. The pictures of Masaccio then were not thought of as providing solutions to new or to aesthetic problems or conveying new truths about man, society or the ancient world. Rather they taught the old truths better.

The example of Masaccio suggests that the great originators had something to offer to their patrons. Should we go further and conclude that the very originalities of Renaissance art were not merely something that could be made tolerable to patrons, but which had been devised in order to please them? Wackernagel suggested that there was a gulf of taste between patron and 'romantic' artist. In this he was perhaps affected by the so-called 'bourgeois–artist' dualism, to be found amongst the poets and artists of Germany, summed up in the image of Thomas Mann's character Tonio Kröger, an artist returning home to gaze estranged upon the complacent bourgeois he had left behind.

The modern artist is affected by opposite conditions to those which occupied him then. Now the artist is subject to the influence of powerful market forces against which he is inclined to react. The artist may define his artistic objectives by contrast to what is expected of him. Down to the High Renaissance, weak 'market' conditions encouraged the painter and sculptor to attract renown by offering better solutions to his patrons' problems. Thus viewed, the artistic achievements of the Renaissance would be seen less as developments tolerated by patrons, or 'saleable' to them, than ones expressly designed to earn their approval.

Attention, however, had to be won before a work was commissioned. Many of the artists now celebrated as geniuses must have been those original talents who knew how to catch the eye. Not merely flowers but also geniuses are born to 'blush unseen'. Artists had to persuade patrons of the viability of a work, its conformity to their wishes and parry criticism. This required power of argument. There are anecdotes to suggest that the most original artists were the ones who possessed these qualities.

There are two stories of Leonardo persuading Florentine magistrates to allow him to raise up the Baptistery of San Giovanni and divert the course of the river Arno. These are testimonies to his power of argument, especially since, as soon as he had left the room, the officials realised that the Baptistery project was impossible. These were not tricks and deception, or cases where artists were persuading patrons to measures which were contrary to their interests. When artists were successful it was because they had persuaded their patrons that their projects were precisely designed to suit their needs.

Persuasion also involved humour, tact, guile, imagination and honesty. When the king of Naples told Giotto that he would make him the first man in Naples, the artist retorted that he already was since he lived in the first house inside the walls. The conventional taste for the inverting of familiar relationships may be detected here, and even an echo of ancient painters described by Pliny who could speak to emperors as their equals. There is also, however, a hint here of the successful artist knowing how to talk to a patron. The success of other great artists like Mantegna and Giovanni Bellini may have lain in the fact that they knew the nature and limits of their abilities and had the honesty to say so: how, for example, to seek or refuse commissions on classical subjects.

An artist might need guile for his scheme to be accepted. When the consuls of the Cloth Guild in Florence expressed reservations about Donatello's statue of St Mark, the sculptor persuaded them to erect the statue on the understanding that he would re-carve it *in situ*. In due course he displayed it unaltered and convinced all doubters. Donatello appreciated the necessity of deference to the understanding of patrons and knew their actual ignorance. He grasped how differently a statue would look when placed at that height for which it was designed.

Something similar is recorded by Vasari of Michelangelo's giant statue of David. The chief Florentine magistrate, who had commissioned it, criticised the nose and the artist pretended to re-work it. He dropped dust through his hand, chiselling the air and the complacent patron declared himself content. More telling perhaps is the story of how Brunelleschi convinced Giovanni de' Medici that he should rebuild the whole church of San Lorenzo. Brunelleschi is said to have remarked (ed. Milanesi, ii, 369):

> I am amazed that you, being a leader (*capo*) do not order the spending of a few thousand scudi and build the body of the church . . . if [the noble families of the neighbourhood] saw you begin they would follow with their chapels; especially since when no other memorial remains of us but ruins, they bear witness to the man who built them (*di chi n'è stato autore*) hundreds or thousands of years before.

This was itself artistry. Here were reasons to convert Giovanni, and ones which he could use to persuade lesser patrons to participate. These arguments, like the best rhetoric, also contained a compelling truth. If Giovanni undertook the commissioning not of a part of the church in alliance with other local families as was customary, but of the whole structure, then those other families would be compelled to join in Giovanni's scheme. Such families would be established in a new relationship to the Medici not as their equals but with Giovanni as *capo*. This was the time when the Medici were establishing their power in Florence and to the front amongst their supporters were the leading families of their quarter of the city. Here are to be found two of the most celebrated departures from tradition in architecture – the commissioning of a whole church by a single lay patron and a new style in which it was built – which were solutions devised by the artist to the problems of the patron.

Yet the artists of the time did not conceive themselves as the subservient supporters of a patron, nor vie with each other to be ever more useful to him. Whilst it is an error to see the artist as a figure isolated from society, he came, from the middle of the fourteenth century, to offer something on his own terms to which the patron must respond. The Renaissance artist supplied the needs and solved the problems of his patrons, but he stood a little apart from them.

In itself the imagination required by the artist to capture his patrons' attention by devising solutions to their problems set him aloof and conferred a certain identity. Perhaps it enhanced artistic self-respect or a notion of power. Whatever the reason, from *c.* 1350 traces are to be found of an idea of the artist distinct by life-style and sentiment from the countryman, artisan or unfeeling merchant. This is separate from the slow enhancement of the artist's status. It was a distinctness in the artist's 'self-idea', which set him a little apart from the vulgar herd, and which may have prepared the way for his social advance.

Manetti's *Life* of Brunelleschi attributed the success of Brunelleschi and Masaccio whilst in Rome to the fact that neither had family cares, paid attention to what they ate or how they dressed. Vasari observed that Donatello cared nothing for money, keeping it in a basket in his studio where it was regularly pilfered. This carelessness was shared by the fourteenth-century painter Bufalmacco who was accustomed to squandering the money he had earned.

Such artists also felt themselves apart. Sacchetti and Vasari have preserved accounts of incidents in which Giotto and Bufalmacco ridiculed insensitive or vulgar patrons. A petty individual (described as a man 'of little account' and 'a rough artisan' (*grossolano artefice*)) asked Giotto to paint a shield for him bearing his coat of arms. Giotto, believing the man to possess none, painted ridiculous objects and, following litigation, won his point, although the customer was made to pay less for the shield than Giotto had demanded (Novella 63).

Vasari has two stories of Bufalmacco ridiculing countrymen (*contadini*) who failed in different ways to appreciate the value of his art. One ordered a painting too large for its location, and the artist bent the legs of his figures to accommodate them. Another rustic neglected to pay for the Virgin and Child which he had ordered until Bufalmacco turned the child into a bear, whereupon the patron was brought to heel.

There are parallels here to Vasari's tale of a dispute about a bronze head made by Donatello for a Genoese merchant. Cosimo de' Medici, who had arranged the commission, mediated, but when he sought to raise the price towards that demanded by Donatello, the Genoese remarked that since Donatello had completed the work in a month, the price would represent a payment of more than a florin per day. On hearing this, Donatello seized the head and hurled it from the battlements of the Medici Palace to the street beneath. Deeply insulted, the sculptor declared that the merchant was the sort of man who could wreck a year's work in a single second, understanding better how to deal in beans than in bronzes, and he refused to re-do the head for double the price.

A number of points emerge from these anecdotes. There is the fiction that art has a price and yet is beyond price. Money is to the fore in all these stories. The last episode proclaimed the conceit of Donatello (or of Vasari) that, as an artist, he did not care for this world. All these stories concern disputes over the asking price for works of art. Arguably, prices were too high, for Giotto was awarded less than he had asked, whilst Cosimo was seeking a compromise which would have fallen short of Donatello's bill.

There is a social dimension: the artists' adversaries were rustic or contemptible. It would, however, be false to see these as expressly social conflicts. The artists curried favour with the great, and poured contempt upon the little men. It was because of the manner in which these rude patrons approached the artist that injury was done and ridicule returned. They insulted because they presumed to judge art as a mercenary object. We are not dealing here with cases of social solecism: 'nice people don't mention money'. What was wrong was not the mentioning of money, but the *judging* of the work in terms of it. What made Donatello angry was the suggestion that his work should be measured according to the industry he had expended upon it. Why should that mean 'ruining a year's work in a single second'? Donatello was not disputing the fact that the head had taken a month's work. He seems to have been implying that this was to ignore what today we would call the 'hidden costs'. The work had taken far longer in gestation than in its birth. It took, as it were, eleven months to prepare and one month to make.

To judge the work of art by the time spent on its construction was to ignore the intellectual preparation and the artist's skill, and so demean his art. The presuming of knowledge by the ignorant was also the fault of one of Bufalmacco's rustics, who commissioned paintings for walls too small. The sins of Giotto's artisan were social, but there is also something of the same faulty assumption of the artist's ignorance or compliance. The point of the story was that these elements were reversed: Giotto understood his art and the worth of his patron better than the latter understood the artist or his own worth.

The artist therefore saw himself as more than an artisan. This improved idea of himself had a social aspect. Perhaps the artist may have considered that he was 'better' than artisans in status as he was better than them in his art. Certainly there is an implication that the social betters of artisans would appreciate art as the vulgar would not. The idea begins to form in our minds at this juncture that the impudence and even 'bohemianism' of Renaissance artists may sometimes have been a ploy whereby to gain the attention of patrons. By pleading unworldliness they could call on the latter's concern and encourage their largesse. By being unpredictable they could enlarge their freedom of manoeuvre. The story of Cosimo de' Medici's attempts to shut Filippo Lippi in his house and how the latter escaped to pursue his amorous pranks, until Cosimo realised that genius could not be 'contained', may be interpreted in this way. Being 'difficult' was also a way of stealing attention from rival artists, courtiers and men of letters.

The anecdotes recorded by Vasari of other-worldly artists are not just good stories or literary stereotypes. Behind them did not lie many ancient models. Pliny's accounts of Apelles and Protogenes almost certainly did strengthen bohemianism (see below, p. 93) but they fell on fertile ground. This was formed by the sudden rise in the great artist's position and the competitive struggle he experienced to achieve commissions. From Bufalmacco via Donatello, Brunelleschi and Filippo Lippi to Cosimo Roselli and Leonardo da Vinci, it was in competitive Florence that these tendencies were chiefly observed.

'Attention seeking' cannot be separated from creative endeavour. Competition led also to innovation in order to please patrons. Innovation required imagination; imagination needed study and reflection. This involved solitude which bred absent-mindedness (cf. R. Wittkower, 1961). As we have seen, innovation also required artists to persuade patrons of the value of innovations.

In passing we notice how these innovators were from unusual backgrounds. Donatello had been brought up in the home of the Martelli family, associates of the Medici. Brunelleschi and Leonardo were sons of notaries. Did these connections enable them to speak the 'same language' as their patrons? It would have given them the *savoir-faire* to know which arguments would convince and how to be agreeable. Sometimes it afforded them other skills: Leonardo was a musician and Michelangelo a poet and, according to tradition, it was owing to his musical talent that Leonardo was invited to the court of Milan.

Relative privilege describes the position of these great artists. They were of higher birth than many lesser artists, but they were not rich, nor did they spring from the ruling class. They had access to it whilst they were able to draw on the more sedentary skills of the studios and workshops. They did, however, depart from tradition by their receptiveness to new ideas. Here their advantaged position was crucial because it allowed them to undertake 'research'. Manetti informs us that Brunelleschi was able to sell a small farm in order to pursue his studies in Rome. The ability to spend time improving their skills was a necessity in the formation of creative artists.

The painter and sculptor wished to have their art recognised and enjoy respect for the knowledge which lay behind it. If these were withheld the artist could ridicule the patron. Bufalmacco's painting of the Virgin's bear suggests that honour was conferred upon the patron either by the right relationship with the artist or by the commissioning of the appropriate work of art itself. Yet it is not self-evident why a ridiculous and indeed sacrilegious picture should have brought ignominy upon the patron rather than upon the artist. The implication is that a work of art was thought to be the patron's, in the sense that he had conceived it, whether by devising its scheme or by the appropriate rapport with an artist.

Renaissance art, therefore, was the outcome of a subtle relationship between artist and patron. It was not produced by the romantic artist isolated from society, whose values and tastes he defied; nor yet by the command and determining control of patrons. Rather it sprang from the artist's understanding of the needs and wishes of his patrons. That understanding, however, was only possible if the right relationship existed between the two.

What this was is indicated by a story of Giotto's relations with the papal court. The Pope had sent a courtier to seek examples of work from painters in Siena and Florence. Giotto, without mechanical aid, drew him a perfect circle. The courtier believed that Giotto was poking fun at his enquiries, but the artist urged him to send the drawing to Rome and see if it was understood. In the event the Pope and courtiers with 'understanding' (*cortigiani intendendi*) appreciated how far Giotto surpassed the other artists of his time.

Knowledge came to form the common ground where patron and artist could meet, and before long that became a self-conscious understanding: the notion of the connoisseurship of 'fine' art. Thus Vespasiano da Bisticci observed of Niccolò Niccoli that he

> not only favoured men of letters but he had an understanding of painting, sculpture and architecture, in all of which he had the most complete knowledge. And he lent the greatest favour to the work of Pippo di Ser Brunellesco, Donatello, Luca della Robbia, Lorenzo di Bartoluccio and with all of them he was very intimate. He had a universal knowledge in all fine things ('*cose degne*') on account of the universal judgement he possessed of them.
>
> (*Le vite*, ed. A. Greco, ii, 237)

Niccoli's attitude is also interesting as showing that the idea of connoisseurship and 'art for art's sake' began early. In fact, it went back (like so much else in the Italian Renaissance) to Petrarch a century before. In his will (drawn up in 1370) Petrarch bequeathed a painting of the Virgin by Giotto to the lord of Padua remarking that 'the ignorant do not understand the beauty of this panel, but the masters of art are stupified by its beauty'(para. 12: Mommsen, 1957, pp. 78–80). There was in fact a widespread attitude, shared by writers and intellectuals in the fourteenth century, that the finer points of art could only be appreciated by the learned or the wise (cf. Larner, 1969).

The artist's 'art' became the meeting-ground of artist and patron. It was fashioned by the former's talent for pleasing his patron and by the latter's appreciation that artistic skill was the appropriate standard by which to estimate the value of art. Connoisseurship suited the vanity of patron and artist alike. It proved to the former that he was 'getting his money's worth'. It accorded with the latter's 'self-idea' that he was more than an artisan. His rewards, however, were the less than fine ones of money and status.

Artistic innovation emerged immediately from the right rapport between artist and patron, but this was shaped by the ideas influencing them. The essential thing was the freedom allowed the artist and, as we have seen, the avenue to this was that the artist's mind should be taken seriously. The names of Petrarch and Niccoli suggest that it was intellectuals who mediated this to the two parties. In tracing the origin of this decisive change it will be necessary to leave the familiar territory of artist and patron for the history of ideas, especially ancient ideas which were coming into vogue.

The ability of poets and *literati* to perceive an intellectual quality in works of the great artists partly arose because they were responsible for it. The lives of fourteenth-century artists are ill recorded, but several of the most original painters and sculptors were open to intellectual influence. According to the tradition received by Vasari, Dante had suggested the schemes for Giotto's paintings at Assisi, Naples and Ravenna. Ambrogio Lorenzetti studied letters, was friends with learned men and was a 'gentleman and philosopher' more than a painter. Petrarch consorted with Simone Martini and commissioned work from him. Brunelleschi, Donatello and Masaccio in the early fifteenth century were closely associated with the humanists.

In some of these cases, moreover, there is the possibility of a connection between the artistic novelties and the ideas of the poets and philosophers. The originality of Donatello, Brunelleschi and Masaccio partly lay in the classicising character of their work, and this was inspired by the ideas current in the humanist circles with which they associated (perhaps in Masaccio's case directed via the example and work of Donatello). Piero della Francesca (1410/20–92) and Mantegna were influenced by Alberti's theory of composition. Simone Martini and Lorenzetti furnish the first known instances respectively of portraiture and landscape painting produced since the ancient world. Martini's portrait had been done for Petrarch, and we may suspect in Lorenzetti's landscape the influence of 'learned' men.

By the *Quattrocento* artists were seeing themselves as intellectuals. Cennino Cennini wrote that they should imitate philosophers and theologians; Alberti said that they should associate with orators and poets; Leonardo da Vinci declared that painting was philosophy. Some aspects of the intellectual quality attributed to artists arose from obvious causes. Study was required to imitate Roman work and understand the anatomy of animals. Intelligence was needed to execute more formal notions of design. The research that prepared the way for perspective involved a considerable knowledge of mathematics. Far more important than any of this, however, were ancient traditions. These had a powerful effect both upon the artist and the patron. They led the artist to develop his imaginative faculties and the patron to conceive it as his duty to commission works of art for the public good. Therefore, whilst art developed as the artist sought to please his patrons, intellectual traditions were influencing both parties.

Chapter Nine

The Influence of Humanistic Ideas

1. Ancient rhetorical ideas

Creative artists advanced their skills in the Renaissance as they grasped that material effects reflected invisible forms. Action, gesture and expression flowed from the soul of the individual concerned, whether the subject was the Virgin Mary, a saint, a contemporary individual or a battle scene. This perception was believed to spring from the artist's power of self-scrutiny and his capacity to project himself into the soul of his subject. It was not theorists, but imaginative artists like Raphael and Leonardo who recorded their belief in these ideas. They derived ultimately from the Ciceronian idea of *phantasia* (*fantasia* in Italian) and the notion - preserved by Cicero - that the artist could perceive the mind of the gods.

A letter of Raphael refers to his conceiving of a painting as an idea within him: 'certa idea che mi viene alla mente' (Bottari, 1757, i. 83). This notion, as it might be called, of the birth of the picture in the soul, implied a subjective view of the act of creation. Before the date of Raphael's letter, a still more personal view had been expressed by Leonardo. He was fond of the dictum 'every painter paints himself'.

He was alluding in an idiosyncratic way to the artist's capacity for self-esteem (M.Kemp, 1976, pp.311–23). The formula is first recorded in a collection of aphorisms some generations earlier when it was attributed to Cosimo de' Medici (A.Wesselsky, 1929, p.150). It probably owed its origin to Ficino's Neo-Platonism and at first it was understood to mean that a painting expressed the soul of the artist (A.Chastel, 1959, pp.102–4). All these expressions, however, show that by the early sixteenth century the work of art was thought to exist first in the artist's mind.

Whence had this idea originated? One element was artistic practice itself and the pursuit of originality. Another was imagination: to envisage how a scene might be and how that fantasy could be given material form. Imagination called for solitude: thus Michelangelo walked in the hills of Carrara and Leonardo in the Alps. *Fantasia* was also a specific idea with a pedigree.

The idea has been followed from the poetry of Dante to its first significant re-appearance in the treatise on art by Filarete. It can be traced in the works of Francesco di Giorgio and Francesco Colonna before it became more common around 1500. It has been argued that it was not until Neo-Platonism became widespread that the idea of *fantasia* or the more general notion of the artist as a divinely inspired genius attained currency (Kemp, 1977). The conjunction of Dante's idea of poetry with Neo-Platonism produced a strong current in the *Quattrocento*. Yet *fantasia* had not been forgotten since Dante's time. Italian intellectuals did not need to await Neo-Platonist writings for an idea of the artist as the beneficiary of divine inspiration.

Dante's legacy and classical ideas of the artist were already influential in the early *Quattrocento*. Boccaccio in his *Life* of Dante described the poet abandoning the sublime *fantasia* of the *Divine Comedy* – by which he meant its lofty poetic conception – and later resuming that *fantasia* (ed. A. Solerti, p.57). In this same work Boccaccio set forth the divine character of sculpture and painting. Sculpture had arisen, he said, in an effort to portray the divine essence. Zeuxis had formed in his mind a true image of Helen, which 'so far as art is able to follow genius' he had contrived to paint. In this passage he also likened the fine arts to poetry.

Elsewhere Boccaccio claimed that Giotto had revived the ancient idea of painting which, like poetry, appealed to the mind. This comparison of painting and poetry was to be taken up by Alberti (*De Pittura*, ed. C. Grayson, p. 104) and later commentators. The analogy hints at Boccaccio's source, which was the comparison of the two disciplines in Cicero, Seneca and Horace. An instance of this has been quoted from Aulus Gellius (see above, p. 16). Horace's famous view of the two arts is summed up in the oft-quoted phrase *ut pictura poesis*. It was, however, Cicero and the Elder Seneca who produced a theory emphasising the elevated nature of art and the divine character of the artist. Each of them praised the Greek sculptor Phidias for his capacity to give birth in his soul to the idea of his subject (*Controv.*, 10.5.8):

Phidias did not see Jove; he made him, however, as the Thunderer; Minerva did not stand before his eyes; his soul, however, was worthy (*dignus*) of that art and conceived the gods' appearance in his mind and exhibited them.

Three elements can be discerned in this judgement: the 'worth' of the painter, the grandeur of his subject and the conception of that subject in the painter's soul. Another dimension is added to them by remarks in the rhetorical writings of Cicero and Quintilian, such as Cicero's *Orator*, (ii, 8–iii, 10):

> Writing of that kind is so beautiful that it is not outshone . . . by that which it expresses as is an image (*imago*) by the face. It cannot be perceived either by the eyes, the ears or by any of the senses, but thought and mind can grasp it. Thus with the likenesses of Phidias (of which we have seen nothing more perfect of the kind) and with those paintings I have named we can however conceive of something more beautiful. Indeed that artist when he was sculpting the form of Jove or Minerva did not look at any person from whom he drew a likeness, but in his mind there dwelt the very form (*species*) of beauty itself and thus fixed and intent he directed his hand to create the likeness. These forms of things are called 'ideas' . . . by Plato; these, he says, always exist and do not change . . . therefore whatever is to be examined by means of reason and disputation must be related to the ultimate form and species of a thing.

The artist was therefore attributed a visionary character by Cicero as one who could penetrate the flux of things to the ultimate forms represented by divine ideas. Italians of the *Trecento* and *Quattrocento* did not need to await Neo-Platonism for a notion of the visionary artist working under divine inspiration.

These influences were strengthened in the fifteenth century by Neo-Platonism. Plato himself had belittled art as imitating a semblance of reality. But Plotinus, the greatest of his later followers, had a very different idea. For him the artist contained within him a spark of the Divine Soul and so could reproduce its beauty (*Enneads*, V, viii, 1). Neo-Platonist ideas on art may have reached Florence in the early fifteenth century. There is a passage suggesting this in a letter of Chrysoloras, the Byzantine scholar, who introduced Greek studies to the early humanists of Florence. He invoked the artist's soul which enabled him to reproduce in inanimate form an image of another soul (*phantastikon*). Is this not the Platonising idea of *fantasia*? (cf. Baxandall, *JL. Warburg and Courtauld Institutes* (1965), 197–8; (1971) 82, 151).

Ancient ideas helped also by furnishing aids to the practice of imagination. There is a passage in Quintilian which shows that the key to this development lay in the imaginative skills taught by the ancient orators as well as in the theory of *fantasia*. Quintilian wrote that the power to conjure up distant objects could be achieved by harnessing the day-dream:

> . . . when for example while the mind is unoccupied, and we are indulging in chimerical hopes and dreams, as of men awake, the images of which I am speaking beset us so clearly that we seem to be on a journey, on a voyage, in a battle, to be haranguing assemblies of people, to dispose of wealth we do not possess, and not to be thinking but acting, shall we not turn this lawless power of our minds to our advantage? To make a complaint that a man has been murdered shall I not bring before my eyes everything that is likely to have happened when the murder occurred? Shall not the assassin suddenly sally forth? Shall not the other tremble, cry out, supplicate or flee? Shall I not behold the one striking, the other falling? Shall not the blood, and paleness and last gasp of the expiring victim present itself fully to my mental view? Here will result that . . . 'illustration' and evidentness which seems not so much to narrate as to exhibit, and our feelings will be moved not less strongly than if we were actually present at the affairs of which we are speaking.

(Ars Orat., VI, ii, 29, tr. J.S. Watson)

Together with the notion of *fantasia* this rhetorical stress upon the power of imaginative sympathy was the chief intellectual source for the enhanced idea of the artist's worth and the associated notion that he was a visionary. The altered idea of the artist is first to be seen amongst patrons, but from the start their attitudes influenced artists to whom they communicated them. Moreover, it is possible that this ancient theory of imagination developed the artist's actual imagination.

One particular ancient author, whose writings deeply affected the attitude of Petrarch and later humanists towards art, was Pliny whose *Natural History* contained chapters on art. Cicero, the Elder Seneca, Quintilian and Plotinus furnished a lofty and vague idea of the artist; Pliny produced a more specific and thorough-going account which was widely read in the fifteenth century. It was down to earth and yet it stressed the reverence held in antiquity for painting and sculpture and the capacity of the Greek artist to see into the mind of his subject.

2. Pliny

The interest in Pliny's account of ancient art had been quickened by Petrarch; and in the *Quattrocento* the text became widely used by the humanists. Pliny did not suggest that the artist could penetrate the mind of the gods, but he did show how he could reveal the soul. Pliny recorded the notion (first attributed to Socrates) that the painter and sculptor perceived and depicted the soul through their observation and reproduction of the human face. It was probably from reading the *Natural History* that the Renaissance was made familiar with it. Pliny also illustrated how the artist could ennoble human life. In addition, the *Natural History* supplied examples of the high prestige enjoyed by the Greek artists, the 'intellectual' conception of ancient art and a certain idea of the artist set apart from ordinary folk.

Many stories are told in the *Natural History* of artistic monuments erected to celebrate the gods or public heroes such as athletes, generals and tyrannicides, or else to mark the conquests of cities. Conversely, criticisms are recorded by Pliny of artists working for the adornment of private palaces (*N.H.*, xxxv, 119), and of rulers like the Emperor Tiberius who bore off public works of art to decorate his own apartments (xxxiv, 62–3; cf. xxxv, 26).

Pliny showed the artist's capacity to see into the mind of man and humanise him as well as celebrate his 'public' role. The tyrant Phalaris, who had employed a bronze-founder to cast a bull as an instrument of torture, had, for Pliny, degraded 'the most human art' (xxxiv, 89). This 'humanity' is another name for the 'naturalism' of Greek artists recorded by Pliny. Their perception of the soul was also praised. Aristides of Thebes had been the first 'to paint the soul' and express the emotions (xxxv, 88). For similar reasons Euphranor's portrait of Paris was revered (xxxi, 77):

> . . . it may be grasped from it at once how he was the judge of
> the goddesses, the lover of Helen and the slayer of Achilles.

This is close to Boccaccio's judgement of the achievement of Phidias.

The stories in Pliny of the artists' fame are, however, what caught the eye of artists and patrons of the fifteenth century. There are many anecdotes of the good relations enjoyed by artists with Greek rulers or Roman emperors. Often repeated in the Renaissance was the account of the intimacy of Apelles with Alexander the Great. Apelles alone was commissioned to paint Alexander's portrait and he was given his master's mistress as a gift. Apelles was also allowed licence, ordering Alexander to be silent when he spoke of things of which he was ignorant (xxxiv, 85–7).

The idea that the artist was an intellectual set apart from his fellows helps to account for the high esteem enjoyed by famous artists in the ancient world. Painting and sculpture were perceived to be a theoretical 'art'. Phidias had been the first to demonstrate the *ars* of sculpture (xxxiv, 34–35) and Polycletus brought sculpture to a theoretical level (xxxiv, 56). There was knowledge in the 'art' which could be extracted from it. Thus Pomphilus was celebrated as the first artist to achieve perfection in all fields of knowledge including mathematics, without which mastery of the fine arts could not be attained (xxxv, 78).

Conversely, unfinished works were valued more highly than completed ones; this was partly because the artist's intentions could be readily glimpsed in them (xxxv, 145). The practice of art therefore involved induction: from his observations the artist induced certain laws or rules; these he embodied in the work of art. Polycletus executed a certain statue known as the Canon, 'seeking the elements of art from it as from a certain law and he was the only man judged to have made his *ars* in an actual work of art' (xxxiv, 55).

Artists were esteemed partly because they were seen as intellectuals: their's was an 'art' precisely because intelligence could be observed in it. Fame was also associated with the idea that the artist must be accepted (by implication revered) as living on a plane of his own. In this realm he was immune to ordinary appetites and fears. Apelles was allowed to silence the irascible Alexander the Great and Protogenes lived on lupin seeds whilst engaged on a commission. Once he continued painting amidst a besieging army around his native city (xxxv, 102–5).

Artists sometimes affected to believe that their paintings were priceless: Zeuxis gave away some of his works because they were beyond price (xxxv, 62). This aloofness was a pose: even Apelles and Protogenes were subject to the whims and loyalties of their fellow countrymen and their works did have a price, as they well appreciated. Pliny informs us that Zeuxis amassed great wealth by selling those paintings which he did not give away (ibid.). Nevertheless, artists were accepted as breakers of convention: as bohemians at court and as defiers of the normal rules of good behaviour.

There are many elements here which were transmitted to Renaissance Italy. At the heart of them is an idea of the artist enjoying favour with the powerful and set apart by knowledge and disposition. There was not, in Pliny, the idea of the artist as a visionary – which is to be encountered in Cicero and Seneca – but his artists saw truths hidden from ordinary folk. This helped to forge the divine notion of the artist current in the Renaissance just as much as the more grandiose ideas of the rhetoricians.

In Renaissance Italy did these ideas supply something that was lacking or enforce existing traditions? Were they decisive in giving birth to a new idea of art or merely adjuncts to experience, justifying – even limiting – what was already observed? The most authoritative treatment of humanist conceptions of art, Michael Baxandall's *Giotto*

93

and the Orators (1971), firmly opts for the latter view. Beginning from certain assumptions about language, Baxandall insists that language is 'a conspiracy against experience . . . being a collective attempt to simplify and arrange experience into manageable parcels' (p.44). In this scheme of things art is and was an expression of experience: most Renaissance artists were influenced not so much by ancient texts as by 'visual things' (p.133). At the same time, Baxandall has collected an impressive body of material concerning the lively understanding by the humanists of the ancient idea of art and he acknowledges their revival of the 'facilities' and 'possibilities' of ancient aesthetics (pp.6–7,116–20).

The premise that language limits experience can be debated. If we assume that language is a vehicle of thought rather than a determinant of it, can we not make better sense of the material gathered by Baxandall and recognise the influence of ideas upon Renaissance artists? Few artists were probably influenced directly by texts or by 'grammar'; their ambitions may nonetheless have been deeply touched by ideas. Artists, humanists and everyone learn from experience and that knowledge is limited by language. We learn from experience because we think, and we think because we *have* language. Without the latter it is not possible to think or learn from experience, except following the manner of Pavlov's dogs. This is a necessity from which none can escape. What particular ideas shaped the thinking and art of Renaissance painters and sculptors is feebly recorded.

Certainly it is not likely that there were many artists who were directly familiar with the niceties of humanist thought. Mantegna and Piero della Francesca may have been affected by Alberti's theory of composition. These, however, are telling names, being those of two of the most original artists of the fifteenth century. It is those men, very few in number, on whom attention should be focussed. It was the original discoveries of such creative talents which gave Renaissance art its importance. Brunelleschi, Alberti, Piero della Francesca and Leonardo in his later years, may have read humanist texts. More often they and their like would have known of ideas at second hand, because they were the friends of humanists. Mantegna was acquainted with Alberti, and Luca della Robbia, Ghiberti and Donatello with Niccolò Niccoli. It is equally noticeable how frequently the original artists of the *Quattrocento* worked for patrons who were protagonists of humanist ideas. Mantegna worked for the cultivated Gonzaga dukes Ludovico (1412–78), Federigo (1441–84) and Gianfrancesco II (1440–90), whilst Leonardo was in the service of the humanist prince Lodovico Sforza (1452–1508), and Verrocchio and Botticelli undertook commissions for Lorenzo de' Medici (1449–92) and his cousin Pierfrancesco de' Medici (1430–76), both devotees of Neo-Platonist culture.

Did such *avant-garde* patrons tolerate the artistic novelties or influence them? Painters and sculptors like Simone Martini, Gentile da Fabriano, Masaccio and Donatello had the opportunity to learn from Petrarch, Palla Strozzi, Cosimo de' Medici, Niccolò Niccoli, and their like, an idea of the awe in which famous artists had been held in ancient Greece. What could be more flattering than that princes and patricians were interested in their work? In an annotation to his copy of Pliny, Petrarch compared the respect accorded Simone Martini in his own day to the favours given Apelles in ancient times (M. Baxandall, 1971, p.62). Petrarch is likely to have passed on this absorbing thought to Simone Martini whom he employed. He must have communicated also a sense of that intellectual importance he attributed to art which he expressed in many passages of his writings. He did, after all, employ Martini for purposes central to his work, and it was Martini who executed a likeness of Laura for the completion of which he said the artist must have visited Paradise (see above, p. 44).

Did this serious regard not make artists serious about their own craft and derive rules from their personal practice? This is surely a reason why artists from Cennino Cennini via Ghiberti to Filarete and Leonardo themselves began to compose treatises on it. Petrarch, a humanist who was also a patron of art, and Alberti, a humanist who was an artist, had a special importance in disseminating ideas to the artistic world. Petrarch had given currency to a general sense of the importance of the artist. Alberti transmitted to Mantegna and Piero della Francesca an idea of composition.

The most important conception conveyed to artists was *fantasia*, which patrons and their advisers would have found in Cicero. The notion fell on the fertile ground of the prevailing religious character of art. Religious teaching had already encouraged the imaginative power of the artist. *Fantasia* offered a theoretical defence of imagination, while Pliny and the ancient biographers showed how gestures could indicate the soul or character of the subject. The ancient rhetoricians further revealed how it was possible to nurture the power of the imagination to reconstruct scenes. This was a potent stimulus to the development of portraiture and dramatic representation of every kind.

The revival of the ancient idea of the imaginative artist is an *explanation* of the original achievements of Renaissance art. It was not a literary *trope* and it was shared by artists themselves. Many of the most novel creations in the fields of sculpture and painting were made possible by the artist learning how to perceive the soul animating the body. This process was helped by the revival of ancient ideas of imagination. Classical *fantasia* supplied the stimulating notion that imagination afforded not fictionalised semblances of reality, but real images falling from without.

Ancient ideas therefore affected the act of creation by opening eyes and suggesting possibilities. They taught patrons and the public to have regard for the intentions of the artist and to show themselves worthy of the latter. At the same time the artist learnt how to develop his imagination. Those classical sources had a power of suggestion that is indicated by a comparison of certain passages in Pliny and Vasari. Vasari's account, for instance, of the unfinished statues of Michelangelo for Julius II's tomb, and that of the admiration for the drawing by Leonardo for the never-to-be-completed *Battle of Anghiari*, echo Pliny's remarks concerning the high value set in antiquity upon unfinished works of art.

Equally influential were Plinian stories suggesting that the patron was worthy of the artist. This was to be inferred from the relations of Apelles with Alexander the Great, or of Cteticles with Queen Stratonike. Having been received by the queen without honour, Cteticles painted her in bed with a fisherman who was said to be her lover (xxxv, 140).

There is a revealing instance of how the creativity of Michelangelo was shaped by such ideas. Several of the great artists, like Leonardo and Michelangelo, sought solitude to develop their imagination. Vasari remarked how in the hills of Carrara Michelangelo saw his statues yet imprisoned in the rock. The story is similar to one recorded by Cicero about Praxiteles and makes one think that ancient ideas had shaped Vasari's story. In *De Divinatione* Cicero declared that the famous heads by Praxiteles were not created by chance because they lay already within the unhewn blocks of stone in the quarries of Chios. All Praxiteles did was to chip away at the stone; he did not add anything to it (II, xxi, 48–9).

Yet is this any more than one of so many reminiscences of antiquity scattered through Renaissance letters? It is not a literary *trope*, for the story is not told by Vasari of other sculptors nor is it a manifest fabrication because Michelangelo did seek solitude and visited the quarries at Carrara. Perhaps it is a simple truth. Inspired by the ancient theory of imagination, Michelangelo did conceive within him images of what he took to lie within the rock. Together with the practice of imagination recommended by the ancient orators, this enhanced the artist's ability to conceive the soul behind the face, to imagine how the body might look when animated by great thoughts or (less often) when deflated by misery or death.

Renaissance art, therefore, developed in the fifteenth and sixteenth centuries as artists sought to please patrons, and the latter contributed 'space' so that the former could hone that skill whose exercise was their ultimate satisfaction. This common ground constituted the connoisseurship of art, whereby each party could claim immunity from those material considerations which partly moved them. The claim to appreciate art as an end in itself suited well the needs both of patron and artist, and owing to this the notion found a home.

Intellectuals were given the opportunity to become the orchestrators of religious art and cast themselves as the interpreters and even 'spiritual directors' of the artist. Previously the painter had listened to the cleric and the friars; now he would be guided by the poet and philosopher. Probably intellectuals perceived that they were laying claim to the role of the friar. Afterwards it was to be friars (notably San Bernardino and Savonarola) who would prove the loudest critics of the art produced under the new direction. Intellectuals could furnish artists with programmes for their paintings, especially for the classical subjects which began to be fashionable in the fifteenth century. They could provide a theory to explain the work of the artist and interpret it to the patron. Above all they enhanced the belief that the artist purveyed truth. By this means intellectuals made themselves indispensable to both.

It is easier to understand why artists and intellectuals should have propagated this notion than why patrons received it. Intellectual worth was a notion by which the low-born artist could close the gap with grand patrons and command the latter's respect. The work of art was to be worthy of the patron and the latter deserving of art. Here intellectual and social snobbery were conjoined. Claiming that paintings were to be judged in terms of ideas rather than money appealed to the intellectual snobbery of high-born patrons and at the same time secured respect from them whilst it disciplined the socially unacceptable patron. The story of Bufalmacco bending the legs of figures in a fresco commissioned by a rustic who had insisted on dimensions too large for the room, shows that works of art were conceived as testimonies to the worth of a patron. This assumption is necessary to explain why such a painting brought disgrace upon the patron rather than the artist.

This was why intellectuals and artists advertised the value of art. Humanist interests touched patrons also and this made intellectual snobbery a successful way to impress a patron. But snobbery is an insufficient reason to account for the interest of *avant-garde* patrons in artistic innovation in the fifteenth century, and their preparedness to spend large sums of money in furthering it. From the *Quattrocento*, individuals from several leading Florentine families – (the Strozzi, Rucellai and Martelli, for example, besides the Medici), the lords of Ferrara, Urbino and Mantua as well as certain of the popes – possessed this new outlook on art.

The Florentines (notably Palla Strozzi and Cosimo de' Medici) were earliest amongst these men. Chance may have played some part in the process of dissemination. For example, it was the contacts of Duke Federigo da Montefeltro of Urbino (1422–82) and Tommaso Parentucelli (later Pope Nicholas V) with Florence that encouraged those individuals to carry ideas with them to Urbino and Rome. Also, the new ideas were not contained in these centres, but spread to Venice and Milan. The prominence here of Florence and small courts disproves any notion that this artistic patronage was an aspect of 'court' or civic culture. What feature of patronage was it that could appeal to the patrons of these different cities? An answer to this question leads us towards the ideals of magnificence and magnanimity which ancient writers had extolled.

3. The motivation of patrons: the ideals of magnificence and 'magnanimity'

A notion of magnificence inspired Cosimo de' Medici to commission works of art (especially buildings) and he may have helped convey this ideal to the rulers of other Italian states like Duke Federigo da Montefeltro (see A. D. Fraser Jenkins, 1970). The idea is first to be found in the writings of two Florentines, Leon Battista Alberti and the little known Timoteo Maffei. The former's *Della Famiglia* was written in Florence in the 1430s, and contains references to magnificence, as do the writings of Maffei who was a monk at the abbey of Fiesole, which was partly rebuilt at Cosimo's expense. The idea may have been drawn from classical sources, either from Aristotle or from Vitruvius. Cosimo's great commissions were of buildings and Vitruvius's book on architecture sparingly referred to the 'magnificent' character of ancient temples. Equally, it may have come from Aquinas who employed the term and whose use of it was quoted by Maffei.

New ideas may inspire novel undertakings but why should conventional ones do so? Aquinas was one of the most widely read writers of the thirteenth century and his use of the term makes it improbable that magnificence could have passed unnoticed until the fifteenth century. In fact it has been shown that it had already been applied in the fourteenth century by a Milanese to the commissioning of buildings by the dukes of Milan (Larner, 1971, p. 101). This continued currency makes it difficult to accept that magnificence, unless it had been re-formulated or compounded with novel elements, can explain a quite altered conception of patronage. In any case, would not building undertaken in order to be grand have been inappropriate to Cosimo de' Medici or to the ruler of a small court such as Urbino?

We know that Cosimo remained anxious to appear as a simple citizen, and rejected one design for the rebuilding of the Medici Palace because it was too imposing. The prince of a small territory like Urbino or Mantua might lack the resources to indulge grandiose dreams. Ironically the connoisseurship of some famous fifteenth-century collectors, like Isabella d'Este and Cosimo's grandson, Lorenzo de' Medici, was probably strengthened precisely because they were not wealthy enough to patronise art on a grand scale. Others, like Cosimo himself, who did possess the resources, were given to a high-minded appreciation of artistic things. Could it be that it was such high-mindedness or 'magnanimity' which inspired such patrons to commission a painting or a building?

The term 'magnanimity' is found alongside magnificence in the sources. In his account of Brunelleschi, Vasari remarked of Giovanni de' Medici that he was a greater patron of art than his father because he was 'magnanimous' and ready to spend money. In the Renaissance a broad meaning was lent to the concept of magnanimity which was taken from antiquity. It meant not merely rising above an immediate personal interest, but a general breadth of vision. Cicero had used magnanimity (literally greatness of soul) to denote a search for truth and an independence of spirit, whereby the individual would be guided by the wise man or wise ruler, and he referred to this quality being made manifest in the 'active' life of public service (see above, p. 40). For him the concept was imbued with Stoic qualities, counting fortune for nought.

Greatness of soul, therefore, according to this classical usage, meant placing wisdom above all else and administering the gifts of fortune, such as wealth, for the benefit of one's fellow men. This was the quality which Vasari observed in the patronage of Giovanni de' Medici and also in that of King Francis I of France.

> Now it is true there is nothing by which the spirit [of the artist] is so greatly kindled to glorious achievements (*virtù*) as seeing that they are duly appreciated and rewarded by princes and lords; as was always done in the past by the most illustrious house of Medici . . . and as was the practice (*maniera*) of the said king Francis who may be truly called magnanimous.

(*Life* of Valerio Vicentino in *Lives*, ed. Milanesi, v, 376–7)

The spending of money upon great buildings and works of art by Cosimo and Lorenzo de' Medici was animated by a similar 'high-mindedness'. There is a passage in Lorenzo's memoirs (the *Ricordi*) in which he refers to the vast sums which his family had spent since 1434 upon alms, public taxes and building, which should be interpreted in this way. Such patronage was not done for self-aggrandisement, but to be useful and magnanimous by devoting personal wealth to unselfish purposes. The patronage of art should be seen less as consumption for pleasure, than as a newly conceived duty.

99

By such undertakings, patrons certainly hoped to gain esteem, by using money for the public good. Indeed, when contemporaries employed the term 'magnificence' they usually gave it a high-minded sense. Again this was following ancient usage; for Cicero the *animus magnus* was a close relative of the *animus magnificus* (e.g. *De Officiis*, I,xxiii,79; cf. III,i,1). There is a speech in Bruni's *History of Florence* in which Florentines were urged to follow the example of Rome's expansion, and add Lucca to their dominions for the utility, majesty and glory of Florence. In the public sphere one should seek magnificence and ignore expense.

> Men should not pursue the same purpose in public as in private life. For in the public sphere the end should be *magnificentia* which consists in glory and greatness (*amplitudo*); while in private affairs rather temperance and frugality. Consequently, those who counsel the state (*respublica*) must have a greater soul (*grandiorem animum*) and assume a loftier purpose, not to think of expense and effort but of glory.

(R.I.S., XIX,iii,140)

This was the 'greatness of soul' and the magnificence by which civic conduct came to be judged in the 1400s. Here there were no boundaries between conduct becoming in a statesman and in a patron of art. When efforts were said to be guided by magnificence, contemporary patrons, such as Cosimo, intended by this not conspicuous consumption or splendour, but liberality with a Stoic tinge such as they had read about in Cicero.

This surely is the sense in which Alberti used the term in *Della Famiglia* where the earliest signs of a new attitude have been detected. He remarked that the one 'who fears adversity and gives way to sorrow, who seeks fortune and fleeting things will never deserve to be regarded as strong or of *grande animo*' (Pellegrini, p.202). This is the Stoic idea of magnanimity and can be compared to what Alberti said of wealth. Its only use must be to escape enslavement to it. What he had in mind is indicated by the observation that wealth was to be defended if it was expended for magnificent purposes and the public good (p.210). If fortune gave you wealth it should be used in *cose magnifiche et onestissime* (p.224). The reason was that men are born 'not for idleness (*ozio*) but *cose magnifiche*' (p. 196; cf.pp.110, 190). This amounts to disapproving of wealth when employed for other than public pursuits. Behind this lies the Stoic belief that wealth is a gift of fortune, which should not be depended on; rather men must demonstrate that they have chosen virtue as their end by using money for unselfish purposes.

This should be compared to what Cicero had written of art itself. He praised the keeping of statues of the gods in public places as a high duty of the citizen; like rhetorical speeches they contributed to piety and public virtue (*De Leg.*, II, x, 26). At the time of his exile in 58 B.C. he owned a statue of the goddess Minerva, which he installed in the temple of Jupiter Capitolinus and dedicated it as a guardian of Rome (Plutarch, *Cicero*, 31; cf. *De Leg.*, II, xvii, 42). Cicero was highly critical of leading Romans who collected statues and pictures for private pleasure, considering such men to be ignoble slaves of a desire for possessions (*Paradoxa Stoicorum*, 37–8). The patronage of art, like the possession of wealth, was, therefore, good if it was used to adorn public buildings and for the general good.

The clue to new attitudes towards artistic patronage in the *Quattrocento* is to be found not in an Aristotelian idea of magnificence, but in Ciceronian magnanimity and the similar meaning which Cicero had lent to 'magnificence'. Nevertheless, it remains puzzling why leading Italians should have wished to be 'high-minded'. Cicero again furnishes us with a clue. In *De Officiis* he remarked that 'greatness of soul' arose from man's refusal to be governed except by wise precept or justly and lawfully in the cause of utility, as such subjection conflicted with man's natural desire to be a prince himself (I, iv, 13). Do we not find here the enunciation of a meritocratic principle? In societies where eminence is no longer based upon blood or (as in *Quattrocento* Italy) not yet so, political obligation needs to be fixed by some other principle.

Meritocracy is a system which allows human beings to reach high places if so deserving. It is also one that enables individuals to accept that others should occupy those positions. In 1400, Italian families whose right to rule was not based on immemorial custom, or whose eminence did not rise so far above rivals or subordinates, could base their power upon the merit of magnanimity. When Cosimo spent money building, he would have had in mind the attitude which Cicero expressed when he said that the men who had founded the Roman republic had not demonstrated an avaricious desire for riches or fine possessions: Romulus had become king because of his virtue (*Paradoxa Stoicorum*, 10–11).

It suited Cosimo to count his wealth for little by using it for the public good. The desirability of this attitude is indicated by Cosimo's disparagement at the hands of the humanist Filelfo, who had been exiled from Florence on the Medici's return there in 1434. In his *Commentationes Florentinae de exilio* he compared the wealth of Cosimo to that of the Milanese banker and state treasurer Vitaliano Borromeo (*c.* 1391–1449); the former had obtained it by usury for personal gain: the latter used it with liberality for the good of others (*Prosatori Latini del Quattrocento*, ed. E. Garin, p. 510). In Ciceronian terms Filelfo was drawing a distinction between a man worthy of ruling the state through greatness of soul, and one who was not. Later in the century Cristoforo Landino, who was friendly to the Medici, listed in his *Camaldulensian Disputations* 'greatness of soul', alongside mature prudence, as the quality which had enabled

101

Lorenzo de' Medici to weigh and confront the difficulties before him when he was forced to manage the government of Florence in his youth (Bk. I; ed.Lohe, pp. 10–11).

Chapter Ten

Conclusions

In the relationship between artists and patrons answers are to be found to many of the perplexing problems raised by Renaissance art. Each party could offer the other a guarantee or elevation of their social position. This was not crudely or suddenly accomplished. The initial union of patron and artist brought forth a work of art, but the effects of competition between patrons or artists produced innovation. The desire of patrons to secure the services of certain artists encouraged them to bestow grace and favour; the anxiety of artists to gain the attention of a suitable patron led them to develop an art which could please and gain the notice of a wider public.

The human rather than the legal side of the relationship was important. The quality and originality of a work of art depended upon a rapport between artist and patron. The greatest achievements sprang from artists who sought to please their patrons and from the latter's readiness to understand the former's creative and personal needs. The sensitive patron would also accept the tedious by-products of effort and imagination: irresponsibility and caprice, which in some instances may have been practised precisely to command attention.

A high-born patron could bestow an improved standing by giving land, money, titles or even by his mere approval. To understand how artists could give an equal benefit in return, it is necessary to recall that established authority was very weak in Italy around 1300. The decline of the Holy Roman Empire and papacy after 1250, and the dispersion of ecclesiastical property, pushed Italian cities into political prominence. The great success of the mendicants, the rediscovery of antiquity and the expansion of civic governments were all encouraged by these conditions.

The friars and the communes alike could supply the failings of weak popes, bishops and secular clergy. Franciscans and Dominicans stimulated a religious life based upon self-help. Communes from the thirteenth century adopted ecclesiastical responsibilities: they built or maintained churches, co-operated in the suppression of heresy, and controlled in some detail the life of the Church. At the same time the city-states remained weak and they were led by families with no ancient and undisputed right to govern.

The establishment of ruling oligarchies and dynasties had made progress by 1400, but it was not complete until it was buttressed by national monarchies from beyond the Alps after 1494. Down to that time even the most powerful communes like Florence continued to be replaced by despotisms, whilst powerful lordships like that of Milan could face displacement by a republic, as happened between 1447 and 1450. All the time, small states faced 'predation' and élites suffered rivalry within.

Broken loose from their imperial moorings and unsecured by accepted custom or ancient blood, the would-be governors of Italian cities needed to fix their right to rule. They found it in what is to us the strange combination of contemporary orthodoxy and ancient morals. Governments defended orthodoxy at home and the papacy abroad. Citizens were attracted to the religious self-help of the friars and to the civilisation of antiquity. The latter supplied a common past to which Italians could return and, in the specific notion of *humanitas*, refinement, urbanity and moral views triumphing over vulgarity or rusticity. Both mendicant and classical influences stimulated the idea that art was a peculiarly fitting vehicle to express the moral conceptions of a governor.

Moral value in this context possessed inevitable connotations of social worth. The social class seeking to express itself in moral values was neither republican nor princely: it comprised the rulers of both types of city. Art was civic in that it was largely produced in cities and for city-dwellers. It was not brought forth by the citizenry at large, let alone all inhabitants. We often read in Vasari of citizens commissioning works of art or of masterpieces being located in their houses, yet there is hardly a humble patron recorded there. One such is described in the life of Franciabigio, and Vasari felt it necessary to apologise for the artist accepting a commission from such a man.

So genial was Franciabigio in disposition, Vasari commented, that he did not think any commission too small for him, with the result that the master's hand was sometimes turned 'to objects of very inferior character'. Such were the portraits of a rustic and a *Noli me Tangere* executed for a cloth-maker called Arcangelo in a tower used by the latter as a place of recreation. This tale reminds us that the 'citizens' in Vasari were the leading citizens of great republics. Art was also commissioned in the courts by the prince or the town-dwelling aristocracy. The patronage of art belonged to a governing class, which was almost senatorial. At the same time, the art was not produced for the grand alone but for the city at large. To understand this, it is essential to turn aside and ponder on the religious and classical ideas which were directly affecting fine art.

The weakness of monarchical, episcopal and papal authority and the corresponding ubiquity of heresy forced leading citizens to defend the Church and supply its failings. Oligarchs and rulers became the defenders of orthodoxy, protecting the papacy, suppressing heresy, building and maintaining churches or charitable institutions, and taking on something of the fatherly role of earlier bishops.

Governments and individual patricians were assuming moral duties at the same time. Uncertain of their position within the élite, individuals and families sought to prove their right to govern by promoting the public interest and moral certitude. They supported classical studies as a revival of the Italian past. For the same reason the names of Guelph and Ghibelline continued to be heard for a century after the conflict of empire and papacy had ended. This desire to be moral and patriotic coincided in the patronage of art.

In commissioning art the patron was being the benefactor of religion. In response to the work of the friars, painters were producing heavenly 'visions' before which the devout could pray and seek intercession. The friars had urged their congregations to conjure up in their minds images of Gospel scenes. This mendicant piety evoked the Italian religious art of 1300. There was an essential point of contact between the religious art of 1300 and those ideas of the classical artist seeing the gods or penetrating the soul. Already in 1300 (nowhere more so than in Giotto's work) the painting was becoming a feat of the imagination. Art historians have observed that Giotto's achievement consisted in his applying to painting the homilies of the mendicant preachers.

The friars had urged their congregations to imagine what it would have been like if they had been present at the Biblical events. In observing a scene like Giotto's portrayal of Christ's deposition from the Cross in the Arena Chapel at Padua, there is a far echo of a sermon in which some friar had exhorted his listeners to imagine how those who loved their Lord would have acted. Most Italian paintings before 1500 were religious and this homiletic tradition can be discerned in many of them. Those of the fifteenth century are often described as being secular in tone. The Holy Family are depicted mundanely or in contemporary guise.

Benozzo Gozzoli's frescoes of the coming of the Magi in the chapel of the Medici Palace in Florence have been viewed as a secular portrayal of the *joie de vivre* of the Medici in the *Quattrocento* or even as political allegories. The scenes possess a tapestry-like quality and the Magi have the faces of the Medici family. However, political allegory would have been thought clumsy and indecorous in a chapel. The humanity and worldliness of such paintings recalls the Franciscan tradition. The mundane elements merely strengthened the viewer's ability to imagine himself present at the Gospel scenes. From first to last, therefore, the imaginative element ran strongly in Italian art. Classical ideas of the visionary character of the artist complemented this strain in religious painting.

The clause of Petrarch's will, in which he bequeathed a Madonna by Giotto to the lord of Padua, represents a junction-box in the development of art when intellectuals began to 'manipulate' this tradition of religious art. Both old and new attitudes can be seen there. Petrarch noted that by means of the image his beneficiary might obtain the Virgin's intercession, which was a quite conventional expectation. On the other hand, he observed that whilst the picture was undervalued by the vulgar herd, it was highly esteemed by masters of painting. Not only was it novel for an intellectual to interest himself so keenly in art and think a picture his only possession worthy (as he said) of a lord, but in judging its value he deferred to the estimate placed upon it by artists. Thereafter, patrons slowly began to be mindful of new attitudes. The change can be summed up by saying that whereas previously works of art had been seen as books of the poor, they became objects in which the educated could perceive intellectual and moral worth hidden from others.

With the advent of new classical ideas and of a commissioning of art in which form was left to patron and artist, the sacred images by artists were no longer merely imaginative reconstructions of Gospel scenes. They were records of visions, which by imaginative *fantasia* artists had glimpsed of Christ, the Virgin and Saints in Heaven. In commissioning them the patron made himself the benefactor and even connoisseur of religious truth. This was why Bufalmacco was able to humiliate a patron by depicting the Virgin cradling a bear in place of the infant Christ: the work of art betokened the patron's moral worth. This notion emerged more clearly still in the fifteenth century. Then the ideas of magnificence and magnanimity were used to denote the patron's high-minded giving of money for public building.

The governing classes therefore aided both classical studies and the visual arts out of the same desire to attain moral fitness. Antiquity was Italy's past and greatest age. Ancient ethics furnished Italians with a set of public-spirited values proper to a ruling class. The same classical sources led them back to art by a second route. They found that the ancients also believed that art should exercise a public function, that the artist was a visionary and that it was the mark of moral and intellectual excellence to understand him.

The largely public character of great works of art cannot be explained on the assumption that culture was produced by a largely individual interest in antiquity or by a rich man's taste for splendour and display. The great works of art of Renaissance Italy consisted in churches, hospitals and public palaces, the building of private chapels within churches or in sculptures and paintings designed to adorn such buildings. Princely palaces were also public buildings. The façades of private palaces were public also. There is left only a relatively restricted group of works produced for the interiors of private houses. This is not meant to imply that there is no sense in which the rich did not 'conspicuously consume' or sometimes gather works of art for wholly personal reasons. But these motives were subsidiary and secondary, even when adorning the chambers of private palaces.

Instances of indisputably original works of art, which were designed for private locations such as the sculpture of Donatello and the paintings of Pollaiuolo in the Medici Palace in Florence, do not disprove this. Cosimo and Lorenzo de' Medici were not commissioning art primarily for personal pleasure or to display their wealth. Vespasiano da Bisticci tells us that Cosimo de' Medici, the founder of that collection, thought it his duty to keep painters and sculptors at work lest they be unemployed. For his part Lorenzo used painters and pictures as vehicles to show his own and his city's excellence abroad.

Nonetheless, in Lorenzo's time there was a narrowing of the public scope of art. It was not that a larger private sphere was created outside, but that the enduringly public role of art was defined more tightly. Increasingly in the sixteenth century it came to express public and moral values to a smaller circle of grandees rather than to the citizenry at large. This is how we should interpret the decorative schemes of private houses wherein the great entertained each other, or the palaces where princes received their courtiers.

A sign of this narrowing is that Lorenzo's collections did not escape censure. In 1494, when the family were driven from Florence, Donatello's statue of David, which had stood over a fountain in the Medici gardens, and his sculpture of Judith and Holofernes were brought to the public palace. Pollaiuolo's paintings of the labours of Hercules, the furniture, precious objects and altarpiece from the Medici chapel, various antique busts and the Medici library were also carried there for public use. The great works of art of the Italian Renaissance, therefore, were intended in some sense for the public domain or to express the moral or intellectual excellence of the patron, and their production was encouraged when artist and patron alike conceived that a work of art was being created for high and public ends. Art came forth, therefore, out of a sense of moral duty.

PART III
THE ACHIEVEMENT OF THE
ITALIAN RENAISSANCE

Introduction

Two years after Lorenzo de Medici's death in 1492 the French armies of Charles VIII entered Italy. Twenty-five years later, Luther had begun his protests at Wittenberg. The advent of the Italian wars and the religious troubles in Germany marked the end of an epoch in papal and Italian history. It is often implied that they also ended the sway of the new movements in Italian art and learning. The Renaissance is held to encompass the sixteenth and seventeenth centuries inasmuch as they bear the impact of Italian philology and artistic styles beyond the Alps. It is less accepted that great intellectual changes of the age owed their origin to Italian influences.

A case can, however, be made that this was true of the religious controversies of the sixteenth century. The growth in classical scholarship, historiography and what may be called the human sciences were also on Italian stock. This is not surprising since these latter subjects were the disciplines in which the Italian humanists had worked. Nevertheless, the growth of these subjects after 1500 is often attributed to the Aristotelian traditions of northern universities or to creative energies spurred by the times. With some exceptions, however, the Italian contribution in these fields is not visible to the naked eye. This is also true of the religious controversies of the sixteenth century. A close examination of the master ideas of the Reformers and of alternative causes to account for them does, however, reveal humanist inspiration. Similarly, Italian influence on later philology and the writing of history is evident when it is viewed from a far point: perspective clarifies the traditions behind these subjects. The Italian contribution in all these areas is easier to understand by reference to the formation of a new ideal of intellectual cultivation, which itself was one of the greatest legacies from Renaissance Italy.

The humanists let four dynamic ideas loose upon early modern Europe: a belief in man's intellectual and moral capacity; the judging of its proper limits by reference to the human condition; a finely tuned sense of history; and a highly sophisticated inductive method. Faith in human capacity was not owing to any better understanding of the ancient cliché that 'man is the measure of all things'. It came from the realisation that the educated could attain wisdom without the help of priests or intellectuals. The conception was strengthened by a renewed acceptance of the ancient proposition that virtue *is* knowledge. Behind this lay a belief that knowledge brought an appreciation of the human condition. These attitudes constitute an idea not of individualism but of what may be called 'man in society'. They implied both a set of assumptions about humanity and a procedure for analysing human actions. They filtered out of Italy by many routes, one of the most important of which was the early sixteenth-century writings of Machiavelli and Castiglione. They formed the means by which (in Italian or in translation) such attitudes reached a wider European public.

The notion that all men could achieve wisdom helped to forge a new ideal of intellectual life. At the same time, the judging of actions in terms of moral choice affected the writing of history. When the humanists combined this with a new sense of period or perspective they were able to advance the technique of historical explanation. The feeling for periodisation sprang from the loss felt by Italian intellectuals for ancient Rome. As well as the discovery that the Romans had an idea of cultural evolution from an earlier Greek world, this accounts for many of the philological triumphs of the Italian scholars.

It was this which enabled them to understand afresh the history of texts and lay the groundwork of later classical scholarship. The same ideas, reinforced by a regard for what men actually did (a formulation drawn from the ancient rhetoricians), enabled the humanists to launch a new understanding of man in society. Consciousness of human motivation accelerated the development of biography, whilst a new perception of the social factors influencing human development spread. The humanists' confidence in man's capacity was therefore a qualified one. They might have expressed it by saying that man could achieve moral greatness by the exercise of reason, but he could not evade the necessities of Fortune. This belief, and the dilemmas it raised, deeply influenced the religious controversies of the sixteenth century.

Chapter Eleven

Man and Society

'I ndividualism' and 'Man and Society' are respectively Victorian and modern clichés which die on our lips. Their use seems to reflect an inflated notion of the Renaissance which is out of date. If conceptions of the individual have ever changed we are inclined to think that this happened over a much longer period and by social pressures rather than the circulation of ideas. Such sceptical and material doubts have silenced the voicing of expressions which in fact deserve to enjoy continued currency. It will be argued that the humanists found in ancient literature a novel idea of the individual as well as of man in society.

The discovery was not occasioned by any social change other than the phenomenon of lay intellectuals and artists having their eyes opened by ancient wisdom and reflecting upon their own situation. The original achievements of the humanists in the fields of classical scholarship and historiography sprang from a novel historical consciousness. Because they perceived antiquity and their own age differently, the evolution of culture was seen in a new light. This applied also to ideas of the individual. Biographers, artists and humanists eagerly took up techniques from classical sources which showed them how to grasp human psychology and they reflected on their own make-up.

The clearest instance of the latter is to be found in Vasari's *Lives of the Artists*, in which the author, who was himself an artist, pondered the achievement of certain artists in its relation to their personalities. The humanists were able to accomplish things the ancients never knew in various fields by contemplating themselves. Vasari was discovering truths in contemporary activity. This is what Machiavelli and Castiglione also attempted. They were the most important writers in Italian in the early sixteenth century. Vasari, Castiglione and Machiavelli all celebrated the Italian world and Vasari and Machiavelli sought to explain it also. They sought furthermore to make Italian reality an ideal by means of the ancient technique of induction. The works of Castiglione as well as of Machiavelli (notably *The Courtier* and *The Prince*) acted as a vehicle by which older humanist ideas were carried beyond the Alps. The humanists in short discovered and elaborated an ancient approach to the individual and society and aspects of it were to reach a wide European public.

1. An inherited idea of man, society and civilisation

As the threads composing the ancient idea of wisdom are traced to antiquity they become entangled. The neat formulae with which historians describe ancient morals fail once the sources are examined. The Latin moralists and their Greek forebears were not 'civic' thinkers and the epithet of 'pagan ethics' raises questions. Renaissance scholars have placed too much stress on the over-quoted words of Aristotle that man was a 'political animal'. Aristotle's dictum can by no means bear all its accustomed weight and Greek thought cannot wholly be construed in terms of it.

 . Some light is cast on Aristotle's opinion by a remark attributed to Demosthenes. He is said to have wished that in his youth he had known of the evils of public life; then he would have chosen the alternative road towards death (Plutarch, *Life of Demosthenes*, chap. xxvi). This statement does not mean that Demosthenes conceived only of the *polis* or of death. He held to a sharp distinction between public and private life. The deepest root of the preference which ancient thinkers displayed for 'public' activity was a belief in man's social disposition, and this is what lay behind Aristotle's view. Because of the prominence of city-states in the Greek landscape there was a tendency to equate public activity with life in the *polis*. Hence Aristotle's employment of the word 'political' – the adjectival form of the word *polis*. Nevertheless, there was nothing invariable or necessary in this equation. By 'public' life the ancients had in mind a life of public office and not the values expressly of a non-monarchical community.

An intriguing recent theory deserves attention at this juncture. The claim has been advanced by J. G. A. Pocock that there was a republican tradition linking Aristotle, the Roman philosophers, Renaissance Italy and early modern political thought.[1] The starting-point of the tradition is alleged to have been the Greek city-state described by Aristotle, and

---

1. J. G. A. Pocock, *The Machiavellian Moment* (1975).

which Pocock has labelled the Aristotelean *polis* or republic (these terms are used interchangeably) (pp. 3, 66, 67, 75, 84, 99, etc.). This *polis* incorporated universal moral values so that for the Greeks the good man and the good citizen were one and the same (p. 74). This conception then passed via Rome to Renaissance Italy where it was reborn in Florence around 1400.

However, the notion that the Greeks had a fundamentally civic idea of man in society or that there was a single republican attitude over two millennia is equally open to doubt. The Greeks could and did distinguish between citizenship and virtue. When Zeno of Citium, the founder of Stoicism, observed that human beings were all a flock feeding on one pasture, he was referring to the moral interdependence of man arising not from cities but nature. Moreover, it is hazardous to think that fifteenth-century Florentines, Roman moralists and Greek philosophers had one conception of a republic, so that we can use republic and *polis* interchangeably.

When Roman writers of late antiquity discussed the 'republic' they did not generally mean the same thing as Greeks had by the *polis*: the *res publica* of Latin writers was a far looser term. It might mean no more than what we would call public affairs or the state, and indeed the Roman Empire was happily called the Roman republic. This loose usage is found also in the Renaissance and early modern times. As Hexter has observed (1979, pp. 292–3), Bodin and Seyssel casually applied the term to monarchy. In fourteenth- and fifteenth-century Italy the word crept into use as a synonym for commune and was contrasted to despotism. Generally it did not possess ancient or modern connotations of a self-conscious republicanism because in law there was only one republic, which was the contemporary Roman Empire, which we call the Holy Roman Empire. In fact what connected Aristotle, Rome and Renaissance Florence was not civic conceptions but a universalist outlook that man belonged with the gods.

The ancients passed on certain master ideas to the humanists. These included a belief in the moral greatness of man, his capacity to discover truth (moral as well as natural) by means of reason and what might be called a worldly perspective. The Greeks interpreted all ethical and metaphysical topics by reference to what they could see around them. Happiness lay in adjusting desires to the hard facts of life – not to what we ought to do according to some abstract standard. God was to be discovered (if at all) in the constant principle governing the world behind the superficial flux.

They constitute a specific enough body of ideas for the humanists who came to possess them to be distinguished from the scholastics of twelfth-century Europe. They are, however, sufficiently vague to encompass classical thinkers of a widely differing stamp. Man's 'moral

115

greatness' could be applied to various teachings of the Stoics and Epicureans. Often the notion was interpreted to mean, in the words of the modern philosopher Bergson, that 'man discovers himself when he is measured against an obstacle'. Yet that sentiment could serve as a justification both for self-sacrifice and successful egoism.

Finding moral truth by reason signified in a short passage of time Socrates' search for truth by means of definitions and Plato's theory of Forms. The ancient idea of human psychology and potential was still more diffuse. Measuring desire against necessity focussed on potential, but this could be lent either a gloomy or an optimistic colouring. Historians and biographers stressed the vain and selfish instincts of men on which the outcome of events turned. At the same time, the Neo-Platonist belief in the divine capacities of man and the confidence in reason combined to produce an idea of the perfectibility of man amongst the Roman educationalists.

According to Quintilian, man was born for intellectual endeavour as birds were born to fly, horses to run and wild animals to be fierce. Dull boys were created by poor teachers (*Inst. Orat.*, I,i,1). Mental capacity was a gift bestowed by divine Providence (ibid., I,xii,19). Equally, human achievement depended upon free choice (I,iii,8). Accordingly the reach of the human mind was great (I,xii,24; cf.I,iii,8–9), but its development required the teacher to harness the will by recognising and nursing the disposition of individuals (I,iii,1; cf. I,ii,15–16; I,ii,30; II,iv,10f.).

It is wrong to exaggerate these divergences amongst classical thinkers. One attitude to man and society linked selfish and selfless ideas of moral greatness as well as directing different views of human potential. All ancient thinkers believed in man's social nature. Even Zeno of Citium and Epicurus, who are commonly said to have circulated conceptions of man's selfish pursuit of inner harmony or pleasure, subscribed to a thoroughly social view of man. For Zeno humanity was most aware of community when oblivious of personal needs. Epicurus believed in social evolution.

All the ancient moralists searched for knowledge of the good life. Whilst only Aristotle held that virtue was knowledge, all philosophers believed that wisdom meant discovering virtue through knowledge of the human condition. This gave ancient ethics a markedly different aspect to the Christian morals which followed them. They did not preoccupy themselves with moral obligation and ask what were the proper grounds, or extent, of duty. Rather they looked to what we might call the art of the possible. How were human desires and goals limited or determined by fortune – whether the desires of fellow men, the conflicting wishes of the individual, or the interventions of fate, disease or death? Accordingly, questions asked by them concerned such matters as whether discretion was the better part of valour, or if utility could be combined with honour; how far virtue was attainable when events were controlled by necessity and whether it was better to pursue a public life or one of private seclusion.

Despite the divergent conclusions of the moralists, the humanists inherited from them a distinctive vision of man in society. Its common assumptions were a belief in the sociability of man and a 'worldly' way of regarding his goals and duties. The emphasis upon the personal and the actual dispositions of men were further threads in late Greek ethics. The belief in human sociability implied that humanity could be understood by looking at how man behaved in society. This was a powerful stimulus to historical writing and to what might be called sociology.

Regard for the common ways of men drew attention upon vice as well as virtue – upon the faulty 'strategies' with which individuals set their course. Ancient biographers and historians perceived that individuals steering with vain hopes would come to grief. For this reason the gulf between the viewpoints of ancient moralists like Quintilian and biographers such as Plutarch was more apparent than real. It was not man or his nature so much as right reasoning that determined whether or not human paths could be directed towards knowledge and perfection.

Emphasis distinguished those ancient writers who portrayed the base appetites of men and those who drew their noble likenesses. In this respect it was stress that set Plato and his school apart from Latin moralists like Cicero. The latter incorporated Platonist elements in his philosophy (see above, p.32) and he combined this with the Stoic theory of man participating in the rational mind of God. He differed in stressing the common dispositions of man from which these airier elements could be refined.

The metaphor of refinement hints that there was a further common denominator which today would pejoratively be called élitism. Classical ideals of ethics, education, politics and civilisation were for the few. The human ideal of the moralists concerned mankind rather than an élite, yet it could only involve the few. When ancient writers described the baseness or perfectibility of man they were referring to potentialities: all *can* be fine or base. Inevitably, however, it was only the few who would possess the capacity, opportunities, teachers or knowledge which could make for perfection; the hoi-polloi would remain base or bestial. The Greeks fashioned two momentous ideas on this same ground of virtue. One concerned the individual; the other the progress of society.

By a short step biographers and painters employed virtue to estimate the motivation and actions of individuals. Trivial gestures could lead the imagination of both writers and artists to hidden character.

In the most illustrious deeds there is not always a manifestation of
virtue or vice, nay, a slight thing like a phrase or a jest often makes
a greater revelation of character than battles where thousands fall,
or the greatest armaments, or sieges of cities. Accordingly, just
as painters get the likenesses in their portraits from the face and
the expression of the eyes, wherein the character shows itself, but
make very little account of the other parts of the body, so I must
be permitted to devote myself rather to the signs of the soul in
men, and by means of these to portray the life of each.

(Plutarch, *Life of Alexander*, i,2–3; tr. B. Perrin)

This was a method of perceiving the individual, which the humanists
and Renaissance artists rediscovered.

Virtue also afforded a means of weighing human progress. Virtue was
shared by man with God; it was a perfection of nature. Natural gifts were
bestowed on man for his use and man imitated nature by using reason
(Cicero, *De Leg.*, I,viii,25). According to this view it was virtue which
gave rise to society. It enabled human beings to discover the fruits of
the earth, and then by turns clothes, housing, crafts, an ordered way of
life, wealth, speech and society itself (Cicero, *Disp. Tusc.*, I,xxv,62). The
Renaissance inherited this idea of man and society. The most important
expressions of it came only after 1500 although the idea of virtue as a
key to the individual had been canvassed long before.

2. Individualism and the cult of creative personality

Jacob Burckhardt devoted the second part of his *Civilisation of the
Renaissance in Italy* to 'the development of the individual' and he
described a great change in human awareness during the Renaissance.

In the Middle Ages both sides of human consciousness – that which
was turned within as that which was turned without – lay dreaming
or half-awake beneath a common veil. The veil was woven of faith,
illusion and childish prepossession, through which the world and
history were seen clad in strange hues. Man was conscious of himself
only as a member of a race, people, party, family or corporation –
only through some general category. In Italy this veil first melted
into air; an *objective* treatment and consideration of the State and of
all the things of this world became possible. The *subjective* side at the
same time asserted itself with corresponding emphasis; man became
a spiritual *individual* and recognised himself as such. (Middlemore's
translation.)

Burckhardt attributed this change to growing wealth, the development of culture, the role of the Church and above all to the Italian city-state. Although liberated by the ending of party conflicts, the individual remained insecure because of political strife. Alike in republics and despotisms, the prevalence of revolution and exile as well as the brevity of political favour led men to develop their inner resources, a cosmopolitan outlook, and to live life to the full.

Against this background an individual ideal arose of the 'universal man'. By this phrase Burckhardt meant not universal knowledge merely, but art as the expression of the individual personality, private education and manifold accomplishments. Corresponding to the inward cultivation of individual talent lay the outward distinction of a modern idea of glory. This rested on the social equality of the Italian commune and ancient notions of fame.

The desire for glory found expression in a new patriotism and novel literary forms. Civic pride encouraged the commemoration of local leaders, poets and scholars, and led also to the writing of biographies of famous men. Jealousy, however, equally stimulated a sense of the limits, failures and folly of ambition. Thus the short story, satire, burlesque, invective as well as wit and parody put down new roots as monuments to the development of the individual.

Since Burckhardt expressed his view, much effort has been spent in showing successfully that 'individualism' was known in the preceding centuries. Burckhardt exaggerated his case. The brilliant phrasing of his thesis and the arresting generalisations with which he prefaced the detailed exposition won him, as it were, the intellectual battle and lost him the campaign. The statement that in the Middle Ages men had been conscious of themselves only under the 'common veil' of a corporate identity conjured up an eye-catching and imaginary background. Consciousness of individuality is as old as the First Person Singular. More particularly, the principle of 'individualism' in the natural world was accepted by the scholastics. It was a commonplace of theologians that God, working through nature, had differentiated individuals one from another.

Distinctions of terminology are helpful. By the free development of the individual Burckhardt had meant both the appearance of striking personalities and an idea of individual development. It is sensible, however, to separate the strands: the novelty of the latter is more immediately plausible than that of the former. Different results, moreover, may be obtained by considering the separate senses of the notion itself. Individualism as moral autonomy, the assertion of the will, and subjective feeling may have seen new developments in *Quattrocento* Italy but these developments had been foreshadowed in the twelfth century. A clearer novelty consisted in the exploration of individual personality as the engine directing the outward actions of men. Did Burckhardt himself supply any evidence which could support this?

He remarked that Italians forged a new notion of their inward and outward 'physiognomy' and adopted private education as a means of nurturing talent. The ideal, however, to which he drew attention was that of the 'universal' man. Burckhardt noted that fifteenth-century sources used this phrase to denote the many-sided accomplishments of Leon Battista Alberti and Leonardo da Vinci. Alberti was an athlete, scribe, musician, painter, architect and philosopher. Leonardo was a musician, lover of nature, and scientist as well as a painter. Perhaps referring to these extraordinary men was a mistake, for it may raise doubts whether they could have been typical or even widely influential.

The diverse talents of such men were unusual but our knowledge of them partly derives from a contemporary belief that talent could be explained by disposition and habit – such as Leonardo's walks in the Alps or Alberti's physical capacities. Perhaps all ages are obliged to view the world through a veil and possibly the Renaissance was wearing one which was the beginning of our own. Burckhardt's theory as it stands cannot be saved, but in respect of artistic personality (which he somewhat neglected) there is evidence to show that the Renaissance did evolve an ideal for the individual.

Ironically it was the German-speaking world of the late nineteenth century (from which Burckhardt sprang) which possessed a cult of the romantic artist, but it was only after his time that it led scholars to explore the personalities of artists and the documents which recorded them (Wackernagel, 1938). It could be said that we owe to the Renaissance our habit of valuing the artist more highly than the work of art. Men such as Michelangelo and Pontormo in the 1500s not only made a cult of their feelings, but conceived their art as an expression of themselves. In fact there are earlier signs of this cultivation of the artistic personality.

The personal tastes and whims of artists (notably Bufalmacco) were thought a worthy topic for humour in the stories of Franco Sachetti. Manetti in his life of Brunelleschi observed how the latter's creative achievement grew from his personality or life-style. This story belongs to the early *Quattrocento* and, if the later accounts of Vasari are to be believed, there were several artists of the early fifteenth century whose personalities (as Wackernagel noticed) isolated them from society (see above, pp.82–4). What is still more remarkable in these accounts is that patrons accepted and even approved of the eccentric behaviour of such masters.

The cult of the artistic personality has been explained as an expression of the changed working practices of the artist, brought about by the weakening of the guilds and the artist's need to pursue his creative ideas in solitude (cf. R. Wittkower, 1961). As well as working habits and, as we saw before, the encouragement of an imaginative art and attention-seeking behaviour accounting for bohemianism, patrons and writers may have come to believe that eccentric behaviour was associated with original achievement. There were creative talents like Giotto, Masaccio and Raphael who, as far as is known, completely conformed to convention. There may have been artists before who, like Donatello, destroyed a work of art when they failed to be given the price they were seeking for it, but if so these actions must have been thought foolish or self-defeating. Was what had changed acceptance or encouragement of behaviour? Nevertheless, it is likely that the altered attitude fostered and multiplied the 'personalities'. One reason for this which is evident at once is that a work of art was seen as the product of one mind or personality. In the words which Politian expressed (and which afterwards were taken up by Leonardo da Vinci): 'every painter paints himself' (*ogni dipintore dipinge sè*).

To Burckhardt's evidence, then, of a new consciousness of personality and the idea of the universal man must be added the cult of the artistic personality. The chief instances of 'bohemianism' come from Vasari's *Lives of the Artists*. That work also reveals an understanding that the creativity of the artist sprang from his motivation and circumstances. Vasari possessed a talent here which has not been recognised: it constituted a new ideal of individuality. In introducing certain of the lives, Vasari set forth explanations of artistic achievement.

Occasionally the causes advanced were banal. He attributed the success of Desiderio da Settignano and Domenico Puligo to nature and grace. Nor are we surprised to learn that Agostino and Agnolo of Siena's excellence (cf. the life of L. Vasari) was the fruition of long implanted seeds, even though he seems to have meant by this that the seeds of talent in one generation bore fruit in a later one.

Often Vasari drew attention not to birthright or nature but to material circumstances and human effort. The achievements of Gaddo Gaddi, Vellano of Padua and Pisanello, for instance, were traced to the imitation of earlier masters. Much weight is placed in the *Lives* on the family situation, inclination and skill of the artist. Giuliano da Maiano and Ghirlandaiao were able to perfect their talents because their fathers allowed them to pursue their callings. The art of Starnina, Antonio Veneziano and Perugino was helped by exile or foreign sojourn. Studious application after early idleness played its part with Baccio da Montelupo; the nursing of ability by study was effective with Dosso whilst Alberti united theory with practice.

Vasari subtly adduced his explanation. He was willing to accept that these same causes could frustrate the attainment of excellence. Andrea del Sarto, Fra Bartolomeo and Rosso were discouraged by the presence of Michelangelo in Rome (*Life* of Rosso). Similarly, the development of Uccello and Verrocchio was stunted by their copying of earlier masters.

Vasari's comments on artistic excellence amount at times to a psychology of achievement. Perhaps it was because he was an artist himself, capable of reflecting upon his own development, that Vasari was able to pass beyond trite reflection. Instead of regular allusions to nature, genius or training, he sometimes drew attention to motivation. The talents of some artists were fully drawn out owing to their pleasing character: thus Simone and Lippo Memmi, Lorenzo di Bicci and Don Bartolomeo. The unprepossessing personalities of Dosso and Battista Dossi atrophied their skills.

The relationship between character and attainment was explored further in terms of competition. Giottino, Franciabigio and Donatello broke new ground in striving to surpass other masters. Conversely Raffaello da Montelupo achieved less because his diffidence and hatred of conflict made him refuse large commissions. Baldassare Peruzzi and Andrea del Sarto failed to fulfil their promise because of timidity, simplicity and faintness of heart.

Ambition and the desire to excel were the engines which fuelled labour and overcame difficulty. The progress of Benozzo Gozzoli and Perugino was likened by Vasari to the ascent of the religious zealot towards perfection by a laborious and painful path. They rose because they were driven: Perugino and Raffaellino del Garbo were determined to escape poverty or humble beginnings. Artistic success (like excellence in the religious life) demanded abstinence (*Life* of Torrigiano) and some were too ready for a life of pleasure (*Life* of Domenico Puligo and account of Silvio Cosini in *Life* of Andrea da Fiesole).

Exhortation and reward were essential. Taddeo Gaddi's talents were fostered by encouragement. The corollary again applied: Sogliani achieved excellence because of melancholia and we are told in the description of Boccaccino da Cremona that no artist could receive a greater injury than to have been highly praised in his youth because this dulled his appetite and rendered him vulnerable to later criticism, or immune from it. For Vasari the artist's main incentive was the wish for 'honour and profit'. This phrase (familiar in the political life of Tuscany) was applied to artists too numerous to mention. It referred to the desire for fame and for those material rewards which usually accompanied them.

This sense of the psychological influences which shaped cultural achievements owed its origin to ancient biography and to contemporary experience. Vasari's judgements were probably influenced by comments made by Plutarch in the preambles to certain of his lives. In the *Life* of Demosthenes, for example, Plutarch observed that it had been conducive to the intellectual development of orators like Cicero and Demosthenes that they had been born in cities with libraries (chap. 2). He also attributed Demosthenes' achievement to his poverty. This induced him to undertake studies which a well-born boy might have avoided (chap. 4) and pursue a career in order to recover his private property (chap. 6).

Vasari may have applied the same perceptive approach; he was not imitating ancient opinions. He was himself an artist and could look back upon his own career. He seems to have asked himself what had inspired some artists to originality and worldly success and others to fail. Perhaps as much in himself as in ancient biographers he divined that the answer lay in motivation. Writers of lives of eminent men already grasped that the same truth applied to scholars.

Vasari's psychological approach cannot quite be paralleled. The work of art excited a curiosity which did not extend to the output of scholars. Bohemianism may have been encouraged by the cultivation of imagination and as a ruse to elevate the artist above his servile origins (cf. above, pp.82–4). Nevertheless, the situation and even the idea of the artist, poet and scholar were not fundamentally different. Vespasiano da Bisticci declared that scholarship would fail if those honours were lacking which would inspire men to seek rewards (life of Alfonso of Naples). Contemporary and ancient sources compared painters to poets and philosophers and their achievements supplied an ideal for an educated class to follow. Boccaccio described the poet as a theologian and a seer because he could penetrate by his imagination into secret and future things. This attitude led men to look at the biographies of poets for clues to their creativity.

The poet and scholar, as well as the painter, were purveyors of wisdom. They furnished ideas for patrons and everyone to follow. Patrons were being supplied with an ideal to whose value they could testify in their own lives. The Renaissance, besides focussing upon the life and times of the creative personality, advertised the lives of men whose actions bore witness to the teachings of philosophers. Those great men were the patrons of the poet, philosopher and artist.

There was a pattern for this in the *Lives* of Plutarch, which presented the virtuous teachings of the philosopher alongside the fine deeds of illustrious men. The glory and fame sought by fifteenth-century Italians meant their ability to embody the virtue recommended by poets and philosophers. This notion of pursuing virtue was not quite the tearing asunder of a veil which separated man from reality. It represented the replacement of one ideal by another. Nevertheless, it was an ideal which moulded the way individuals behaved.

The heroic and chivalric notions current since the age of migrations had lain in glory and fame. Yet unsupported by ancient literature and philosophy they could not hope to dislodge Christian ideals. Now the situation was reversed. The humanists, like the poets, appropriated the classical culture which had formerly sustained theology. A great impetus was given to a vision of man in society which, whilst never un–Christian,

123

was sharply different to the learned nostrums fashionable since antiquity. Poets, philosophers and the artists gave currency to an art of how to live and drew morals from the way their patrons actually lived. The achievement lay therefore not in fostering or creating individualism or even an ideal of the individual where none had existed before, but in propagating a certain conception of virtue whereby every man's life could be judged.

The idea was attractive and powerful because it was realistic. Its starting point was the human condition and personal disposition. Guided by this principle, the Greeks had possessed a steady vision which enabled them to fix virtue according to the struggle of reason to comprehend the human flux, and estimate how mood, deed, gesture and expression reflected a struggle between appetite and reason within the soul. This and the tracing of creativity to character and circumstance was the individualism which the humanists and artists of the *Quattrocento* discovered or revived.

3. Machiavelli and Castiglione

Machiavelli and Castiglione were the most original and influential Italian writers of the early sixteenth century; they also embodied the rhetorical tradition. In the dedicatory letter to *The Courtier* Castiglione asked for his book to be compared to famous ancient authors who had written about *perfection*. Plato had thus described republics, Xenophon kings and Cicero orators. Castiglione himself would delineate the perfect courtier.

Castiglione should also be likened to contemporary humanists: he was doing for the courtier what Machiavelli had done for the prince and Alberti for the family. Poggio and Landino had described the duties and moral dilemmas of the citizen. Many humanists from Petrarch to Benedetto Accolti had written about illustrious contemporaries. These writers set forth an art of living for a governing class drawing upon the ancient sources for their approach and deriving their material from their own Italian world. Alberti has a special position amongst these figures, having been the first to treat such a subject in the vernacular. Yet Machiavelli and Castiglione hold pride of place for the novelty, respectively, of their conclusions and subject-matter.

3.1. Machiavelli

Machiavelli's political thought is customarily seen as the activation, in one sense or another, of a pagan morality; sometimes as the attenuation of a republican tradition, or as a contemporary political science. The first view was most articulately expressed by J. H. Whitfield and has been renewed in a highly individual manner by Sir Isaiah Berlin. They have held that Machiavelli believed in public life and a strong state as these principles had been understood loosely in the ancient world. At the same time, Berlin has argued that Machiavelli assumed that public morality was not applicable to private behaviour: what was moral in the public sphere became immoral as a code of private ethics. In this sense Machiavelli propounded a 'dual' morality.

The 'republican' view of Machiavelli's thought represents a particular version of the general theory associated with that name. J. G. A. Pocock has claimed that Machiavelli fell into a tradition which looked back via ancient Roman writers to Aristotle and Polybius. Having been revived by the civic humanists, this standpoint was expressed in the *Discourses* of Machiavelli. Equally *The Prince* represented the 'deformation' of the same tradition: in an age in which citizenship had decayed, morality became the sole affair of the prince. Croce and Olschki have called Machiavelli a political scientist who described rules of politics independent of morality. For Skinner, Machiavelli was a moralist who disagreed with several tenets of the ancient moralists.

If, however, Machiavelli is aligned with the rhetorical tradition that has been described above with its anti-speculative and inductive methods, and habit of drawing wisdom from wherever it might be found – the sources of his ideas become clear. This is demonstrated by his principle of studying 'what men do', his historical method, the public morality he espoused and the rules he observed in political life. These form the master ideas of Machiavelli and it can be shown that they derived their essential features from the ancient moralists. It will be suggested later that similar methods drawn from the same sources guided also the great work of Castiglione. Neither, however, was an imitator. Both were applying ancient methods to modern experience. They were also concerned to understand and influence the predicament (as they saw it) of contemporary Italy.

There was occasion earlier to notice that Machiavelli's vaunted principle of studying what men actually do, instead of describing imaginary states like earlier theorists, belonged to the anti-speculative tradition, which ran back via Petrarch to Cicero and ultimately to Socrates (see above, pp.40, 45–6, cf. 47). Machiavelli's historical method also possessed a Ciceronian ancestry. But where Cicero had suggested that ideals could be discerned in the actual history of Rome, Machiavelli's more methodical approach was to suggest that in general it was possible to learn how rulers should act by discovering how they *had* acted. It was startling to approach historically what formerly had been treated as a moral question. Moreover, since he observed that the great princes of the past had attained power by acting immorally, an amoral observation became an immoral command (see Stephens, 1988).

Machiavelli employed the same method in the *Discourses*. The work takes the form of a commentary on Livy's history of Rome, but Machiavelli cast his eye upon other states. He was concerned with political prosperity and claimed that its causes could be discovered in the early development of Rome. The city's secret had lain in the political, moral and military participation of its citizens. It is easy to think that this answer contradicted the message of *The Prince*. In fact the 'contradiction' is a testimony to the vigour of Machiavelli's historical method and to the different focus of the two works. History proved that states sometimes succeed by monarchical and at other times by republican institutions. Machiavelli may have believed that the republic was most desirable for an uncorrupted people, but that monarchy was inevitable and even best for a citizenry whose virtue had been lost (Whitfield, 1947).

There is evidence, though, that Machiavelli believed in the moral vigour and political strength of states rather than in specific constitutional forms. His ideal was a morally healthy commonwealth based on martial strength rather than on republican tradition. He expressed as much admiration for the monarchy of France as for the republic of the Swiss. Both possessed moral vigour; the one embodied in its aristocracy, the other in its peasant soldiers. The military might of each class sustained a different form of government. Moreover, he was preoccupied with what *is*, rather than with the best form of government which smacked of that concern of older writers with the 'ideal' which he scorned.

The basic conception therefore of both *The Prince* and the *Discourses* is historical and moral. Machiavelli's very method was historical: deciding what should be done by reference to what *had* been done in the past. The approach was moral rather than republican in that the overriding standard of a constitution's form was its guiding spirit, or morale. This historical approach had been drawn from Cicero.

The clearest expression of an historical method in Cicero's writing is to be found in his *De Re Publica* where the historical evolution of the Roman state from its origin towards perfection was described (see above, p.32). The bulk of this major work was not discovered until the nineteenth century but Machiavelli and earlier humanists could gain access to the historical idea of politics from other writings, notably the *Dream of Scipio* (Book VI of *De Re Publica*) and above all the historical interpretation of language in Varro's *De Lingua Latina* and of law in Cicero's *De Legibus*. Further, there was the historical idea of jurisprudence in the legal opinions enshrined in the *Corpus Iuris Civilis*.

These texts did not provide a simple historical or republican approach to politics or law. The purpose of studying history was not just to understand present institutions by examining how they had come to be. The Ciceronian and Varronian point was that through history things *tended* to perfection. That perfection resided in the uses to which they had been and could be put. This is the spirit of *Scipio's Dream*, where Scipio conceived of delivering Rome. This is also the theme of the last chapter of *The Prince*, where Machiavelli exhorted the Medici to liberate Italy.

The attainment of perfection was possible if laws and institutions harnessed the energies of the people. Such a state, guided by public spirit, was deserving for Cicero of the name of a *respublica*, whether it assumed a republican or monarchical form. The Ciceronian concentration upon moral vigour, rooted in good laws and customs, is the source of Machiavelli's concern for the strength of states whether they were principalities or republics. Machiavelli was not a republican who flirted with despotism, or one who thought a republic 'ideally' best. He simply believed in the Ciceronian *respublica* or, as we might say, the state.

Thus political ideas changed as they became attached to ancient ethics – as represented by Varro, Cicero, Seneca and the Roman legists. Political theory did not become detached from morals. Instead it became moral philosophy both in that it emerged from a study of the ancient moralists and because political thinkers (even including Machiavelli) were prescribing moral ends for the state – or more precisely immoral and historical beginnings tending to a moral end.

Machiavelli's achievement mirrored that of the humanists in general. This was to revive the methods and conceptions of the Roman moralists, but parcelled in a new historical consciousness. This novel awareness accounts for the ability of the humanists to comprehend antiquity in unprecedented ways; it also constitutes one of their greatest achievements. A sense of history had allowed Petrarch to conceive of antiquity as a lost world and appreciate better its values. At the same time this viewpoint gave a new idea of historical development – the periodisation of European history. The preoccupation of the humanist historians and of Machiavelli with understanding the situation of Italy forced ancient ideas into a new mould. As we shall see, the humanists forged an idea of historical explanation and a modern approach to historical method. Machiavelli equipped himself with an historical understanding of social change which can be considered the beginning of modern sociology (on all this see Chapter 14 and cf. Chapter 13).

It seems likely that this historical consciousness is also the root of the original way in which Machiavelli deployed the ancient moral approach to political thinking. In this respect he took over and completely recast classical ideas. He disagreed completely with the ancient moralists but he took all the elements of his thinking from them. His political thought laid down an art of living for the prince, in which the classical principles of reason, the moral greatness of man and the extraction of rules from experience by induction were combined with an idiosyncratic interpretation of *humanitas*. From the ancient ideas of man in society he fashioned a view of his proper immorality.

Machiavelli had a gloomy opinion of human nature, believing that half of the world's affairs were governed by Fortune. Equally he assumed that the key to sound government was the exercise of reason. It could determine why ancient Rome had prospered and account for the success of one ruler and the failure of another. For Machiavelli the successful prince possessed moral greatness as well as reason because he could use his power for good. In *The Prince* a scheme of things was set forth which was rationally achievable and whose end was moral. The guiding idea, however, was not pagan morality, but the inductive method of the Socratic tradition. In the early chapters certain historical facts of how principalities have been acquired and maintained are outlined (chs 1–11). These successes are then traced to policy, chiefly military self-sufficiency (chs 12–14) which in its turn is shown to depend upon the ruler's personal conduct and outlook (chs 15–19). The lessons are applied to the contemporary Italian situation (chs 24–6).

The goal set by Machiavelli for the prince was an ethical one, but this does not make his vision as a whole moral. The prince's goal was certainly ethical in that he was to use his power to allow his subjects to be prosperous and safe (ch. 23), make laws and institutions to that end (chs 24 and 26) and finally act as a saviour, driving the barbarian foreigners from Italy (ch. 26). Equally, in earlier passages Machiavelli had stressed that successful princes behave immorally: they should, for instance, 'take little account of faith' (ch. 18).

This contradiction arose not because for Machiavelli the end justified the means, but because for him the end was made possible by the means (see Stephens, 1988). He did not say that a moral end, such as liberating Italy, legitimated methods that would otherwise have been immoral, such as, for instance, killing subjects. Morality did not cast a benign light over all: he insisted that the means were (and remained) immoral. He was at one with the ancients in believing that man was made of vice and virtue. For him virtue was to be refined out of vice; morality too was fashioned from immoral materials. Princes had risen to power and would continue to do so by selfish and cruel means. This poor beginning, however, could be turned to a good end.

Reason, virtue and vice therefore governed the political thought of Machiavelli. The causes of political success could be discovered by reason, but the moral end success made possible was only reasonable when the selfish appetites of men were acknowledged. Machiavelli was employing the concept of *humanitas* in an idiosyncratic fashion. According to the ancient view, man's savage and bestial nature was drawn up by reason to higher things. Once reason was applied, a refinement began towards humanity and even divinity. In Machiavelli's scheme the application of humanising reason was delayed until man's savage nature fell within his field of vision. Since he said that princes should *be* bestial until they had secured power (and only then be turned to humane purposes) he was recommending immorality. He did this by deploying one element of ancient thought against another.

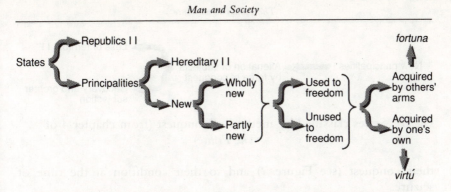

Fig. 6   The classification of states (from chapter 1 of *The Prince*)

Machiavelli's thought demonstrates the ancient idea of induction still more strongly. His famous method of studying what men 'do' instead of what they should do, is directly in the tradition of Cicero who had criticised 'abstract' theories. This, moreover, is what Machiavelli practised. In the first chapters of *The Prince* he established 'rules' which he had discovered.

Beginning from his assumption of the fickleness and faithlessness of men, Machiavelli inferred rules for the prince to follow. These included both general and specific rules. It was a 'general' rule (*regola generale*) that a man to whom a prince owed his power would be ruined by that prince (ch. 3, ed. Burd, p. 199). It was an 'infallible rule' that a prince must trust in himself or a single adviser (ch. 23, p. 352). The French king would have maintained his power and reputation in Italy more easily if he had observed the 'rules' of Machiavelli (ch. 3, p. 195). Contrariwise, it was not possible to give a 'certain rule' concerning how a prince could win popular favours because this varied according to the 'subjects' (ch. 9, p. 240). Similarly, Machiavelli sometimes gave 'a precept' (ch. 20, p. 329) or described the *modi* to be followed by a prince and the *termini* within which he must work (e.g. ch. 3, p. 199; ch. 14, p. 281; ch. 22, p. 348).

Besides these 'rational' inductions from experience *The Prince* supplies a rational classification of states. Machiavelli describes what can be called rules for concluding the strength or weakness of states from policies pursued by their rulers. These are so 'categorical' that they can be expressed in diagrammatic form. In chapter 1 there are what may be called rules for the classification of states. Prospects open up from policies and these depend upon political conditions. To be still more systematic, Machiavelli mentioned even republics and hereditary principalities which he excludes from his discussion (see Figure 6).

Chapter 4 analysed 'mixed' principalities, by which was meant a state where a territory was annexed to an old one. Here there are two types of classification. Mixed states are described according to the nature of

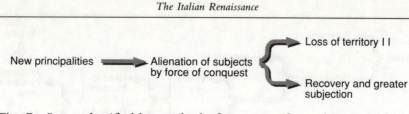

Fig. 7   States classified by method of conquest (from chapter 4 of
The Prince)

their conquest (see Figure 7) and to their condition at the time of seizure.

In chapters 4, 5, 7, 8 and 9 the security of the state is inferred from the sorts of princely policies, and the latter determined by the 'necessities' of the situation (see Figure 8). Most revealing of the high place given to induction by Machiavelli is that his notorious 'immorality' derives from it. In the early chapters of *The Prince* he looked at how rulers had come to power and concluded that it was by military strength unsoftened by moral scruples. He then told princes to go and do likewise. In first describing and then prescribing immorality he was detailing rules which he claimed to have derived from the experience he had observed.

The original view taken by the humanists of the ancient world, as well as their essential contributions to classical scholarship and historiography, sprang from a perception of their historical situation. Much the same historical outlook allowed Machiavelli to balance one ancient idea against another and ask novel questions. The different elements with which he juggled were *humanitas* and induction. Cicero had claimed that the orator should attend to what men actually thought, felt and did and avoid the imaginary prescriptions of the theorist. Here was a powerful encouragement to induction. Yet Cicero also admitted that man was raised from a brutish level by reason. Moreover, he condemned leaders who had made Rome great by cruelty or deceit.

From his different perspective Machiavelli was able to shake these contrasting elements into a new pattern. Must the thinker who avoided abstractions and focussed on what was done not have acknowledged that Rome was actually made great by cruelty and deceit? By alleging this Machiavelli was claiming new territory for the inductive method as well as welcoming evil. He brought man's bestial nature (which the ancients would have called *feritas*) within his field of vision and induced rules from its operation.

Machiavelli was detaching reason from 'right reason'. Cicero's strictures against abstraction and praise for how men acted fell short of recognising evil on rational grounds because for him all reason was rooted in the right reason of God. Reason could not, therefore, acknowledge actions other than those directed to higher ends and divine reason. Machiavelli saw no necessity in this assumption and

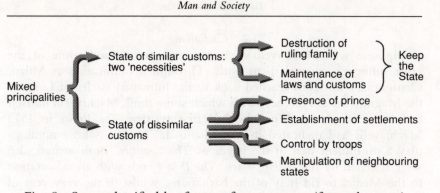

Fig. 8   States classified by forms of government (from chapter 4
of *The Prince*)

busied himself inducing rules from whatever men did, howsoever
brutish.

In allowing reason to describe inhuman ends Machiavelli opened the
way to a science of society based not upon what man's nature essentially
was (whether viewed metaphysically or according to the 'physical' or
biological assumptions of the Greeks) but upon a narrow view of what
men *did*. Thereby one strand of ancient thought, having been separated
from others, was launched into a grimmer future: something had been
lost. Machiavelli had not discovered truth but a technique; later these
two things would be confused. In laying bare the technique Machiavelli
was the distant forebear of social science. He did not detach politics from
morality in that he promoted moral ends. He was not a moralist for he
approved of immorality.

In expanding the scope of rational induction to include man's brutal
actions Machiavelli nevertheless prepared for an unimaginative and
narrow social science. It was not to be limited or dour because it
detached man or society from morals as a Christian might understand
that phrase, but because intellectual scrutiny of humanity was separated
from 'physical' considerations as Aristotle would have conceived them.
Man's nature, his *physis* – the animating principle that differentiated men
from animals, grass or matter – was now forgotten. The beginning of
social science was not a modern imitation of natural science or the science
of Aristotle, but Machiavelli's use of induction.

The study of man in society on ancient principles was tackled in more
conventional ways during the early *Cinquecento*. The most important of
these in the vernacular lay in the work of Castiglione. He also applied
induction to man, but he coupled it with a less novel scheme of morality
and in the short run he exerted a stronger influence than Machiavelli. At
the same time, Castiglione's concern with life at court was one which
greatly interested the educated classes of Europe.

3.2 Castiglione

Castiglione was Machiavelli's exact contemporary and some of the same influences shaped them both. Through his education at Milan, Castiglione's horizons reached back to the humanist circles of Lorenzo the Magnificent at Florence, with which some think Machiavelli himself had been associated. When he had first written *The Prince* in 1513 Machiavelli had dedicated it to Giuliano de' Medici, whose opinions play a prominent part in the pages of *The Courtier*. Both writers also were touched by the Italian Wars. *The Prince* ends with an exhortation to the Medici to rid Italy of the barbarians, whilst in the very year of *The Prince*'s composition Castiglione had cast his own prince, Francesco Maria della Rovere, as the saviour of Italy in the *intermezzo* to a play which he produced at the court of Urbino.

Nevertheless neither the conception nor the subject-matter of these works are the same. They also appear to have been influenced by different models. Machiavelli was impressed by Cicero and the Roman historians, whereas Castiglione's obvious classical sources were Plato and Aristotle, though in fact, as we shall see, he too used Cicero. Machiavelli's style was pungent whereas Castiglione employed nonchalance and charm. Furthermore, the methods proposed respectively for princes and courtiers diverged widely. *The Prince* has serious topics, and *The Courtier* is in large part given to lengthy expositions of jokes, sports and love.

The essential purpose and achievement of *The Courtier* is difficult to state. It describes the courtier's service and leisure. Yet Castiglione's originality did not lie in this: there was already a code of loyalty, service and even entertainment furnished by the aristocratic manners of the courtly world. The courtier is also attributed high moral purposes in Book IV. How can this be squared with the exhaustive examination of sports and humour which bulk large in earlier parts of the work? What indeed can the Platonising paean to love and beauty in the finale have to do with the prosaic pastimes and banter of a contemporary Italian court described in other passages? Pondering these difficulties it is natural to wonder whether any single purpose or literary model organised the whole of Castiglione's famous work.

In fact, the harmonious link between these discordant passages is that ancient tradition which had shaped Machiavelli. The same classical writers had given them the idea of inducing truth from 'what men do'. The formula which Machiavelli applied to *The Prince* – 'a long experience of contemporary affairs and a continuous reading of the ancients' – could extend to Castiglione, who wished to fashion experience according to similar ancient models.

At a first reading the jokes and pastimes are the least digestible elements in Castiglione's work; yet they constitute the contemporary experience at its base. There are hints in *The Courtier* that personal experience should be held in high regard. One character is made to say 'reasons do not appear good to me that are contrary to experience' (Bk III, ed. Cian, p. 321; tr. G. Bull, p. 226), and experience is twice held preferable to authority (Bk III, tr. Bull, p. 207, 248). Furthermore, accounts in the text of courtly amusements are a form of commonplace experience. There is evidence, too, of assumptions or attitudes seeming to derive from daily life.

Opinions vary (Bk I, p. 53).[2]

The crowd pays more attention to the first-comer than to the last (Bk II, p. 116).

First impressions of people are affected heavily by expectations (ibid., pp. 142, 244–5), physical aspect (ibid., p. 137) or nobility (Bk I, p. 56).

Nobles are more virtuous than commoners because they have more wish for honour and fear of shame (ibid., p. 54).

Non-Tuscan nobles should not be expected to use the vocabulary of peasants simply because the latter are Tuscan (ibid., pp. 79–80; cf. p. 85).

Women have to be chaste so that men can be sure of the legitimacy of their children (Bk III, p. 241).

Women (if begged) refuse to submit (Bk III, p. 245).

Women like to be begged (ibid., p. 267).

Women acquire lovers in order to demonstrate their beauty (ibid., p. 261).

We hear in these opinions echoes of the banal observations and prejudices of the Lombard and Umbrian courts. The grounding of *The Courtier* (notably the first three books) in ordinary experience and assumptions is illustrated by the similes which Castiglione employs. Throughout the book the life of the perfect courtier is likened to that of the merchant, soldier and doctor. A decision whether the courtier should disobey the prince's strict command is compared to the strategy of a merchant who risks a little in order to gain a lot, but does not do the opposite (Bk II, p. 133). Placing a bad man in the company of worthies is like the 'passing off' by a trader of a debased coin in a heap of good ones (ibid., p. 173). There is imagery from the worlds of medicine (ibid., p. 108; Bk IV, p. 289), soldiery (Bk I, p. 66; Bk II, pp. 123–4) and blacksmithery (Bk III, p. 240; Bk IV, p. 341).

Still more frequently, metaphors are drawn from nature and art. The bees gather pollen from different flowers; the sea breaks unavailingly upon rocks; a ship is becalmed before a dying wind; torrents pour in contrary streams from the Appennine divide and large rivers dwindle

2. The references are to the translation of G. Bull.

into channels (Bk I, pp. 66–7; Bk III, p. 255; Bk IV, p. 295; Bk I, p. 75; Bk III, pp. 265–6). The art of the courtier and the court lady resembles that of the painter and musician (Bk I, p. 69; ibid., pp. 70, 77, 82; Bk II, pp. 114, 138).

A number of Castiglione's images self-evidently come from contemporary practice. At this point we are far below the high moral and intellectual purposes claimed for the author. Nowhere is this more true than in Castiglione's long account of pleasantry and wit. The great parade of jokes covers a tenth of the whole work. Closer inspection reveals that the array has been subjected to an intellectual process. The jokes are classified as well as described. They are divided into narrative, witty and practical kinds (Bk II, p. 157f.). In turn the narrative jokes are broken down into verbal extravagance, folly and oafishness (ibid., p. 160), the witty ones comprise the ambiguous, the unexpected, play on words, 'hoisting the petard', irony, cleverness masquerading as folly, gravity and self-ridicule (ibid., p. 166f.), and even the fewer practical jokes are sub-divided (ibid., p. 187).

A general principle of clarification, order and demonstration has been employed: jokes are identified, sub-divided and general rules deduced, as to the nature and effectiveness of humour or the limits of its proper use (ibid., pp. 186, 195). A character is made to say in the discussion which precedes the jokes that humour is a topic which 'may be taught and has some method in it' (ibid., p. 152), and it is implied by the outcome of the ensuing discussion that this method or 'art' is that which is demonstrated by the classification of jokes.

In one passage Castiglione declares that the orator should employ words in popular use (Bk I, pp. 76–7). It may be said that humour and oratory begin, respectively, with the jokes and words in popular usage and proceed by clarification and logic. This is true of Castiglione's design as a whole: the courtier's perfection 'can be determined through informed and reasoned argument' (ibid., p. 53).

Demonstration through clarification and division was an Aristotelian method. Similarly, Castiglione's arrangement of his discussion of the court lady is repeatedly described as a *disputa* (Bk II, pp. 201, 202; Bk III, pp. 257, 276; Bk IV, p. 283), a term deriving from the Schools. His approach throughout is 'dialectical' in that a thesis is commonly posed, an antithesis opposed to it and finally a synthesis reached, generally the Golden Mean.

Nevertheless, it would be quite wrong to think of *The Courtier* as an Aristotelian work. The influence of Aristotle upon Castiglione was keen. The mark, however, of Cicero lay deeper. Woodhouse has detected the effect of *De Oratore* upon the structure of the work (Woodhouse, 1978). Another respect in which this is true is that Castiglione expressly declares that his purpose was not to apply 'the precepts of . . . philosophers' (Bk I,

p. 87): this is an echo of Cicero, who urged the orator to use the language and belief of the people and avoid the prescriptions of philosophers.

Ancient rhetoric lay still closer to the heart of Castiglione's method in its approach to the commonplace. His materials were the prejudices, humour, vocabulary and common values of his own lay world. This base matter Castiglione worked, by art, into a philosophical form by applying to it a rational method. Reason made sense of the disordered impressions, attitudes and activities of everyday experience. This was the Ciceronian approach. The 'ordering' of ordinary experience might serve as a description either of Cicero's rhetoric or of Castiglione's *Courtier*. Like Machiavelli, Castiglione applied the inductive method to what men actually did. Where the former's terrain comprised a ruler's brutal road to power, the latter's was the 'foolishness' of the court (cf. Bk III, p. 223). From Aristotle came the idea of clarification and the Golden Mean, while Plato supplied the transcendent themes of love and beauty at the close of the book. Typical of its time was the tendency to draw comparisons with, and examples from, the ancient world. Yet all this was merely a dressing for a Ciceronian approach.

Castiglione gave weight to contemporary actions and opinions by yoking them to the *dicta* and *gesta* of the ancients. *The Courtier* supplies an index of examples to quote for polite and sophisticated conversation. There is mention of classical writers changing earlier vocabulary (Bk I, p. 76), ancient orators who dared to disagree with their forerunners (ibid., p. 82), and examples from antiquity of soldier-scholars (ibid., p. 89), famous painters (ibid., p. 100), true friends (Bk II, p. 137), brave women (Bk III, pp. 226–7), and loving wives (ibid., pp. 229–31).

In addition, *The Courtier* contains examples of women responsible for the greatness of Rome (ibid., p. 233), ancient rulers praiseworthy for their continence (ibid., p. 243), or marred by small failings (Bk IV, p. 287) and tyrants who feared for their lives (ibid., p. 301). There are references to rulers, sages and painters of antiquity such as Alexander the Great, Bias, Xenophon, Alcibiades, Apelles and Democritus. In this way Castiglione gave scholarly substance to commonplace activity and attitude by relating them to the intellectual method, or the deeds and sayings of the classical world.

After experience had been 'rationalised' it needed to be refined for Castiglione was describing the courtier's perfection. The four books of *The Courtier* represent a course in perfection similar to that which Alexander the Great had effected in changing barbarous people 'from a brutish to a human way of life' (Bk IV, p. 321). The dancing and music discussed in the early books were ways of engaging the lower instincts of the prince and courtier until this could be transformed into the precious object of true knowledge (Bk IV, pp. 302–3). The latter represented the subordination of emotion to reason (Bk IV, p. 327), of the active to the contemplative life, of war to peace (Bk IV, p. 303) and sensual to Platonic love (Bk IV, p. 334). This transformation reveals the heart both of Castiglione's intentions and achievement.

There are here all the elements of Ciceronian *humanitas*, whereby man was elevated from a brutish to a human condition by reason. In this process emotion gave way to reason and the brute to the man, whilst the active life was governed by the contemplative. What appears at first sight to be Plato's influence was in fact Cicero's. The method as well as the idea of perfection came from Cicero, though the latter in his turn had taken 'perfection' from Plato. Castiglione's Platonising, which goes further than anything he is likely to have discovered in Cicero's writings, reflected the Greek fashions and erudition of the early sixteenth century.

Castiglione's other method of changing the base into the precious was perhaps the reason for the enormous success of *The Courtier* in sixteenth-century Europe. Kings and courtiers knew already how to dance and make music and even how to exercise prudence in conducting their affairs. The best courtiers instinctively understood how to be nonchalant. Nor can the style and elegance of the work in itself be considered a sufficient explanation for its popularity. The seductiveness of the book was its art of raising ordinary things and commonplace assumptions to a high plane. Like Machiavelli, Castiglione found in Cicero the means of applying reason to experience and inducing rules and morals from it. The discovery of morality and truth in what courtiers actually did was a captivating pedagogy which modern scholars fail to notice when they castigate the 'idealism' of the book.

Chapter Twelve

The Intellectual and the Ideal of Intellectual Cultivation

Ancient wisdom combined with a change in the intellectuals' role to transform the idea of intellectual life during the Renaissance. These influences were first seen in fourteenth-century Italy; after 1500 they made their mark in northern Europe. The change was that laymen overran the cultural citadel of the Church. Learned culture had been monopolised by clerics from the days of Gregory the Great (d. A.D.604) to the life-time of Petrarch. During that epoch any advanced knowledge of the classics or progress in disciplines based upon them, had been almost completely in the hands of clerics; this began now to change.

A new professional corps of intellectuals did not replace the old. Petrarch did much to establish the new ideal of cultivation and he was in clerical orders. Erasmus (1469–1536), who performed a similar role in moving Italian ideas beyond the Alps a century and a half later, was a monk and later a priest. In each case a cleric prepared the way and laymen followed. Even afterwards the change was incomplete: while laymen became expert in classical culture, scholastic philosophy and theology maintained their primacy in the still clerical universities. Furthermore, ancient ideas themselves discouraged the formation of a new cadre of lay intellectuals. The greatest sign of the change indeed was the appropriation of the ideal of wisdom and learning by the aristocracy.

There was a classical principal of truth being a universal property. Seneca had declared that men should listen to philosophers, but follow the lessons of their own experience rather than formal precepts, because wisdom was common to mankind and to be found in all places (see above, p. 36). The accessibility of wisdom prepared the way for the clerical intellectual to be replaced by the layman and the 'amateur'. As the path of the intellectual's formation is traced forwards from the activities of Petrarch (see above, p. 42–4) both these processes can be observed.

Certain figures represent stages along this intellectual route. As we shall see, the Florentine patrician Niccolò Niccoli (*c.* 1364–1437) seems to have been influenced by Petrarch's ideal of the scholar, and was an 'amateur' possessed of such enthusiasm that he made his life into an intellectual labour. He was to some extent joined by other leading Florentines like Palla Strozzi and Cosimo de' Medici and together they helped to focus and pass on a new ideal. A great patron of the later *Quattrocento*, like Federigo da Montefeltro, was as much their heir as professional lay scholars such as Politian or Erasmus. The latter deserves especial attention for he acted as a channel by which the ideal of the intellectual was carried north. Although a churchman, he broke ground which laymen later worked. The lives of Niccoli and Erasmus (like that of Petrarch before them) allow us to investigate the passage of intellectual cultivation to the lay world.

Vespasiano da Bisticci's life of Niccoli shows him to have been a connoisseur, collector, bibliophile and an expert in orthography. It records that Niccoli brought sculpture and other fine things (*cose degne*) to Florence. He had a knowledge of painting and sculpture as well as architecture, and possessed 'universal judgement' (*universale judicio*) in all the fine arts. Niccoli collected medals, ancient bronzes, marble heads, antique vases, inscriptions, mosaic tables, famous paintings and other *cose degne*. Indeed he was *universale* in all such things. Furthermore, Niccoli was intimate with artists like Brunelleschi, Donatello, Luca della Robbia and Ghiberti.

Niccoli might be called a friend of the arts. Arguably he displayed in this an originality surpassing that of the more famous Cosimo de' Medici whom he may have influenced. A new notion of patronage is implied by his actions: Niccoli did not employ artists; instead he made them his friends. He was novel in holding works of art to be worthy of judgement and discrimination. Niccoli did not commission but rather collected, and he may be considered a candidate for the title of the first modern connoisseur.

There are a number of distinctive traits in Niccoli's personality. He placed an unusual importance on collecting books. Much was sacrificed by him in order to assemble a library, and he copied manuscripts himself. He was responsible for bringing to Florence and having circulated there the first complete text of Cicero's *De Oratore* which had recently been discovered at Lodi. Previously only fragmentary versions had been known. He spent his father's inheritance in buying books. Moreover, Niccoli seems to have thought that his library might exercise a semi-public role. If he discovered any classical text that was not in Florence he took pains to procure it;

by implication this was for the benefit of the city. Vespasiano says that Niccoli kept his books for the use of others rather than for himself, hoping that a public library would be formed from them after his death.

Niccoli seems to have envisaged a second public position for himself as the friend of young scholars. He was a patron of students, and the wise elder of all young aristocrats in the city who might possess a scholarly disposition. Vespasiano declares that he kept open house for studious young men and gave them private reading to undertake, followed by discussions. At least one of these youths had been recruited in the street, for in his life of Piero de' Pazzi, Vespasiano recorded that Niccoli met him in the city and engaged him in conversation 'seeing that he was a very attractive youth'. He urged him not to waste his good qualities and breeding but rather win esteem by pursuing letters. He even sent a scholar to work as his tutor.

There is a hint that Niccoli also associated gentility with 'good' taste, criticised what he took to be the 'materialism' of his contemporaries, and aspired to 'universal' knowledge. Vespasiano remarked that besides Niccoli's fastidious eating habits (dining off ancient plates) no house in Florence was better decorated or supplied with *gentili cose*. This may seem odd when we recall that Niccoli exhausted his patrimony on his collections. Perhaps he had discovered that, with his house full of genteel possessions, the man of good taste could find a place in high society which his want of substance otherwise would have denied him.

Niccoli rejected conventional values. He refused opportunities of making money and spent what he had inherited. He embarked early on a commercial career, but when his father died he devoted himself to study. Farms bequeathed to him were sold in order to buy books. Niccoli only kept enough back to maintain himself. In the end he was compelled to rely upon the generosity of Cosimo. Niccoli abandoned trade; he also declined marriage out of fear that his studies might be impeded.

The rejection of wedlock and business seems to be related to Niccoli's scorn for the 'material' outlook of his fellow citizens. He would not hold political office, especially the 'colonial' governorships in the Florentine dominions, because they were food for vultures. Vespasiano reports that by vultures Niccoli meant men who spent their time in taverns and devoured the substance of the poor. Similarly, Niccoli despised those who only cared for their bodies and who even doubted the immortality of the soul. It was, he said a great misfortune of many that they only think of governing their bodies and do not wish to think of the immortality of the soul as opposed to their unbridled wills and wish to see that soul sit in a chair and think it is so very substantial that they can see it.

(Le vite, ed. A. Greco, ii, 232)

Niccoli felt a great hate for such people and for any who doubted the truths of Christianity.

This distinctive personality had one more facet. In something like Burckhardt's sense, Niccoli was a 'universal' man. He was considered to possess a universal judgement, skill and knowledge not only in letters but in the visual arts. He also had a knowledge of all parts of the globe, having in his house a map of the world (*universale*). We may add to this that Niccoli wished to bring to Florence a complete corpus of ancient writings and that his erudition was so wide and his own literary standards were so high that he was always ill-content with his own efforts, whilst other writers never failed to consult him.

Some of these remarkable views may have sprung from one individual's personal talents and proclivities. Niccoli was a zealot for the antique; conceivably emotional tendencies led him away from marriage, and it may be that he was one of that breed who hammer the establishment in order to enter it on their own terms. Nevertheless, the general influences of Petrarch and the Greek revival are to be sensed on Niccoli. His idea of a public use for his books was surely inherited from Petrarch. The latter had revived the ancient notion of a public library, and he had planned to use his own manuscripts as the basis of a Venetian library. Nearer to home Boccaccio had bequeathed his books to the library of the Florentine convent of Santo Spirito. This was a torch which Niccoli seems to have taken up and passed on to Cosimo de' Medici.

Do we not also hear an echo of Petrarch in Niccoli's concern for good handwriting and the correct copying and transmission of classical texts? Niccoli's own written work (to which Vespasiano does not refer) was on Latin orthography and he has been given the credit for creating the later italic script whilst Poggio Bracciolini established what became known as Roman script. These were answers to the call made by Petrarch several generations before for a return to a clearer form of hand, like that of antiquity (he quoted Priscian) and away from those then current (cf. B. L. Ullmann, 1960, pp. 60, 77).

One of the most intriguing achievements of Niccoli and his circle was to have attributed a new importance to artists and works of art. Almost the only known example of this sort of attitude before him was furnished by Petrarch. The latter was the friend of well-known artists and he thought a painting by Giotto the only possession he had worthy to leave in his will to a lord. Petrarch's concern for things and situations worthy of lords fitted easily with the poet's contempt for the vulgar and his scant respect for communal and civic institutions. He complained of the disadvantage of writing poems in Italian which the common people could understand, and when Boccaccio reproached him for living in the courts of despots, Petrarch replied complacently that they were good for him.

Do we find here the origin of Niccoli's regard for works of art as *cose degne*, his attack upon the vulgar tongue and his scorn at holding civic office as the occupation of avaricious men from the alehouses? Petrarch's influence may be detected with some confidence in these quarters, and possibly in Niccoli's celibacy. The latter's refusal to take a wife lest it hinder his studies might seem to owe something to Petrarch's advocacy of the solitary life and his renunciation of sensual passion, however much Petrarch himself had failed to live up to this ideal and the very requirements of his ecclesiastical orders.

Niccoli made a work of art out of his own life as a pattern for the man of letters or 'civilised' individual. In all this there were two strands that did not derive from Petrarch. There had been many cultivated clerics before Petrarch and there had even been a few lay scholars before Niccoli. However, he combined lay scholarship with clerical virtue. He was a layman, he was a scholar and yet he renounced marriage and directed wealth to higher ends. This might have sprung from the germination in the different soil of the Florentine ruling class of Petrarch's teaching; it also owed something to further study of ancient sources. The permanent heirs of the lay philosophers of the ancient world were destined to be the educated laymen of modern times. A particular influence on this was the knowledge of Greek traditions that was beginning to advance in Florence in Niccoli's time. It is hard not to hear echoes in Niccoli's 'fathering' of the young patricians of Florence of the guidance given by Socrates to the young men of Athens.

The strains of the new scholar-personality we hear in Niccoli can be paralleled in other Florentines (a few Tuscans amongst them) whose lives were immortalised by Vespasiano. For instance, Sozomen of Pistoia took a most 'un-bourgeois' view of money and employment. He gave up his superfluous wealth to God or spent it upon books. He astonished a cardinal by brusquely declining to tutor his nephew because he did not need the money. On another occasion he gave up his teaching for a year since it interfered with his writing. To this end he lived frugally on his savings, which he kept in a purse on his hat-stand. Vespasiano describes Sozomen's abandoning of work as springing from a wish to lead the life of a philosopher.

Similar attitudes are attributed to Ser Filippo di Ser Ugolino who retired late in life to the abbey of Settimo so as to lead a quieter, more devout and studious life. In this he was 'like an ancient philosopher'. Ser Filippo was resistant to female charm, moderate in his food and drink and devoted all spare time to study. This takes us back into the circle of Niccoli. Ser Filippo was the friend of Maestro Pagolo, another man of letters, who was intimate with Niccoli, Cosimo de' Medici, Leonardo Bruni, Ambrogio Traversari and Giannozzo Manetti. All these figures, according to Vespasiano, did not care for pleasures of the senses or for eating and drinking like the ignorant herd. Maestro Pagolo himself, who was a Latin and Greek scholar, was reputedly a virgin, and a vegetarian; he had chosen to lead a simple life, sleeping beside his desk.

Similar stories are told about several of the younger Florentines at that time. So as to commit themselves to letters, Cipriano Rucellai and Niccolò della Luna never married, whilst Donato Acciaiuoli had the reputation of having known no woman until his marriage. As we have seen, one of the members of this younger generation, Piero de' Pazzi, was led to abandon his wanton pleasures for the other-worldly delights of letters under the influence of Niccoli. During solitary walks at his villa at Trebbio, Piero was able to learn by heart the whole of the *Aeneid* and many orations by Livy. This practice of solitude doubtless owed something to Petrarch who had combined elements of monastic contemplation and of classical *otium* in his praise of solitude. In the early *Quattrocento* the idea was secularised for the benefit of the lay intellectual under the more direct guidance of ancient sources.

The notion of connoisseurship, the search for truth wheresoever it might be found and the idea that artistic creativity required solitude, helped to shape the idea of art and letters for the future. However, there was a side to the Petrarchan ideal that was soon to give way before antique ideas. The opposition to marriage owed a good deal to Petrarch and ideals of Christian scholarship. In Niccoli's own lifetime this older attitude to marriage was already being replaced by a positive one more in tune with ancient sources.

The ideal of individual cultivation had passed from Petrarch, who was a philosopher and a poet, into the hands of citizens. Florentines like Niccoli and Cosimo de' Medici in their turn prepared the way for the 'philosopher–rulers' of the next generation. To this class belonged Federigo da Montefeltro, duke of Urbino, Lionello d'Este of Ferrara, and Cosimo's grandson, Lorenzo de' Medici. The latter was the party despot and even *de facto* ruler of Florence, since princes felt him to be one of themselves. Petrarch had advertised to Italians the contemporary value of a knowledge of antiquity; the citizens of Florence, like Boccaccio, Niccoli, Palla Strozzi and Cosimo de' Medici had appropriated this learning. Now through their efforts and success the idea passed to rulers.

Of course not all princes were philosophers and probably none were so learned as Lorenzo de' Medici, who was actively involved in the

Plate 1 Simone Martini: *Virgilian Allegory* (Full captions to the illustrations are given in the List of Plates, p. vii)

Plate 2   Crucifix at S. Chiara, Assisi (formerly at San Damiano, Assisi)

Plate 3   Leonardo da Vinci: *The Virgin of the Rocks*

Plate 4 Perugino: The Battle of Love and Chastity

Plate 5 Justus of Ghent: *Federigo da Montefeltro and his son Guidobaldo listening to a philosophical discourse*

Plate 6 Masaccio: *Holy Trinity*

Plate 7   Masaccio: *St Paul*

Plate 8   The facade of Or San Michele, Florence

learned life of his time. He was interested in the Italian vernacular and he was himself amongst the finest Italian poets of his day. Perhaps in this devotion to the vernacular as well as in his enthusiasm for architecture he had been influenced by Alberti. In addition, Lorenzo was a patron of the arts. Princes no longer felt excluded by the learning of the Church. They felt they had become accomplished in letters, or could become familiar with them.

The spectacle of scholar–princes received mixed applause. It was probably easier for a solider like Federigo da Montefeltro to be a philosopher than for a man of leisure like Lorenzo de' Medici. Indeed, it can be argued that it was Machiavelli's purpose in *The Prince* to advise the Medici of his own day against imitating the example of Lorenzo, whom he may have thought was too learned and unmanly for his city's good (Stephens, 1986). Conversely, it may have been Castiglione's intention in *The Courtier* to counsel Francesco Maria della Rovere of Urbino, who was a rough soldier, to follow the philosophic example of his Montefeltro forebears, notably Federigo.

The first of the philosopher–kings of northern Europe is to be encountered some two generations after Federigo da Montefeltro's death in 1482. In one of his letters Erasmus commended Henry VIII's authorship of the *Assertio Septem Sacramentorum*, the broadside which Henry had fired at Luther (see below, p. 211). Erasmus was anxious to deny rumours that he himself was its author. He did so by calling attention to Henry's talents as a horseman, mathematician, musician and theologian. Erasmus observed that the king was a student of Aquinas, Biel and Duns Scotus (*Op. Epist.*, ed. Allen, no. 1038). Erasmus had not written Henry's defence of the sacraments but his ideas had deeply influenced the king and a number of those thinkers around him who had helped in the work. The notion of the wise prince which Erasmus thus helped to shape was a particular formulation of a general idea of cultivation. For Erasmus, as for his intellectual forebears in antiquity, like Plato and Cicero, rulers must be virtuous. For this they needed knowledge, which should be taught them by philosophers. There was therefore an ideal of cultivation particularly appropriate to the leader, governor or prince.

While Erasmus channelled the idea of the prince to northern Europe, he himself became a pattern for the intellectual. It was one which others imitated, but like Petrarch who had begun the Italian movement a century and a half before, Erasmus himself was a cleric. He had taken monastic vows and lived for some seven years after 1486 as a monk at Steyn near Gouda in the Low Countries. He did, however, leave the monastery to enter the service of the bishop of Cambrai. Later he received a papal dispensation allowing him to put off monastic dress. Afterwards he wore the habit of a priest (he had been ordained in 1492) but he lived in the lay world.

Erasmus twice held positions in universities. In 1511 he was appointed to a chair at Cambridge and from 1517 to 1521 he lectured at Louvain. For many centuries to come the universities were staffed by clerics and Erasmus would not have been able to enjoy his academic income or that which he received from an English parish had he not been in orders. All the rest of his income, however, came from tutorships, pensions, gifts and royalties. Between 1496 and 1498, whilst living in Paris, he was tutor to the sons of a Lübeck merchant as well as to two Englishmen, Thomas Grey and Robert Fisher. Similarly, when he went to Italy in 1506 it was as tutor to the sons of the Italian physician to King Henry VII. Later in his Italian sojourn Erasmus tutored Alexander and James Stewart, the natural sons of James IV of Scotland. In subsequent years he continued to receive an annuity secured on his English living but the remainder of his income – other than during the spells at Cambridge and Louvain – came from the generosity of laymen. The Emperor Charles V and the duke of Cleves gave pensions, and Erasmus was the recipient of sums of money from English and German bishops, and from various nobles. Finally, Erasmus received substantial royalties from his publishers. All the while he lived as an itinerant scholar in the cities of the Low Countries and the Rhineland.

Erasmus's position might be described as being in the Church but not of it. This was reflected in his writings and his view of the intellectual. His public was not made up of the clerical intellectuals who had dominated northern European scholarship from the ninth to the fourteenth century. Unlike them, Erasmus did not live in a special institution. He was not teaching young men so as to produce a new generation of 'professional' *clerici* in the cloister or the university. Erasmus stood in relation to the clerical scholars of former times as the friars had been to the monks. Like the friars, he lived in the world; and his writings, so various in their scope, were directed to the edification of all.

Surveying the bulk of Erasmus's writings, the first place is occupied by translations and editions of ancient texts. These included the Church Fathers and Latin and Greek pagan texts. Perhaps in this category should be placed one of the most famous of all his works, an edition of the Greek New Testament. Philology was another of Erasmus's keenest interests and was the essential tool for his textual work. The chief examples of this are his *Adagia* (familiar quotations from the classics), the *Colloquia* (imaginary conversations as an aid to literary elegance), and the text-books of style and pronunciation, the *Copia, De Constructione*, the *De Recta Latini Graecique Sermonis Pronunciatione* and the *Ciceronianus*, a critique of excessive Ciceronianism.

In the *Anti-Barbari* Erasmus justified the claims of philology based on the classics as an aid to a Christian life. The *Enchiridion Militis Christiani* (*Education of a Christian Knight*), the *Institutio Principis Christiani*, the

Ecclesiastes and the *Complaint of Peace* are political tracts inasmuch as they concern the conduct of government in Church and State or the education of their leaders. The *Praise of Folly* stands in a class of its own as Erasmus's most famous and idiosyncratic work. Self-evidently moral writings were fewer, chiefly *The Institute of Christian Matrimony*, *The Christian Widow*, the *De Libero Arbitrio*. Finally, there are Erasmus's letters, published in numerous editions during his lifetime.

In fact, the *Praise of Folly* and the 'political' writings were moral treatises and many of the epistles and 'philological' writings had a moral point. Erasmus was concerned in his writings on princely rule and on matrimony to encourage a wisdom based on what Petrarch had called 'learned piety'; in short, the wisdom of the ancients. In the *Anti-Barbari* Erasmus had defended the relevance of ancient literature to a rational Christianity. In the *Praise of Folly* and the *Complaint of Peace* he recommended Socratic ignorance as a way to wisdom. There, in the *Anti-Barbari* and in many passages elsewhere a cosmopolitanism is enunciated drawn from Christian principles and the universalism of the Stoics. The union of faith and a commonsense reason is the theme of his foray into theology, the *Ratio Verae Theologiae* and of the *Method of Study*. The stories and quotations in the *Colloquies* and *Adages* supplied specific illustrations of the moral tracts. Most of Erasmus's writings were therefore ethical.

All of them had an educational purpose. His treatises on style were textbooks and his *De Ratione Studii* was pedagogical. In fact, there was a loosely educational point behind all his works. Erasmus made his translations into Latin for a public which did not know Greek. He sought to educate boys simultaneously in morals and philology by means of the *Colloquies*. His treatises on princely rule and marriage were intended to teach princes and high-born women. The *Praise of Folly* was meant for a still bigger audience.

In attaching so high an importance to morals and education, Erasmus betrayed the influence of the Italian humanists. Nevertheless, the audience of Erasmus was much wider. The cultural climate of northern Europe, Erasmus's own disposition and the advent of printing help to explain this. When the ideas of the humanists were transplanted their envelope of Italian patriotism fell away and Erasmus added a cosmopolitanism of his own. A great number of his works were immediately printed and the majority were produced *for* the press. None of the Italian humanists down to Politian worked for the press in the way that Erasmus wrote for the Basle printer Froben. This was a pattern for the future.

Erasmus is an arresting figure and he was an ambiguous model for the intellectual class of early modern times. As a cleric he depended only in part upon the benefices of the Church. Working at different times in the monk's cell, in castles, university quadrangles and in the town houses of printers he addressed men and women, boys as well as adults, clergy and laity. He never discarded his clerical garb but he left the cloister and belonged to lay society. Erasmus was thus able, though a cleric, to create a pattern for the lay intellectual of the future. This is illustrated by his letter on the life of the English theologian John Colet (1467–1519), often called his *Life* of Colet. Colet himself was a cleric but mundane in his outlook and Erasmus was anxious to point to the high estimate Colet placed upon the value of the lay world.

Colet is depicted as leading a virtuous life in which he avoided the temptations of sin by sacred studies, prayer and philosophy. He shunned laymen so as to avoid their worldly tastes, notably their rich banquets. Colet's 'other-worldliness' is given a less traditional air when Erasmus adds that he turned away from lay company because the eyes of the world were fixed upon him, and he believed it was harder to gain favour than it was to lose it by slander. Domestic economy was thus given a Renaissance colouring.

The tinge is heightened by Colet's views on building. He preferred frugality and learned conversations to magnificence. He did, however, use his private fortune to erect a 'magnificent' school at St Paul's in London. Afterwards he raised a magnificent house attached to a Carthusian monastery to which he planned to retire with some friends (amongst them Erasmus) to study philosophy. We are shown in short a wise orator designed on ancient principles: Colet's highest pleasure was the 'society' of friends in which good conversation in pursuit of wisdom could be enjoyed.

Colet possessed a Renaissance attitude to scholastic philosophy, education and the laity. Amongst friends he would attack the Scotists as sterile 'logic-choppers' and lambasted Aquinas, despite Erasmus's defence of him, as a man who had rashly sought to explain all things by employing profane philosophy and an arrogant spirit. Colet was siding with the humanists, who had argued that moral philosophy was a better road to Christian truth. They preferred a Socratic ignorance to the claims of the schoolmen to know all things.

Colet's new learning showed itself in his view of education and moral leadership. Quintilian's influence is discernible in Colet's belief that the best hope for a healthy state lay in good education. His principle that boys should be admitted to his school on the basis of 'nature and intelligence' and good pupils rewarded by high places in the class recalls Quintilian. The latter's ideas had already been taken up in early fifteenth-century Florence, particularly by the civic humanists.

Even more striking is Colet's belief that religious life was the high-minded life of the lay scholar. For Colet the most fervent adherents of the evangelical life were not monks but the members of the Platonic Academy of Florence. Laymen versed in pagan wisdom were therefore held to be more religious than monks. This arresting judgement was accompanied by a lofty view of marriage. For Colet, married people were more virtuous than single clerics. Accordingly he chose married citizens as governors of his school. Erasmus adds that Colet's attitude to marriage sprang partly from his conviction that concupiscence was a less venal sin than pride, hate, slander, vanity, avarice or ambition.

As clerics who elevated the importance of lay values and concerns, Erasmus and Colet were transitional figures. In this they call to mind the example of Petrarch. In Cicero's *Letters* Petrarch had found the pattern for a circle of friendship in which scholarly companions pursued their studies to a common end. The ideal was a lay one, rooted amongst the philosophers and patricians of the ancient city-states. Petrarch himself was a cleric, but his immediate heirs were the civic officials from whom the humanists were recruited and the patricians for whom they worked. From similar sources and with the Italian example in mind, Erasmus had helped to pass this ideal of the intellectual life to northern Europe.

Erasmus shared his ideas with an extremely wide circle of intellectual friends whose diversity is shown by a provision in his will. His friend and collaborator, Froben, was to publish an edition of his works and copies were to be sent to certain beneficiaries. Colleges and universities with which Erasmus had been associated were named at Bruges, Cambridge, Louvain and Tournai. Amongst these were colleges noted for the advancement of the new humanistic learning, such as Queen's College, Cambridge and the Collegium Trilingue at Louvain. Two libraries benefited, one of them the Royal Library in Spain. The bishop of Trent and a number of English bishops were also listed. Lay beneficiaries included Sir Thomas More, the senator of the town council of Mechlin, the President of the Estates of Holland and Ferdinand of Austria. Erasmus was the heir of Valla and Petrarch, but he was more cosmopolitan in his outlook and choice of friends than either of his great Italian forebears.

Italian humanist thought reached Erasmus in a single stream, but afterwards branched out. There was no single group who inherited Erasmian *humanitas*, textual criticism and the ideal of the scholar which accompanied them. The chief reasons for this were the composite character of the Italian idea of literary studies, the different traditions of northern countries and the Reformation. 'Literary studies' had been a loosely conceived programme which contained two very different elements. The recovery of ancient culture had been combined by Petrarch with a zeal to learn from its wisdom. These two things, moreover, were seen from a patriotic Italian viewpoint. In time the strands separated. That happened after 1520, when the Reformation began to have its effect.

The universities were a great obstacle in the way of *humanitas* enjoying free sway in northern Europe. In Germany, the Low Countries, France and Britain, universities dominated the national culture as those of Italy did not. To a considerable extent this was also true of the similar institutions of higher learning in Spain, Switzerland, eastern Europe and Scandinavia. 'Humane' letters made a deep impression on northern universities. They changed their teaching and *curricula* and attached new functions to themselves such as the Collegium Trilingue at Louvain devoted to the study of the three languages of Greek, Latin and Hebrew. Nevertheless, literary studies, as the Italian humanists had understood them, did not dislodge the traditional Aristotelian-based thinking of the universities. The humanists had turned their back upon such thought rather than having sought to overturn it. Their intellectual base, moreover, was an imperfectly defined and protean segment of ancient philosophy. Accordingly, it was easier for the traditional disciplines to absorb 'the humanities' than the other way about.

One further reason that Erasmus's successors no longer pursued *humanitas* like the Italians lay in the Reformation, which renewed theology (ironically with the help of humane literary studies) and fostered clerical interests and sectarian divisions. The humanist dream of humanity united by reason and wisdom dissolved with the cosmology of the Reformers and the national rivalries they opened up. Philosophy, as it were, rose up again from the cities of men and returned to the stars. Erasmus and the Italian humanists did have successors but their influence is hard to follow as it flowed into narrower streams.

Textual criticism of the Bible was appropriated by the Reformers and *humanitas* was killed by a Pauline puritanism which trumpeted the notion that wisdom was a worldly folly. Philology and 'humane' studies did trickle through Protestant theology, doctrinaire puritanism and the new Catholicism of the Counter-Reformation. Though later sixteenth-century Europe was divided, it did share this disguised legacy. Meanwhile, court poets took up Petrarchan and ancient poetry whilst classical studies became the preserve of the professional and amateur grammarians. Historiography and political theory came to be shared by assorted companions – lawyers, bureaucrats, university-trained philosophers and theologians from the seminaries.

The early modern heirs of the Italian humanists were so scattered that it is sometimes hard to recognise them. In classical scholarship the French academic Joseph Scaliger (1540–1609) and the Florentine patrician Piero Vettori (1499–1585) were humanists *après le mot*. The Spanish Jesuit Juande Mariana (1535–1624), the Dutch Calvinist Hugo Grotius (1583–1645) and the French royalist Jean Bodin (1530–96) all look back to the work of the Italians or to the sources discovered by them. Despite working in what seem now different disciplines, historians so various as August de Thou (1553–1617) in France, Camden (1551–1623) the English antiquarian and the Dutch man of letters Peter Cornelius Hooft (1581–1647) descended from the humanists.

The learned academicians and aristocratic circles also shared a certain outlook inherited from the past. Through the conflicts of the late sixteenth century it is strange to see such men corresponding, and even visiting each other's countries, crossing the 'iron-curtain' of Reformation Europe. They conceived of themselves inhabiting a 'republic of letters' in which reason united scholars in a commonwealth, as it had before them for Erasmus, Petrarch and Valla. The somewhat mordant opinion with which Paolo Sarpi (1552–1623) from one side of the fence judged the Council of Trent as a force which had helped to perpetuate the division of Europe may be compared to the viewpoint of Hugo Grotius. A Dutch Calvinist who had been born and educated in Holland, he wrote his great work of law and political theory, the *De Jure Belli ac Pacis* (1625) to demonstrate the superior rights of mankind over those of nations. The Stoic cosmopolitanism of Erasmus had not died with him; a shallow current ran on via the Republic of Letters down to the Enlightenment.

There is one group in northern Europe which can claim to have been more faithful than any other to Italian ideas. The humanists had chiefly been drawn from the circle of state servants, lawyers and private tutors, or from the patricians whom they served. The same classes furnished the truest heirs of the humanists in early modern times. Budé (1467–1540), Althusius (1557–1638) and Grotius were lawyers and teachers of law. Others were civil servants or courtiers and patricians. Sir Thomas More was a royal servant and several of the most famous historians were from royal or aristocratic circles, like Hooft and the Frenchman Davila (1576–1631). The great English historians after 1600, Francis Bacon (1561–1626) and Edward Hyde, Earl of Clarendon (1609–74), were the same sort.

Standing well back, the chief effect of the Renaissance upon intellectual life was to ensure that there were no successors of the medieval class of clerical intellectuals. Knowledge of the classics and the ability to judge moral and theological questions were carried from a professional class of intellectuals into the lay world. In this sense the humanists themselves (a layman like Valla as much as a Petrarch or an Erasmus) were transitional figures. The real Italian ice-breakers were men like Niccolò Niccoli, Federigo da Montefeltro or Lorenzo de' Medici. The humanists had opened a way for them and the future was to belong to their successors amongst the learned rulers and aristocrats of northern Europe.

Kings imitated Italian princes in sponsoring humane letters – such as the Regius professorships established in England and France, notably those created by Francis I which became the Collège de France. Aristocrats pursued most zealously of all the humanist ideals of education. The aristocratic mode of life combined hard physical activity with polite conversation. The ancient ideal of educating the 'whole man' could be adapted readily to it.

The 'Country-House' society of the aristocrat was akin to the villa world of senatorial Rome and similarly *mondain*. The ethical dilemmas aired by ancient writers could be used to address their own problems. Preparing for death is a universal problem, but the rich man understands better than the rest how to prepare for poverty whilst in the midst of plenty. The Stoic remedy of *thinking* yourself poor and powerless was well understood by nobles.

The private domain also allowed the genteel to appreciate the senatorial view of pagan Rome. The ancients liked to distinguish *otium* from *negotium* – that is to say, the life of cultured leisure from that of public business. This had been commonly equated by Roman writers with life at the villa and at Rome. In the early sixteenth century, capital cities and royal courts developed together because the court came to reside in season at or near the capital.

Moreover, aristocrats were inclined to cast a jaundiced eye at the goings-on at court and capital which they could not escape, and it was easy for them to appreciate the biting irony with which a senator like Tacitus recited the events of Imperial Rome. The abuses of tyrants and their rise or fall was as well known to them as to the younger Seneca, and the Stoic philosophy which had guided him during his precarious service with the Emperor Nero was suited to console them also in the slippery world of confessional and court politics. Stoic philosophy was no doubt all the pleasanter when pondered in a salon full of Italian books and antiques. The anchorage of ancient wisdom in this mannered world helped guarantee its early success, but also a long-term failure.

Chapter Thirteen

Classical Scholarship

The humanists came to appreciate ancient ethics by delving in the classical rhetoricians. In the course of this work they developed a critical philology. They had also a voracious appetite for the literary remains of antiquity. Scholars like Petrarch, Poggio, Valla and Politian attained a practical expertise in ancient language, style, handwriting and erudition. In the case of Valla this was combined with a philosophical interest in grammar which he had learned from classical rhetoric and legal sources.

The echoing fame of these figures reached the nineteenth century and the work of Voigt and Sabbadini. For them the humanists had simply discovered and revived the ancient world. Since then, historians have become much more conscious of the contribution made by scholars before and since the Renaissance to the survival and recovery of classical literature. This change of viewpoint is nicely illustrated by the judgement of a leading modern work on the classical tradition.

> Time and again during the medieval period we come across scholars who look for rare manuscripts and then copy them or have them copied. The work of Petrarch and his circle was in this tradition which had been the glory of Tours and Monte Cassino. If the invention of printing had not supervened, their labours would have had to be repeated again and again as had been the case after similar efforts in the past.
>
> (R. Bolgar, 1954, p. 263, cf. 280)

Petrarch and his friends *did* constitute a circle and there had been similar coteries before, yet nagging questions raise themselves. Was the nineteenth-century belief in the original work of the Italian humanists wholly imaginary? Were the discoveries of Petrarch in Verona and Liège, or of Poggio in Germany and France, no different to those in earlier centuries? Were Italian achievements only made to seem different when their results were put in print?

A case can be made that the centre of the stage has been neglected for the wings. The humanists *did* play the major role and scholars of the ninth, twelfth and sixteenth centuries were subsidiary figures. Moreover, the conceptions and achievements of the Italian humanists were different by order from those of their forebears whilst early modern scholars continued the work of the humanists. The permanent success of the latters' work was accomplished not by printing it but because of its novel methods and approach.

Modern classical scholarship is the science of a dead civilisation; it was the humanists who had first seen the past in this way. Because they did so they saw its literature and monuments as the limited and knowable artefacts of a lost world. Furthermore, an altered view of the past gave the humanists' endeavours a newly systematic and coherent character. The problem then is to understand how the humanists depended upon the classical traditions preserved through the medieval period and where they advanced beyond them.

Nevertheless, older claims about the humanist achievement were exaggerated. Their work was not based on classical sources, as the thought and letters of the preceding centuries had failed to be. Medieval scribes and scholars misinterpreted, departed from and advanced beyond the culture of Latin antiquity, but these were movements about a base. Greek, Arabic and vernacular contributions were secondary. The Latin thought of the Middle Ages was an evolution of the Christian culture of late antiquity, notably of the Church Fathers. This diet was leavened by a few of the best known orators, poets and historians. These authors provided a preparation for the writings of the Church Fathers. There were, however, two attempts to drink directly at the classical sources during the Carolingian age, and again in the twelfth century; the Italian Renaissance continued these efforts.

The humanists were in no sense discovering or popularising classical texts which had been lost from one age to another, like the Dead Sea Scrolls. Perhaps no more than eight manuscripts had survived from antiquity down to the fourteenth century. With these exceptions, what the humanists used and 'discovered' were works which had been copied since the fall of Rome. Manuscripts survived down to the Renaissance because they had been copied since the fifth century: indeed, there were copies of those few texts which survived in ancient codices. This Italian dependence upon medieval copying can be glimpsed from a map recording the chief places of discovery of classical texts by the Italian humanists (see Figure 9). They were in the monastic and cathedral libraries established since antiquity.

Only two libraries, Monte Cassino and Bobbio, can be considered Dead Sea Caves. From the sixth century down to the thirteenth century Monte Cassino had remained the unique depository of Varro's *De Lingua Latina*, Seneca's *Dialogues*, the later books of Tacitus's *Annals* as well as his *Histories*, the *Golden Ass* of Apuleius and the *De Aquis* of Frontinus. Bobbio afforded a draughty home for some ancient poets, grammarians and technical writers like Valerius Flaccus, the first-century Roman epic poet; Rutilius Namatianus, the fifth-century Latin poet from Gaul; Charisius, the late fourth-century African grammarian; and Manilius, the Roman poet of the first century B.C.

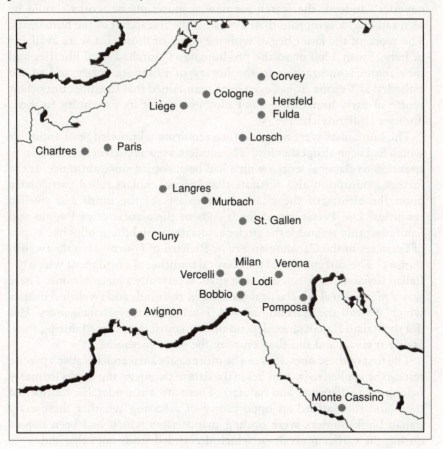

Fig. 9   Sites of discovery of classical manuscripts

Monte Cassino and Bobbio are exceptions proving a general rule that books survived because they were copied, and most of this copying was done in northern Europe. Apart from the lost manuscript of Valerius Flaccus from Bobbio (which may have been an early medieval codex), all these other works were preserved at Monte Cassino and Bobbio in medieval versions. Even in these centres ancient manuscripts which were not copied tended to disappear. Thus, Bobbio was the last place known to have preserved copies of the lost *Letters* of Fronto and the *De Re Publica* of Cicero (now surviving only in palimpsests). In general, the spots where the humanists found manuscripts were in the heartland of the Carolingian Empire and many of the names represent monasteries established at that time. The Italian humanists depended upon the resources of transalpine libraries almost more than those of Italy.

Their classical work did not proceed, however, by means of 'discoveries'. Indeed, the search for new manuscripts or works should be seen rather as a symptom than a cause of the researches of the humanists. The work of the latter began with the study of those that were available in Italy. From 1260 or so the pre-humanists searched local libraries and they found some rarities in the library of Pomposa abbey and in the cathedral at Verona. It has even been maintained that the most important centre of early humanism was Padua because of its proximity to those libraries (Billanovich, 1953).

The humanists were not therefore acquiring a knowledge of antiquity which had been altogether lost. The modern view is correct that they drew attention to classical works which had been copied since antiquity. Is the further assumption also accurate that Italian scholars relied particularly upon the efforts of the classical enthusiasts of the ninth and twelfth centuries? Did Petrarch and his friends or the associates of Poggio and Salutati simply resemble the circles associated with bibliophiles like Lupus of Ferrières in the Carolingian age or Richard of Fournival in the twelfth century? The current idea of the classical tradition as a bridge, of which the Italian Renaissance formed the last span, is certainly a plausible one. There was a marked zeal for classical learning in the ninth and twelfth centuries which we call the Carolingian and Twelfth-century Renaissances. But did the Italian Renaissance depend upon manuscripts copied during these earlier revivals and did they employ the same methods?

The first of these questions can be more easily answered because a precise test can be applied to it. This lies in the date of the surviving books formerly belonging to Petrarch and Salutati. There are a considerable number of these and they afford an opportunity of assessing whether these early Italian book-hunters were finding manuscripts which had been copied during the earlier revivals or which descended from ones that did.

Many of Petrarch's manuscripts passed into the collection of the dukes of Milan, whence they were removed by King Louis XII to

France in the sixteenth century. Altogether at least sixty items have been identified from the two hundred or more which Petrarch once possessed. Many of Salutati's books reached the Medici library and one hundred and eleven have been traced by B. L. Ullman from a collection that contained perhaps as many as eight hundred volumes. A large enough sample survives for a clear idea to be obtained of the date of these humanists' books.

If books from Salutati's library are assigned to the centuries in which they were copied, it is possible to produce a chart revealing their paleographical character (see Figure 10). The most striking fact to emerge from the chart is that books written after 1300 form more than twice as high a percentage as those of the twelfth century. Salutati's books in the latter category were more numerous than those of the thirteenth century. The nearly complete absence of Carolingian books is also noticeable.

More can be made of these figures by considering the texts which they contain. Ullman has noticed that the twelfth-century manuscripts are mostly Church Fathers, while classical authors and texts of scholastic philosophy become more prominent amongst the *Trecento* books. Figure 11 shows how just these comments are.

The Christian authors of antiquity (as a percentage of the total) drop dramatically from some 48 per cent to some 17 per cent, although as the number of fourteenth-century manuscripts is so much greater, the actual number of manuscripts only drops from just under twelve to just under ten. At the same time, the percentage of pagan and medieval authors increases. The notable fact here is the decline in the prominence of the patristic manuscripts to the benefit not of pagan texts but of thirteenth- and fourteenth-century ones.

Overall the *Frecento* manuscripts comprise medieval rather than ancient Christian authors. Conversely, the group of pagan authors is relatively large both amongst the twelfth- and fourteenth-century MSS. Nearly half of the books in the medieval category (ten out of a total of some twenty-one) are scholastic writings, and Petrarch is the only other fourteenth-century author with as many as three volumes. If we add the three manuscripts of Aristotle and Proclus, which make up the group of medieval translations of classical sources, the point is enforced.

What can be concluded about the debt of an early Renaissance library? As far as classical texts are concerned, Salutati would seem to have been indebted to the Renaissance of the twelfth century but not to that of the Carolingian age. Since we have a considerable number of Petrarch's manuscripts we are able to check this impression. Salutati was a generation younger than Petrarch and it is possible that his library reflected a spate of copying which had sprung from a renewed interest in collecting. Petrarch's books are more scattered than those of Salutati,

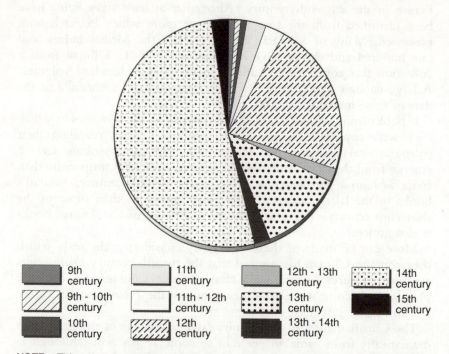

9th century		11th century		12th - 13th century		14th century	
9th - 10th century		11th - 12th century		13th century		15th century	
10th century		12th century		13th - 14th century			

NOTE: This chart is based on B.L. Ullman, *'The Humanism of Coluccio Salutati'* (Padua, 1963), ch. IX. The figures differ slightly from his own summary, *op. cit.*, p.264. In assigning manuscripts to one century, illuminations, palimpsests, corrections, erasures and foliations of other dates have been ignored, and where Ullman has expressed doubt the most probable date has been followed. In calculating what percentage of a manuscript is occupied by a text, blank folios have been ignored. Manuscripts of composite date have been divided on a percentage basis and assigned to the appropriate century.

Fig. 10 Surviving books from Salutati's library, by date of copying

though most of them passed via Pavia and Blois to Paris (see Figure 12 and notes thereto).

Some 40 per cent of the fiftyeight MSS are fourteenth-century codices; no other century can begin to rival this number. Thus far, Petrarch's books conform to the pattern of Salutati's. There is, however, a much smaller contingent of twelfth-century manuscripts. Instead there is a fairly steady progression: some 8 per cent are tenth century, 11 per cent are eleventh century, and 22 per cent are of the twelfth century. There is only a slight retreat in the thirteenth century (to 19 per cent) before the big increase of the fourteenth century.

If attention is restricted to the classical manuscripts, this picture is confirmed. There are $4^1/2$ manuscripts of the tenth century,[1] $5^1/2$ belong to the eleventh, $11^1/2$ to the twelfth century, $4^1/2$ are of the thirteenth century and 16 are from the fourteenth century. Thus analysed,

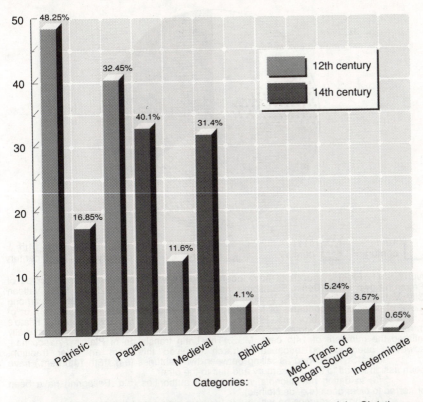

NOTE: 'Pagan' authors includes grammatical and logical writings of the Christian era to the death of Pope Gregory the Great (AD. 604) and 'patristic' authors covers the same period. The category of 'medieval' authors includes all subsequent authors.

Fig. 11   Subject matter (by %) of twelfth- and fourteenth-century manuscripts from Salutati's library

the twelfth century makes a bigger contribution than in Salutati's library. However, this is largely explained by a relatively greater number of Church Fathers amongst the twelfth-century books. A more meaningful guide is perhaps to restrict our gaze to pagan classics. Doing this, there is an almost complete uniformity from the tenth to the thirteenth centuries. It is only in the *Trecento* that there is a big increase.[2]

Certain important points emerge from these figures. Of the fifty-eight

1. The fractions arise because MSS which have been catalogued as falling between two centuries (e.g. the twelfth and thirteenth) have been assigned half to the one century and half to the other.

2. Four such MSS survive from the tenth century; two from the eleventh, 5 1/2 from the twelfth and 4 from the thirteenth; 14 1/2 are from the fourteenth.

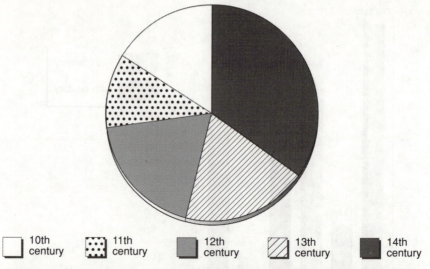

	10th century		11th century		12th century		13th century		14th century

NOTES: (1) Eight manuscripts have been excluded which either consist of copies of Petrarch's own works (Berlin, Staatsbibliothek, Hamilton 493: Paris, B. N. lat. 5784; Vatican City, Vat. Lat. 3195-6, 3357-9; Venice, Marciana, XIII, 70), or letters of Petrarch among those of other correspondents of Moggio dei Moggi (Florence, Med.-Laur., liii, 35), or of Greek texts (Milan, Ambrosiana, 198 inf.; Paris, B. N., Lat. 7780; 2 volumes = L. Pilato's translation of Homer executed for Petrarch). The inclusion of these would have artificially inflated the numbers of 14th cent. MSS. The Latin translation of Plato's *Phaedo* has, however, been inluded because Petrarch received this from an older tradition.
    (2) MSS described as falling between two centuries (e.g. 13th-14th cent.) have been assigned half to the one century and half to the other.
    (3) In dating manuscripts, more recent authorities (e.g. Pellegrini) have been preferred to older ones (e.g. de Nolhac).
    (4) For the sources on which this figure is based, see the note appended to the bibliography (p.237-8)

Fig. 12   Surviving books from Petrarch's library, by date of copying, up to and including Petrucci

MSS which contain Latin texts other than Petrarch's own, no less than forty are classical, whether of pagan or Christian writers. Very few are of 'medieval' authors. There is an Isidore, a Gerald of Wales, an Aquinas and there is Hugh and Richard of St Victor, but little else. In this light the large number of such authors in the library of Salutati appears to reflect his personal tastes and, perhaps, a secondary stage in the development of humanistic interests. The scholars of the fifteenth century read these texts in order to disprove their arguments and to refine eclectic knowledge. Petrarch's books confirm this: in his time there was less of an interest in the writers associated with the French Schools than there was afterwards.

A second important point is that the Italian humanists did not discover classical texts which were preserved in twelfth-century codices, which in turn had been copied from Carolingian manuscripts. The way in which historians have come to focus upon 'renaissances' in the fourth, ninth and twelfth centuries has led to an underestimate of the continuous copying of books through every century. It might be objected that the large number of fourteenth-century codices in the libraries of both Petrarch and Salutati hides the fact that these would have been copied from twelfth- and thirteenth-century ones. We know, for example, that Petrarch's *Phaedo* (Paris, BN., MSS. Lat. 6567A) was copied from a thirteenth-century codex (Paris, MS. Lat. 16581) and there will have been many more examples of this, including ones transcribed from twelfth-century books. However, the latter do not support the thesis of a textual 'bridge': they would have been copied in their turn from tenth- and eleventh-century ones rather than Carolingian examples.

The thesis of a textual 'bridge' between the fifteenth, twelfth, ninth and even fourth centuries has taken deep roots. There are a number of reasons why it is attractive. There are famous instances where it seems to have happened, the idea of 'renaissances' gives coherence to intellectual history and lightens the heavy load of textual scholars. They can dismiss intermediate and late manuscripts as inferior unless they derive from putative archetypes.

Those classical pagan authors who were popular in the medieval period enjoyed a progressive circulation from the ninth century onwards rather than any cyclical revival in the ninth, twelfth and fifteenth centuries. This was true of Cicero (especially his speeches and philosophical writings), Claudian, Eutropius, Horace, Justinus, Lucan, Macrobius, Martial, Martianus Capella, Ovid, Persius, the Elder and Younger Plinys, Quintilian, Sallust, Suetonius, Terence, Virgil and Servius. It is customary to assume that in the Carolingian age the texts of these authors were typically copied from codices of the fourth and fifth centuries.

But in the cases of Justinus, Pliny's *Natural History*, Quintilian, Servius and Vitruvius, manuscripts had apparently reached Carolingian centres from Northumbria and southern England. There may have been other instances where Carolingian scribes were copying not ancient manuscripts directly but Northumbrian ones which themselves had been transcribed from ancient *exempla*. They may sometimes have based their texts (as in the copies of Martial) on seventh- and eighth-century manuscripts from insular centres on the continent, like Bobbio. In other cases where the Carolingian scribes did copy directly from manuscripts of late antiquity, it would not always have been because they lacked alternative MSS.

The idea of a Renaissance revival of ninth- and twelfth-century books applies better to the rarer classical pagan works. There is an eye-catching instance in the case of the text of Pomponius Mela. It has been suggested that the Italian humanists owed their manuscripts of Mela ultimately to sixth-century Ravenna via the revivals of the ninth and the twelfth centuries (Billanovich, 1956, pp. 319–62). There are a number of rare classical writings where this seems to have happened. The works of Petronius, the plays of Plautus and the *Letters* of the Younger Pliny furnish instances. There were occasions when the Italian book-hunters like Petrarch and Poggio were discovering rare classical texts in Carolingian copies.[3] On others, they encountered them in twelfth-century ones.[4]

It is still misleading to claim that the Italian Renaissance owed its rare classical texts to the Carolingian and twelfth-century revivals. It would be true to say that the care and enthusiasm of connoisseurs in every century from the fall of Rome was responsible for the survival of such works. The preservation of the unique manuscript of Catullus's poems seems to have been due to the interest in it of Bishop Rather of Verona (890–974). Rarities[5] were preserved at Monte Cassino because of the efforts of its two abbots, Richer and Desiderius (ruling respectively 1038–55 and 1058–87). There were more numerous enthusiasts of this type in the ninth and twelfth centuries, but we exaggerate the effect of their work. Sometimes the Italian humanists happened to use a twelfth-century book, but they could have used one of another date.[6] Sometimes manuscripts have been dated to that century (this includes the text of Pomponius Mela cited above) which might as easily belong to an adjoining century.[7]

In short, classical texts did not reach the *Quattrocento* by leaping across chasms represented by the tenth, eleventh and thirteenth centuries, or the Dark Ages. Manuscripts did not survive hundreds of years through ignorance or neglect. Classical texts crossed the Dark Ages because they were conserved; they reached 1300 because they were copied *and* conserved. There was a more general and refined interest in pagan classical texts in late antiquity, in the ninth century, in the twelfth and in the fourteenth centuries than in the intervening epochs. One reason, however, that fewer of them were copied in those intervals must have been because so many were available.

The manuscripts owned by Petrarch therefore draw our attention to a neglected truth: Renaissance classical scholarship was the outcome not of the ninth and twelfth centuries but of a continuous wave of concern, conservation and copying. This had grown progressively from the seventh century and especially from Carolingian times. The

---

3. Hyginus, Silius Italicus, Valerius Flaccus, Velleius Paterculus and the *Annals* (1–6) of Tacitus.

4. Propertius, Cornelius Nepos.

5. Frontinus, *De Aquis*; Varro, *De lingua latina*, the *Histories* and *Annals* of Tacitus and possibly Seneca's *Tragedies* (the oldest complete MS of the latter work may have been copied from a Cassinense book).

6. This was true of Pliny's *Letters*: the Italian humanists used a late eleventh-century codex, but others survived.

7. Cf. R. H. Rouse in L. D. Reynolds (1983), p. 292.

twelfth century had offered only relatively more than the intervening period.

Another way of expressing the point is to say that the pattern of classical tradition is better conveyed by the transmission of the texts of Virgil or Terence, than it is by that of Pomponius Mela. With the former authors the numbers of surviving manuscripts grows century by century from the year 800, showing increasing corruption before systematic attempts at revision in the *Quattrocento*. Rare texts appeared first in the ninth century, but their progress was more patchy. They disappeared and reappeared at various times. Some did not come into view again until the fifteenth century; others made their reappearance in each intervening century.

Whilst the humanists, therefore, did not rely especially upon twelfth-century scholars their work was only possible because of a centuries-long transmission of classical texts. This debt of the humanists to tradition is easier to define than their independence of it. They owed much to inherited learning, but they did bring a wider range of texts into circulation. The works of Manilius, Statius, Propertius, Lucretius, Tacitus, Varro and Frontinus were drawn to the attention of a wider audience. Nevertheless, we would still possess a good understanding of the poetry, history, moral sentiments and practical attainments of the Romans without Tacitus, Lucretius and Propertius. Moreover, the works of such writers made little impression before the sixteenth century. The staple diet of the Italian humanists remained that which they had inherited: Cicero, Seneca, Virgil, Livy, Horace, Ovid and Sallust. However, after 1500 Tacitus and Lucretius were to influence European ideas deeply.

A novelty was the appreciation of little-known works by well-known authors. A great number of Cicero's speeches and letters became generally known. More works were unearthed of Livy, Ovid, Horace and Quintilian. Livy's *History* had circulated fairly widely before, but Petrarch was the first scholar to bring together the different surviving parts of it which had come down separately from antiquity (Billanovich, 1951). The *Metrical Epistles* of Horace had been well known before; attention was directed now to his *Odes*. Ovid's *Art of Love* was famous in the twelfth century, but not his *Ibis*. A more complete edition of Quintilian's *Institutes of Oratory* was also assembled.

These discoveries were the fruit of conscious and sustained effort. Petrarch searched for manuscripts with extraordinary enterprise and zeal. He found them in places as far apart as Verona, Avignon, Paris and Liège, and in libraries as little alike as the papal library, the Chapter library at Verona and the library of the Sorbonne. Moreover, these discoveries were the outcome of thirty years of labour, from 1333 to the 1360s. This was a pattern which Poggio imitated in the fifteenth century in Germany and France, and Aurispa and Guarino did the same in the Greek monasteries of the east.

161

The Italian humanists, therefore, used manuscripts which had been continuously copied, and they directed their attention to texts which had been read in earlier times. They began with the study of well-known authors, such as Cicero, Seneca, Livy and Virgil. Moreover, down to 1500 this remained their staple diet. Nevertheless, while Petrarch began his studies with widely available texts he used them to very novel effect. He and his immediate successors did not set out to discover completely unknown works, because they did not know what had been in circulation down to their own time. They were searching for texts which were unknown to them. Similarly, they were ignorant of paleography. Accordingly, they had no means of judging the age of manuscripts, and in seeking to base their handwriting upon classical script they mistakenly took as their model Carolingian minuscule, believing it to have been the writing of antiquity.

The humanist work was thus a puzzling amalgam of old and new. Fifteenth-century Italian scholars were initially ignorant of paleography and yet they laid the foundations of that science. The word bibliography would have meant nothing to them, but they formed the discipline. Earlier scholarship and transcription aided the humanists and they went beyond it. The search for manuscripts was accompanied by advances in philology and textual criticism. By a close reading of the authorities, the Italians developed a new understanding of the ancient authors. Thus Giovanni de Matociis (*fl.* 1306–20) wrote a tract distinguishing the Elder from the Younger Pliny. Petrarch showed that the two Terences who had been similarly confused were separate individuals. Other scholars wrote commentaries upon ancient authors. There were very significant developments in textual criticism which sprang from a close reading of texts and a wide examination of manuscripts. Through his knowledge of classical style Petrarch demonstrated the falsehood of certain diplomas in the possession of the Emperor Charles IV, which purported to record grants to Austria by Roman emperors. It was on the same grounds, fortified by a knowledge of early manuscripts, that Lorenzo Valla proved later that the Donation of Constantine was a forgery.

The latter was a dramatic demonstration of philological expertise, although later centuries were to accord it an importance which the Italian humanists had not. The collation and emendation of texts by the humanists was a still greater technical triumph. In his manuscript of Livy, Petrarch recorded variant readings which he discovered in other codices. This practice was continued and extended by Valla and Politian. For industry, learning and audacity they were the greatest philologists of the Italian Renaissance. Valla possessed the learning and the personal authority to criticise St. Jerome's translation of the Greek New Testament. His *Adnotationes in Novum Testamentum*, in which the criticisms were set forth, was the foundation of modern Biblical criticism. Valla also emended corrupted or defective texts and his brilliant *Emendationes Livianae* proposed many emendations to Livy's *History of Rome* which are still accepted today. Politian was less polemical than Valla, but he exceeded him in learning and as a systematic critic of classical texts. He seems to have been the first scholar to collate an entire text, comparing two manuscripts word for word. He was also the first to provide symbols to denote the different manuscripts from which the variant readings were recorded.

Meantime attempts had been made to understand and imitate the finer points of ancient writing. The Paduan pre-humanist Lovato Lovati had composed an essay on the metre and prosody of Seneca's *Tragedies* and increasingly thereafter efforts were made to understand all aspects of ancient literature. Poggio's invention of 'Humanistic Script' (which we call Roman), followed from this. The search for correct latinity culminated in Bembo's Ciceronianism a century later.

The advance in textual criticism did not come from any new principle or technical discovery but from a greater assembly and assimilation of knowledge. The Italians discerned forged and corrupted texts because they possessed a fine appreciation of the classical style. The taste for the ancient flavour, in its turn, derived from a very wide reading of ancient literature. With that breadth came a better grasp of the identity and careers of classical authors. This new method was not directed to any unfamiliar end. Its chief application was to elucidate the writings of those authors who had been well known in the twelfth and thirteenth centuries, like Cicero, Seneca and Livy. This is even true of Greek studies, the other area where the humanists extended the classical scholarship of former times: here they did so to cast light upon Latin culture.

Italian studies of Greek became of permanent importance. However, with the exception of Plato's philosophy, their influence was quite limited before 1500. Once again the crucial step forward had been made by Petrarch. Although his efforts to learn the Greek language were unavailing, he did master the alphabet and he possessed a few Greek books. Moreover, the importance of Plato was perceived by him. Above all, Petrarch gave currency to the notion that it was important to understand Greek poetry, philosophy and history, and that this could only be achieved through mastery of the Greek tongue. Once again the new departure was made from the conventional starting-point of the works of Cicero, where the writings of the Greeks were reported and discussed.

Florentines were the first to be spurred into action by Petrarch's enthusiasm. Western scholars had not been wholly ignorant of Greek previously, but knowledge had been severely restricted. Apart from a few individuals, understanding of Greek was limited largely to Rome, where a number of Greeks were to be found, and to the 'Byzantine' areas of southern Italy. Knowledge, however, of Greek thought had been spread by Latin translations in the twelfth and thirteenth centuries. Petrarch and the Florentines began by using western talent. Petrarch learnt his Greek from a south Italian monk called Barlaam, and the first Florentines received their instruction from Barlaam's pupil Leonzio Pilato, who also came from the south. Unfortunately the Greek-speakers of Italy seem to have lacked the imagination and wide culture necessary to succeed as teachers. It was not until Manuel Chrysoloras, a Byzantine envoy, came to teach in Florence between 1396 and 1400 that a real understanding of the Greek tongue took root. Thereafter, Greek formed an increasing part of humanistic studies. In the course of the *Quattrocento* many of the Greek classics were translated into Latin, Greek manuscripts were sought in the east and Greek ideas began to be employed in humanist writing.

The translating of Greek works sprang directly from the teaching of Chrysoloras. Bruni who had been his pupil translated parts of Plutarch, Xenophon, Plato and Aristotle. Later, Valla, who had studied under Bruni, translated parts of Homer and (for Pope Nicholas V) the whole of the Greek historians Thucydides and Herodotus. The work of translation undertaken in Florence by Ficino and Politian had more impact. Ficino completed the huge task of rendering the whole works of Plato into Latin, and Politian translated Homer. The completeness of Ficino's translation and the erudition and poetic talents of Politian explain their immediate impression upon the philosophy and poetry of late fifteenth-century Florence.

Meantime, four scholars had travelled to Byzantium and brought back cargoes of Greek manuscripts. In 1405 Guarino returned with some fifty MSS following a period of study in Constantinople. Aurispa made two visits to the east, in 1405 and in 1421–3, and brought back some 300 books. Filelfo was attached to the Venetian embassy to Constantinople between 1420 and 1427 and claimed to have returned with the works of forty Greek authors. Finally Lascaris (1455–1535), of a Greek refugee family, visited the former lands of the Byzantine Empire in 1491, and came back with some three hundred manuscripts, mostly from the libraries of Mount Athos. To these efforts, supplemented only a little by the palimpsests and papyri discovered in modern times, is owed our possession of the secular literature of ancient Greece.

The story of Greek studies seems to define the achievement of the Italian humanists: from a familiar base they reached new ground. They brought into circulation the manuscripts of Latin authors who had been little known since the sixth century. In respect of Latin scholarship the Italians did better what others had done before. They studied the same authors, but more deeply and critically. Moreover, the new authors they unearthed made a limited impact before the sixteenth century. In bringing

Greek studies within their compass, the humanists certainly reached new territory. Despite this advance the general pattern might seem to confirm that the work of the humanists resembled and surpassed that of earlier scholars. In fact it was different in conception and approach, as we have hinted by saying earlier that the humanists created the discipline of bibliography and paleography, as well as the modern notion of classical studies.

If we ask why historians from Sabbadini onwards were impressed by these achievements, the answer is that they had read about them in the letters of Poggio and his like. The humanists reported the discoveries in such letters, and proclaimed them to the world. A famous example of this is Petrarch's letter to Cicero in which he bruited abroad his feelings on finding and reading Cicero's *Letters to Atticus*. These proclamations are the foundations of a traditional view of humanist achievement. The edifice was not imagined by modern scholars.

Have we been deluded by the vanity of the humanists, or rightly persuaded by their rhetoric? Was it not their capacity for self-advertisement and desire for fame which *made* their work different? Certainly, scholars had written letters before and from those of the Carolingian scribes – Lupus of Ferrières, for instance – it is known that such men traced and copied manuscripts. A letter in which a scholar asked a friend to search for a book, is different, however, from one designed for publication or posterity, in which Petrarch or Salutati boasted of their knowledge or discoveries.

Petrarch's scholarly world was connected with later circles and dissimilar to earlier ones. The Italian humanists, as a whole, formed a large group which encompassed several generations of individuals. All of them enjoyed a place in society quite unlike any earlier 'circle'. They were interpreters of a national culture to laymen, not clerics sharing a common interest in classical antiquity. From this it followed that their work had a systematic and permanent character before the invention of printing.

The notion that ancient texts were the surviving artefacts of a lost age of Rome gave them a finite and recoverable character. That which has boundaries can be the object of exact knowledge. Petrarch, who was the first to conceive of antiquity as a lost age, gave a beginning to bibliography, paleography and philology. Nothing better shows this 'scientific' idea of study and the new departure it represented than his attempt (characteristically inspired by the urging of a friend) to compile a bibliography of Cicero's writings. Antiquity was a relic that might be exhumed and to do so was a patriotic task.

The new systematic approach extended to book-collecting and paleography. Having identified ancient writings Petrarch wished to assemble them. Hence came his novel scheme of forming a public

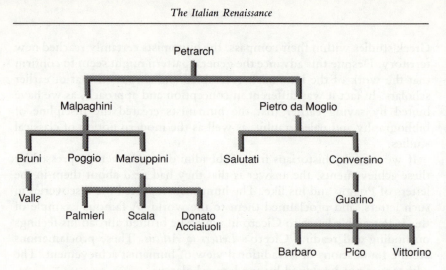

Fig. 13   Petrarch and the late *Quattrocento* humanists

library. At first he collected books for his own use, but in 1362 he thought of bequeathing them to the commune of Venice. Once assembled, different copies of a text could be compared, whilst from extensive examination of manuscripts inferences could be drawn about classical style and handwriting. Petrarch gathered a more complete version of Livy by joining together different manuscripts. He took an important step towards a more accurate text of the work by recording variant readings in different copies. His love of anything antique and loathing for the modern gave him a feeling for ancient style which enabled him to detect forgeries and to emend corrupted texts. There had been extensive knowledge of antiquity in the twelfth and thirteenth centuries, but that activity lacked the systematic character applied to it by Petrarch and his successors.

The humanists were also a permanent movement. As we have seen, through Petrarch's pupils and friends the master's ideas gained currency at Bologna, Padua and at Florence. Figure 13 shows a line of descent which connects the humanists of the late *Quattrocento* to Petrarch via the teaching of Pietro da Moglio and Giovanni Malpaghini, erstwhile assistants and friends of Petrarch.

This was more than a matter of vague influence or familial resemblance: these scholars were united in a programme of study inherited from Petrarch. Moreover, his aims were pursued by others than his pupils or associates. The ambitions of assembling a public library and learning Greek were taken up at Florence, where Boccaccio, Niccolò Niccoli and the family of the Medici were all to form considerable collections and seek to perpetuate them. Cosimo de' Medici eventually was to realise Petrarch's intention of creating a public library. Some of Petrarch's manuscripts passed down: his Livy was inherited by Lorenzo Valla –

a fact in itself of great importance, for Valla inherited thereby Petrarch's emendations and so these, combined with his own, passed into more general circulation.

Petrarch's idea of 'literary studies' as he called it comprised a strange-sounding alliance of ancient and modern interests. Its general purpose was to understand antiquity, to recover its wisdom and to apply the learning (historical, literary and moral) to his own time. This programme was diffuse, patriotic and critical. The wish to understand the ancient world was yoked to the idea of recovering its wisdom by Italian patriotism. Ancient and modern studies were two branches of one historical culture. Petrarch would not have read his sources in a critical spirit had he not perceived the classical past as a lost age.

The humanists owed their critical skill to this sense of history. Because antiquity had gone, its remains could be collected and analysed. Knowing more meant knowing better what there had been and what remained. Everything classical became an antique and scholars could gather the latter together with the collector's zeal. Books, objects and ideas were assembled and arrayed. Manuscripts were collected, and thereby separated parts of texts could be reassembled. Information was extracted from ancient sources to throw light upon the texts. One sort of antique evidence could illumine another. This was the beginning of modern classical scholarship as it was of its ancillary disciplines of bibliography, paleography, epigraphy and numismatics.

The new assembling and ordering of information began with Petrarch. Knowing more brought increased erudition about ancient authors and their language. Petrarch's curiosity about the classical authors led him to Servius's commentary on Virgil: the famous Milan codex of Virgil which Petrarch owned has the text surrounded by Servius's commentary. The marginal annotations prove that he was the first to appreciate its value as a source for understanding Virgil, even though the text of Servius had circulated freely through the medieval period. Finally, Petrarch's improved knowledge of ancient vocabulary and diction enabled him to perceive the change in language from his own time. This allowed him to correct his text of Livy by conjectural emendation and to demonstrate that the Austrian diplomas of the Emperor Charles IV were forged.

Others, however, carried on Petrarch's work of assembling manuscripts, producing better editions of classical texts or commentaries upon them. From Petrarch's new view of antiquity a tradition ran down to the fifteenth century. The increased circulation of classical texts in the *Quattrocento* stimulated efforts to collate manuscripts and to copy *verbatim* the oldest and the best of them. The rapid copying of texts multiplied errors and made it increasingly hard to know from what earlier manuscript the copies had been made. It is to this day a daunting task for the editors of classical texts to analyse *Quattrocento* copies, for they are legion.

This problem already confronted scholars in the fifteenth century and led them to look out and copy the older examples, and where possible the source of the flood. This was the reason why a collation of the *Codex Laudensis* of Cicero's writings (discovered in Lodi in 1421) was carried out seven years later. As Sabbadini discovered, Giovanni Lamola (1407–49) collated the whole manuscript probably because so many corrupt copies had sprung up meanwhile, all of them deriving ultimately from it (Sabbadini, *Storia e critica*, p. 106).

Two further instances of the critical spirit deriving from broader scholarship are knowledge of ancient literary commentaries and inscriptions. Both of these developments receive less attention than they deserve in histories of classical scholarship. There were at least five such ancient commentaries. Apart from that of Servius, they had been little known since antiquity but, having been discovered by the humanists, they spawned a host of copies in the fifteenth century. The commentary of Asconius on Cicero's speeches was found by Poggio at St Gall in 1416, and from his copy and two others made around the same time sprang a mass of copies. Another famous Italian humanist, Giovanni Aurispa, found Aelius Donatus's commentary on Terence at Mainz in 1433, and all the early manuscripts derive from this and other copies sent to Italy. The French scholar, Jean Jouffroy, brought a Carolingian manuscript containing the commentary on Virgil by Ti. Claudius Donatus to Italy in 1438 and all the numerous fifteenth-century copies were made from it or from a second Carolingian book also taken to Italy somewhat later. The more obscure commentaries on Horace and Juvenal were brought to general notice for the first time in Italy by Enoch of Ascoli (after 1400–57) and Giorgio Valla (d. 1500). In addition to these, the commentary on Virgil by Servius was newly appreciated.

This novel regard for the ancient commentaries goes some way to explaining the critical powers of the Italian humanists. These commentaries had a three-fold importance. They introduced the humanists to a considerable body of knowledge about the authors they described. Ancient textual criticism was revealed in them and they must have refined Italian feeling for an historical treatment of texts. The commentaries enabled humanists to compare the extant manuscripts of the classics with ancient knowledge of them. This made Italians conscious of textual evolution and corruption. For the ancient commentator quoted passages not preserved or only transmitted in a corrupted fashion in the manuscripts. This was particularly important in refining an evolutionary approach to the study of texts at a time when paleography had not been born.

By 1500 a rudimentary grasp of paleography was beginning to appear. Indeed, Politian's important understanding of the genealogy of manuscripts and preference for the oldest is traceable to this. The advance was made possible by the realisation that Roman script was uncial, and not Carolingian minuscule as the early humanists had believed. Once this vital step had been taken the humanists at once began to use uncial manuscripts in preference to all others and even to call for future editions to be based upon them.

Of course, there were very few of these ancient books, but contemporaries at once perceived the antiquity of the *Codex Bembinus* of Terence and the *Codex Romanus* of Virgil. Progress here had come about from the study of coins and inscriptions. There is extant a passage in G. P. Valeriano's *Castigationes in Bucolica* (1521) in which Valeriano identified the ancient date of the *Codex Romanus* by comparing its script to the lettering of Roman coins and inscriptions (published by Grafton, 1983, pp. 342–3, cf. 48–9).

The Italian humanists thus refined their critical powers as they came to recover ancient culture. They integrated one piece of knowledge with another, and compared one type of evidence with another. Furthermore, one work by an author could be contrasted to another, manuscripts could be compared to commentaries, inscriptions to books and Latin to Greek literature. This constant refocussing is an important and little acknowledged process which greatly strengthened the critical and historical insights of the humanists.

In addition, professional polemic and Church politics fostered scholarship. It might be thought that these were deleterious influences, leading scholars to waste their time in controversy. Whether or not this is true at all, polemic had a positive effect. Humanists sharpened their wits and techniques in order to defeat opponents. A case could in fact be made that without this incentive acuity would have been lacking. This polemic was a constant feature of the fifteenth and sixteenth centuries. Lorenzo Valla had advanced his emendations to Livy in order to demonstrate the superiority of his talents to those of Panormita and Bartolomeo Fazio (1400–57). One motive of Politian in publishing his *Miscellanea* was to prove that he was a greater scholar than Domizio Calderini (1444–78) or Giorgio Merula (1430/1–94). The scholarly activities of French and Italian philologists after 1500 were also marked by fruitful argument.

Church politics was a more surprising influence: it led to contacts and exchanges of ideas. In the fourteenth century the papal residence at Avignon had brought Petrarch and other Italians into contact with the riches of the French libraries. The ecclesiastical councils of the *Quattrocento* introduced east and west as well as north and south. Sabbadini and A. C. Clark long ago uncovered the routes by which Poggio discovered obscure classical texts in German and French libraries during his sojourn at the Council of Constance. The discoveries of the ancient commentaries on classical authors furnish a specific instance of this.

It was whilst he was at Constance that Poggio himself (aided by another Italian) unearthed and transcribed Asconius's commentary on Cicero. The Council of Basle led Aurispa to Mainz where he discovered Donatus's work on Terence. Contrariwise, the Council of Florence brought foreigners to Italy together with further manuscripts and techniques. Thus Jean Jouffroy brought with him a Carolingian codex of Claudius Donatus on Virgil (cf. A. Mercati, 1946, p. 357f.). Greek scholars attending the Council, such as Bessarion, introduced Italians to Byzantine textual criticism perhaps possessing novel refinements. Bessarion's demonstration of the truth of the Latin doctrine of the Holy Spirit by textual means made a strong impact. His proof that a certain statement in St Basil was genuine because it was found in the oldest manuscripts played its part in sharpening a sense of the historical evolution of texts. It is, however, unclear how far Bessarion was employing western techniques (he was a friend of Valla) against his own countrymen (cf. Mohler, 1942).

It deserves a mention in passing that the Councils affected the ideas of the humanists. The convening of the Councils and their outcome was possible because of international co-operation. They marked the beginnings of a more peaceful era between western powers; they helped to produce it. There were calls for peace between east and west; attempts at a union between the Latin and Orthodox Churches came close to success at the Council of Florence. Some, like Nicholas of Cusa (1401–64), advised peace with the infidel. The Councils also left the papacy in a weakened condition. This is the context in which Valla's call for the papacy to assume a purely spiritual authority should be viewed. The praise of peace over war was made by Politian and both appeals were repeated by Erasmus; from there the ideas were diverted into the armouries of the Reformers.

Thus, by the mid *Quattrocento*, a tradition of systematic scholarship had been well established in Italy owing its origin to a new historical sense. Moreover, it formed the basis of the classical philology of the late fifteenth century and the following one. This last point is not self-evidently true: the character of classical scholarship changed in this period. The advances that happened have been attributed to the influence of printing, the Reformation and the creative energies of sixteenth-century scholars. There were indeed changes after 1500, but they represented a deepening or narrowing of *Quattrocento* efforts. The dependence, nevertheless, of early modern philologists upon the systematic scholarship of the fifteenth century can be glimpsed by bringing two leading figures of the successive periods into focus. This can be done by contrasting the work of Politian with that of Turnebous (1512–65).

Politian was the greatest philologist of the late fifteenth century, and Turnebous one of the leading scholars of an age which possessed no dominating individual. The former's work collating manuscripts has given him a permanent place in the history of textual criticism. He was the editor and translator of Homer. His *Miscellanies* (*Miscellanea*) was a work of extraordinary erudition and a model on which sixteenth-century scholars could base a study of ancient culture. Politian was also the greatest Italian poet of his age. There are certain ideas which animated his scholarship and poetry: he was an adept of Neo-Platonism and propagated an idea of Latin culture as the heir of Greece. Philosophically Politian subscribed to the Platonic notions that the material world was guided by Forms and that love (Eros) was preferable to war (Mars).

The life and writings of Turnebous some sixty years later were different. He occupied a chair of Greek philosophy in the Collège de France. This was itself an institution which had not existed in Politian's day: its origin lay in the wish of King Francis I to encourage classical studies in the French kingdom. Turnebous edited classical texts, notably little known Greek works like that of Synesius. He wrote a verse polemic against the Jesuits, but his métier was classical scholarship. Not a poet as Politian had been, Turnebous also did not wish to disseminate philosophical ideas. We can therefore call him a classicist where it is a half-truth to apply the name to Politian or any of the Italian humanists.

For all this, the intellectual landscape in 1550 was recognisably that of 1490. Philologically Turnebous himself was the heir of Politian. He and his illustrious pupil Joseph Scaliger were in the traditions of Politian's work (cf. Grafton, 1983). Vernacular poetry, inspired by Greek hymns, was being written in Turnebous's time, but by French poets connected to his circle such as Ronsard and Du Bellay. Neither was Turnebous to be found propagating conceptual tenets. For instance, in his commentary on Cicero's *De Legibus* he sought to show how ancient Stoicism inspired it, but he was making no moral point. He was better versed perhaps than Politian had been in the various schools of ancient philosophy and he used his knowledge to a different purpose.

When and why had this change occurred? Its chronology can be grasped by looking back a generation from Turnebous's time to that of Erasmus. Whilst the great Dutch scholar was not a poet he appreciated the virtues of the vernacular. Like Turnebous, he was also the heir of Politian's philology. His *Adagia* was indeed based on Politian's *Miscellanea*. Erasmus also inherited, as Turnebous did not, an idea of wisdom. Most of Erasmus's writing is charged with *humanitas*, which he imbued with a flavour of his own. Like Valla, Petrarch and Cicero, Erasmus believed that it was possible to attain truth by reason. All of them held that knowledge liberated because it produced virtue. Reason led humanity forward to the greater Reason of God.

Erasmus's personal contribution was to place paganism and Christianity on the same footing. The road to virtue and wisdom was by reading pagan ethics as much as by studying the Scriptures. This can be called *humanitas Erasmiana* (see Pfeiffer, 1931). It is one of Erasmus's claims to intellectual importance, and it shows him to have been the product of the *Quattrocento*. In a loose sense, therefore, the mental world of Politian continued down to the days of Erasmus and not beyond them.

The received idea is that Politian had established a new philology based upon a rigorous method of textual criticism: this was the beginning of classical scholarship as it was afterwards known. National feeling and transalpine traditions completed the process. Patriotic instincts encouraged the growth of vernacular literature in conditions where the easy unity of Latin and Italian could no longer be maintained. Finally, the moralising element in the literature and religious sentiment of northern Europe arrested the course of *humanitas*, which was henceforth trivialised or driven into fugitive corners of lay education.

This view makes some things clear whilst others remain obscure. The powerful legacy of Politian does help to clarify the new departures of the sixteenth century. However, the most important work of Erasmus looked back more obviously to the early Italian humanists than to Politian. Evidently *humanitas* could survive transplantation since it featured strongly in the thinking of Erasmus. Equally, the concept was not shared by all the Italians of the earlier epoch. Politian's own work is guided by moral ideas, but not by *humanitas*.

Erasmus's biblical scholarship stood four-square upon that of Valla. The former's Greek New Testament performed a task recommended by the latter. Valla had himself attempted, in his *Adnotationes in Novum Testamentum*, to emend the text of the Latin Bible. Moreover, he had perceived that this could only be accomplished by using Greek manuscripts and preferably by the complete collation of them. There is also an echo of Valla in Erasmus's attitude to the authority and traditions of the Church. Both men believed that these should be judged by reason, which meant in practice the cool appraisal of philology. Were there sources on which the doctrines of the Church could be based, and did these prove official claims? Valla and Erasmus concluded that in important respects they did not do so. The most famous demonstration of this was Valla's tract on the Donation of Constantine. He showed that this document, upon which the temporal authority of the popes had been chiefly based, was a forgery. Erasmus judged the power of the papacy, the wealth of the monasteries and the sacraments of the Church by a similar standard.

Erasmus and Valla ventured these criticisms for the same reason. Neither wished for schism in the Church or any reform on the Lutheran pattern. They desired to purify Christianity by means of reason. Ignorance, error and superstition would be dispelled; the papacy and the monks would become the repositories of spiritual authority. An inner wisdom fed by knowledge rather than external rituals would form the basis of religious life. This spirituality governed by reason corresponded to *humanitas*, and though Erasmus saw it lying more in the spiritual life of the human commonwealth, for Valla its embodiment was Roman law and Latin culture.

Erasmus therefore echoed Valla. In some respects Politian did so himself. In the field of philology Politian's achievement lay in several things, which owed something to Valla. Thanks to his influence the importance of citing textual sources, collating whole manuscripts and studying their genealogy was newly appreciated. He was particularly original in this latter field. No one before had grasped the significance of the age and inter-relationship of manuscripts. Moreover, he argued that the text of an author should be based upon the oldest surviving copy of it. Finally, Politian showed that Latin literature could best be understood by reference to Greece, which had furnished so much of its language and ideas. It was not enough to know Greek; minute comparison was required of Latin and Greek texts.

Politian was a remarkable scholar, and in the habit of citing manuscripts and in tracing their descent he made a bigger step forward than anyone before Bentley (1662–1742). However, he owed his practice of complete collation and of studying Latin manuscripts against Greek forebears to Valla. Valla also furthered critical scholarship by improving the text of Livy by correcting absurdities or supplying missing words from a knowledge of the sense, or of the usage of the author and his times – in short, what is called 'conjectural' emendation.

Valla has recently been consigned to a lower place than Politian in the history of textual criticism on the grounds that conjectural emendation is an inferior procedure to that employed by Politian. Valla, it is said, did not found a school: conjectural emendation is a knack which cannot be taught. It can also be practised successfully by linguists without a strong intellect or historical understanding. Moreover, the textual criticism of Valla was rhetorical in that texts were emended in order to defeat opponents rather than found a profession (Grafton, 1983, pp. 12–13).

These judgements flatter Politian and underestimate the work of Valla. Politian also failed to found a school and philology supported rhetoric in his day much as it had done in that of Valla. Politian used textual criticism to defeat opponents or promote himself, and in his time such criticism was not yet a professional discipline separated from moral ideas. Nor have the great achievements of conjectural emendation been owed to linguists with limited understanding or slight historical knowledge.

Between 1300 and 1540 the most brilliant exponents of conjectural emendation were Petrarch, Valla and Erasmus and in that whole period, with the sole addition of Politian, they were also the keenest intellects and the ones possessing the best historical understanding of texts. These abilities, moreover, formed the roots of their textual skills. They were brilliant at emending texts by conjecture because of their knowledge of the language, customs and history of civilisation. Conjectural emendation is not a technique brilliant in its own day, but subsequently superseded by 'genealogical' or historical criticism. Valla's emendations to Livy were valued in the sixteenth century and ever afterwards. Erasmus first published them and many still find their place in modern editions of the text.

It was not that a better technique became established: these were rather two complementary procedures, both open to abuse. There was a single tradition in textual criticism which had not been established by Politian and which went back even beyond Valla. Within this, the two techniques first competed and finally combined. Conjectural emendation can generate errors if practised by vain, ignorant or undisciplined scholars. With this qualification it has greatly improved texts. No editor wishing to provide texts of practical use can dispense with it, although it must be remembered that such corrections remain conjectures.

The historical or genealogical criticism is also open to wrongful use by inadequate scholars. Basing a text upon the oldest manuscripts is only the best policy if they are the least corrupt; sometimes younger ones have preserved a less interpolated tradition. Moreover, it is only possible to judge whether the oldest is the best by the exercise of precisely those talents which lie behind conjectural emendation: a knowledge of the sense of the text and of language. Judgements here necessarily involve historical understanding. Sometimes it is only possible to decide whether a passage is corrupt by knowing a good deal about the history of language.

Politian, moreover, was not methodical in his employment of collation and the classification of manuscripts. He entered variants systematically in those copies of the text which he happened to possess. When these were printed versions this represented a retrogressive practice. He did not know from which manuscript or manuscript tradition the printer had drawn his text. Yet Politian used the printed version as a 'base' text, a norm from which he noted variants. In this way, as in some others, the advent of printing had a deleterious effect upon classical scholarship. For these reasons, therefore, conjectural emendation has never been a casual skill and manuscript genealogy a critical method. Both were, and are, the outcome properly of one technique and outlook, claiming the same origin in Petrarch.

This Petrarchan outlook might be described as the critical understanding of classical culture and texts. Valla and Politian developed this tradition. In fact, in aspiring to the twin goals of poetry and scholarship Politian was following in Petrarch's footsteps. Like Petrarch, Politian sought a key to Roman literature in Greek culture, and he expected to find moral truth in literary studies. For the former, of course, a direct knowledge of Greek literature had remained merely a dream.

At every stage from 1300 to 1600 the root of new departures in textual criticism was a more critical spirit, which in its turn came from knowing more about authors, texts and antiquity itself. In the hundred years from *c.*1330 to *c.*1430 the most important specific influence was the discovery of new manuscripts. Italian scholars honed their critical approach in the following century by comparing this inherited knowledge from the manuscript tradition to ancient commentaries, inscriptions and the literary monuments of Greece.

The zealous search which harvested these results was possible once Italians had begun to conceive of the ancient world as a lost civilisation whose remains might be restored. Both the new conception and the beginnings of the search were owed to Petrarch. He established a systematic approach to the classics which came to distinguish the work of the Italian humanists from their clerical forerunners, and marked the start of the classical scholarship of early modern Europe.

Chapter Fourteen

Historiography

In writing history the humanists cast their minds back to the Classics as historians had done from the time of Bede (*c.* 673–735) to that of Otto of Freising (*c.* 1111–58) or Matthew Paris (*c.* 1200–59): there was no other available source. However, the humanists like Leonardo Bruni, Poggio, Flavio Biondo and Machiavelli proclaimed that they were using ancient sources in a more authentic way. A low estimate, however, has sprung up of the historical writing of the humanists on the grounds that they revived the ancient pattern of writing history in a mechanical fashion. Naturally this charge would not be weighty if the further assumption was not made that the humanists revived something which was of little interest.

The poor opinion that is held of humanist histories implies therefore a similar estimate of classical historiography, at least that of the Roman period. It is generally supposed that the humanists brought to life something drained of creative power. In forming these views, scholars have been influenced by two discussions in ancient literature. A view of history is set forth in these passages which the humanists are thought to have followed. In his *Poetics* Aristotle contrasted history unfavourably with poetry. He alleged that where the latter imparted general truths the former merely conveyed particular facts (*Poetics*, ch. 9). Ancient historical writing is often said also to have been a rhetorical exercise. In his *Rhetorics* Aristotle himself commended the study of history, but only to the rhetorician who could make use of a study of the results of wars (1.4.1360a). Cicero set forth a rhetorical view of history in a letter to a friend. He exhorted his friend Lucceius, who was composing a history of recent times, to write in such a way that the reader would be moved by the drama, and remedies could be recommended for recent civil disturbances. Cicero also voiced the hope that thereby his own actions might earn praise (even more than truth properly might allow) and the reader pity the vicissitudes of his fortunes (*Epist. ad Fam.*, v, 12).

Some scholars also imply that the humanists had little to learn directly from antiquity: the classical historians had taught their trade to the Christian historians of late antiquity, and they in their turn had passed it on to Bede and his heirs. Accordingly it remained only for the humanists to polish the dry surfaces of familiar texts. In addition, there are few scholars today who will accept that the humanists succeeded in 'secularising' the writing of history. It used to be said that the purpose of Renaissance historians was secular rather than providential, and that they employed new methods of authenticating evidence and new sorts of evidence. Classical models were employed and secular biographies, town chronicles and archaeological treatises were added to the repertoire; moreover, it was all done for lay audiences.

In fact, however, as early as 1207 (or soon after), Villehardouin, a layman and marshal to the count of Champagne, had written his memoirs of the French Crusade for a lay audience; Acerbus Morena (b. *c*. 1100) was a similar figure in Italy. There are twelfth-century examples of lay vernacular chronicles like the annals of Genoa (the *Annales Januenses*) and the *Kaiserchronik* of Regensburg. Petrarch, Valla, Bruni and Biondo did promote an historical writing based on a critical use of sources and employed public records. But the change is only one of degree: Matthew Paris had used public records in thirteenth-century England and Otto of Freising and Guibert of Nogent (1053–1124) had applied a common-sense scepticism to relics and the Donation of Constantine.

The humanists based their works upon the ancient histories of Livy, Sallust, Tacitus and Polybius. Nevertheless, earlier historians well understood the principle of using classical models. In Carolingian times Einhard's *Life of Charlemagne* was patterned on Suetonius, while the *Annals* of Lambert of Hersfeld have been seen as imitating Livy. Sallust was widely admired in the twelfth century. After 1200 there are precedents too for secular biographies such as Joinville's *Life of St Louis*, and city chronicles were common enough in Italy. Moreover, the purpose of works like these was frequently as secular as the subject-matter.

This, however, is to add nuances rather than remove distinctions. The historians of the *Quattrocento* were invariably laymen, and their works were systematically modelled upon a wider range of ancient writing, including Tacitus as well as the Greek biographers and historians. Before 1400 it is difficult to think of any historian but Rudolf of Fulda who had used Tacitus. After 1400 translations from the Greek of Plutarch and Polybius were made for the first time by Bruni (B. Reynolds, 1954), whilst those of Thucydides and Herodotus were executed by Valla (see Alberti, 1957 and 1959).

Moreover, the twelfth-century classical 'models' referred to by modern scholars often describe the exploitation of a source rather than the employment of a model. When William of Malmesbury used Caesar, Pliny, Livy and Suetonius no principle of systematic imitation was being exercised. Furthermore, the commonsense doubts of Guibert of Nogent and Otto of Freising were not the philological scepticism of Petrarch or Valla, which rested upon an understanding of the evolution of language and institutions. Minor distinctions therefore remain between the approach and achievement of the humanist historians and those of the central Middle Ages. The humanists certainly knew more about ancient historians, but did not writers in the twelfth century already know enough to give them the gist of classical methods? The historians of the *Quattrocento* were more critical and learned, but this may seem to be a matter of literary finish.

It can even be argued that writers like Bruni retarded historical method by enlarging the rhetorical element in historical writing (H. Gray, 1963; F. Gilbert, 1965, pp. 203f.). Certainly the humanists inserted speeches in their narratives as a vehicle to express moral sentiments appropriate to the individual or the actions concerned, which are unlikely to have been voiced at the time. In giving currency to a moral idea of history, the humanists were at one with earlier Christian historians who had long since absorbed the moral approach to historical events of the classical writers. If anything, the achievement of the Italian historians like Bruni is seen, therefore, as a retrogressive one, directing the cause of history towards fiction and artifice.

A few have bravely challenged this view. One of the most notable of these is D. Wilcox in his work on Bruni. This study deserves close attention because Wilcox has uncovered a psychological strain in Bruni which is something which students of Renaissance historiography have usually underestimated or misconceived. It also highlights a neglected aspect of ancient historiography which the humanists revived. Great stress is laid in Bruni upon individual motives such as revenge, honour and greed for power or wealth; the motives and appetites of the individual are shared by groups or factions, and infect social classes. Equally the actions of states are interpreted according to their desire for territory, or need for self-preservation (Wilcox, pp. 53–7, 84, 93). Psychological attitudes also effect institutional changes; they in their turn shape the feelings of citizens. In such a way, Bruni interpreted the Ciompi revolution in 1378 when the disenfranchised wool workers of Florence struggled for political reform. In his narrative Bruni subtly wove together the motives and feelings of individuals and groups, mediated and accentuated via political actions and institutions.

Wilcox does not attribute this 'psychological' approach to a source. Polybius (pp. 36, 106) and, above all, Livy are, however, placed in Bruni's intellectual pedigree. The influence of Sallust and Tacitus is allowed less importance than that of Livy (pp. 35–6, 58), but in developing his psychological perspective Bruni is said to have departed even from the latter (pp. 51, 55, 62–3). The implication is that the psychological viewpoint was Bruni's own contribution, though in one instance a debt to Tacitus is acknowledged (p. 73).

These important insights have received less attention than they deserve. The reason for this is perhaps that Wilcox has rightly combined them with a recognition that Bruni's purpose was moral and edificatory, although not uncritical or *a priori* (pp. 29, 40–2, 66, 71–2). Does it not follow that Bruni's psychological insights are an excuse to extract morals from historical events? In short, do we not find here the 'lessons of history', which are commonly said to have been the purpose of Renaissance historical enquiry (see, e.g., M. Gilmore, 1963)? If so, this was following an age-old practice. An example of this was the medieval annotations made to Caesar's *Histories* stressing the dangers of fratricidal war (cf. Sanford, 1944). Was not Bruni merely adding rhetoric and literary elegance to a familiar practice?

To answer this question it is necessary to examine more clearly whether there were ancient sources which prepared the way for Bruni, and how far morals may have had a didactic role in them. The main historians who influenced Bruni were Livy, Sallust, Tacitus and Polybius; to these might be added the biographers, notably Suetonius and Plutarch. As Wilcox has seen, Livy did not obviously furnish the source for Bruni's 'psychological' outlook. The most likely ancient source to consider is Sallust.

Sallust is a telling example because he has always been considered a supremely moralising historian. The ethical framework of Sallust is an obvious one. At the beginning of the *War with Jugurtha* (*Bellum Iugurthinum*) Sallust described ancient Roman values consisting of public wealth and military strength alongside private virtue. These morals were contrasted to the present state of Roman affairs where private riches and luxury reigned. Later in the work the reader is informed that avarice had led to faction, injustice and military weakness (e.g. ch. xxxi). Throughout it, the use of bribery by the Numidian king Jugurtha, in order to gain his ends at Rome, is condemned. His successful employment of bribes is held up as a testimony to the corruption of the Roman people (viii, 2; xiii, 7; xi, 5; xx, 1; xxviii, 1; xxxii, 2).

The moral framework is certainly what appealed to the writers of the twelfth and thirteenth centuries when Sallust became very popular (B. Smalley, 1971). However, while this moral component is prominent, it forms a small part of the *War with Jugurtha* and the *War with Catiline* (*Bellum Catilinae*). Moreover in the *Bellum Iugurthinum* there is a psychological dimension which lies trapped in the moralising preamble and the speeches.

In particular, there is depth to the characters. Jugurtha, though the enemy of Rome and once a 'wretch' (cii, 5), is commonly described in a more complex and favourable light. He is characteristically full of vigour and occasionally allowed self-doubt (lxii, 1). Early in his life Jugurtha had been brave and wise (vii, 5). Through his career he acted courageously, craftily and deceitfully. The imperfections of others reveal moral qualities in the round. Early in life and despite virtuous deeds committed for his country, Jugurtha had been treated suspiciously and insincerely (x–xii). He himself is made to remark in self-justification that the more numerous his acts of virtue the less ready was he to suffer wrongs (xxii, 4).

In Sallust's writing the enemy is not all bad, and friends possess a balance of qualities. The Roman general, Metellus, is brave and renowned and also disdainful or arrogant (lxiv, 1). On one occasion Metellus secured the advantage by employing Jugurtha's own weapon of deceit (xlviii, 1–2). In a later conflict the two adversaries are described as being both great commanders, matched in their personal qualities; being unequal only in money (lii, 1). Roman and barbarian are thus placed on a level footing, while the Roman generals, Metellus and Marius, are divided by envy (lxiii–lxiv, cf. lxxii). Moral ambiguity extends to lesser characters. Lucius Calpurnius Bestia is intelligent, prescient, steadfast, valorous and avaricious (xxviii, 5). A passage in the *Bellum Catilinae* reveals the view of human nature underpinning these judgements: 'Good and bad men alike strive for glory, honour and power; but while the former press forward by the true path, the latter being devoid of good means (*bonae artes*) contend with wrongful and deceitful ones' (xi, 2–3; cf. xxxi, 15).

There is a dichotomy in Sallust between psychological characterisation and the overall theme of his two surviving works. The depiction of character makes sense of motives but does not explain the course of events. In so far as generalisations are made, they turn on Roman virtue. Since corruption was shared by Roman and barbarian its absence cannot account for Roman success. Indeed, when the individual participants are described they are not viewed in this light.

Psychology therefore gives depth and interest to Sallust's narrative, but it does not furnish an explanation of events; as such it is cancelled by his moral generalisations which do not depend on the reported facts. In that sense the explanation of motives is trapped in the moral framework. Here, surely, is the reason why Italian humanists may have been able to discover creative elements in Roman historians like Sallust, which had been ignored by previous writers. The latter had been distracted by the framework.

The incongruity of form and content in Sallust makes it look as if psychological accents had been applied to an existing literary form. Had historical writing absorbed elements from biography which had necessarily concentrated on the individual? Plutarch's *Lives*, which were deeply influential in late antiquity and were revived in the *Quattrocento*, provide immediate evidence to support this hypothesis.

A telling instance is provided by Plutarch's *Life of Cicero*, a work widely admired and imitated in antiquity and in the fifteenth century: Bruni, for example, based a biography of Cicero upon it. In Plutarch's *Life* there is characterisation which is a key to the actions described. Cicero is shown to possess the same mixture of qualities which Sallust gave to his characters. Above all, Cicero is shown suffering from what we would call weaknesses of character. These help to account for the difficulties which befell him. Although he was ready to commend others, Cicero made himself hated by self-praise (xxiv, 1). He was also led on by ambition and cleverness to disregard propriety: he could not refrain from making scathing witticisms at others' expense (xxv, 1). Again this multiplied his enemies (xxvii, 1).

Plutarch seems to imply that the fateful alienation of Clodius and Caesar arose from Cicero's inclination to pursue the line of least resistance. Cicero quietened the suspicions of his wife, who resented his familiarity with Clodius's sister, by agreeing to testify against Clodius in a case brought by Caesar (xxix, 1–2). Having provoked Clodius's hatred he fell into his power. He allowed Clodius to lull him into a false sense of security by accepting the latter's mollifying words (xxx, 3). After giving testimony in Clodius's trial, Cicero had sought to avoid him by accompanying Caesar as legate to Gaul. Later, reassured by Clodius, he resolved to stay at Rome; Caesar was now angered and incited both Pompey and Clodius against him so that he was forced into exile (xxx, 3).

Cicero was injured by conceit. Other passages show the cost of his irresolution and vanity. In the hour of crisis he was unable to decide whether to side with Pompey or Caesar. Having committed himself to the former he regretted his decision, voiced his doubts to his new comrades in arms and earned their hatred (xxxviii). Later Octavian exploited Cicero's vanity and this cost him his life. Cicero was attracted to Octavian through hatred of Anthony and love of honour (xliv–xlv). Plutarch reports that Octavian himself had declared that he had used Cicero's love of power in proposing that they should jointly stand for the consulship. By this means Octavian secured his own position, and Cicero failed to consider that Octavian was seeking merely a temporary alliance. In the event, Octavian came to terms with his enemies and this hastened Cicero's murder (xlv, 5).

It cannot be said that Plutarch's psychological observations amount to explanation of an individual's destiny. Plutarch himself only implies a link between psychology and events. Moreover, the moral ambiguity of his characters arose partly from Plutarch's anecdotal approach. Like other biographers before him, he collected anecdotes about his subjects almost at random, both favourable and unfavourable. Similarly, Plutarch's observations that Cicero incurred hatred by self-praise or unguarded witticisms precedes a long catalogue of anecdotes which illustrate the point. The compiling of anecdotes by the biographer may be the source of the moral ambiguity of later historians like Sallust. Nevertheless, the amassing of anecdotes and the explanation of character was not a haphazard process. A clear purpose lay behind it, as Plutarch made plain in the preamble to his *Life of Alexander*. Trivial acts and gestures were signs which could lead the biographer into the soul of the individual (see above, p. 118).

Such insights were the sources for the 'psychological' technique of the humanist historians, notably Bruni. The latter differed, however, from Sallust and the biographers of antiquity in that he was less concerned with individual psychology than with the motives and morale of the Florentine people. He treated of their hopes and fears, their search for glory, honour and revenge. He is in the line of Sallust nevertheless in furnishing us with an account which at once teaches moral lessons and explains the past.

Viewed from one angle, an historical account which argues that a certain event points a moral is good morals and poor history. From another angle, the approach can offer the material for a convincing and sophisticated historical explanation. In fact, with Bruni as with Sallust it was both. The reason was a simple one: the moral *was* the explanation. Events have happened because human behaviour has determined them: morals have led men to act in certain ways. There also lay the lesson.

What is the grand design of Bruni's *History* which was at once a lesson and an explanation? The contents of the successive books reveal its scope.

Book 1:   Florentine weakness under Roman domination from antiquity to the Holy Roman Empire.

Book 2:   Florence frees itself of the German emperors in the period from the death of Frederick II to the defeat of Manfred.

Book 3:   The unavailing attempts of Charles of Anjou and the Pope to quell factional conflict in Italy, notably in Tuscany.

Book 4:   The Florentine people advance against domestic and foreign enemies with Guelph support in the time of Charles II of Anjou.

Book 5:   The defence of Florentine liberty against Ghibelline enemies with the aid of Robert of Anjou and Charles of Calabria.

Book 6:   The vicissitudes of Florentine liberty in the period of Lewis of Bavaria. Florence secures Pistoia and Montecatini, and loses its liberty to the duke of Athens but then recovers it.

Book 7:   The establishment of Florentine freedom following the tyranny of the duke of Athens.

Book 8:   Florentine liberty withstands mercenary armies, the Emperor Charles IV, the Pisans and the Pope.

Book 9:   Defence of the Florentine republic against the Ciompi rebels, Arezzo, Naples and Giangaleazzo Visconti of Milan.

Book 10:   The prelude to Florence's twelve-year struggle against Giangaleazzo Visconti, ending in Florentine resolve to resist aggression.

Book 11:   Florentine suspicion of Giangaleazzo and unsuccessful rivalry with him to secure the loyalty of neighbouring cities.

Book 12:   War with Giangeleazzo down to his overtures for peace and his death (1402).

The reader is given a narrative of Florentine struggles from ancient Rome to the war against Giangaleazzo Visconti of Milan around 1400. This story also carries an explanation. Superficially this is that Florence prospered and its liberty was preserved *as* it struggled. Bruni observed in the *Proemium* that he wished to record the ascent of Florence to power and greatness. This was demonstrated in the city's civil dissensions, in its resistance to neighbours and finally in conflicts with the duke of Milan and the king of Naples (*R.I.S.*, xix (1926), 3).

Perhaps the most famous modern interpretation of fifteenth-century Italian history has been that of Hans Baron. His thesis was that the republican ideals of Florence around 1400 developed in response to the city's great conflict with Milan under Giangaleazzo Visconti. Republican ideals helped to sustain the morale of the city in its crisis (H. Baron, 1966). In fact, the Baron thesis is a version of Bruni's own. From one standpoint Florence flourished and survived as it resisted foreign tyrants. Equally, success was possible *because* of Florentine liberty: moral values sustained the city and explained its triumph.

A large assumption underlies this thesis and two others surround it. For Bruni, states prosper as they are capable of and willing to resist enemies. To accomplish this they require public-spiritedness, valour and need to prefer glory to wealth. This scheme of values is taken from the Roman moralists. Cicero, for example, had contrasted expedience (*utilitas*), consisting in peace, wealth and power, to integrity (*honestas*), involving a commitment to glory regardless of cost (*De Oratore*, II, lxxxii, 335).

As states struggle and fix their liberty they need to expand and they must also suffer domestic strife. In Book I Bruni advanced the argument that Italian cities were impeded by the power of ancient Rome, as small trees fare poorly in proximity to great ones. This nearness to Rome prevented Florence from growing and encouraged a drain of talent to Rome. Conversely it began to flourish as Rome declined (*R.I.S.*, xix, 6–7). A little later Bruni remarked that republican institutions stimulated growth by harnessing the ambitions of citizens. They did this by offering openings for the latter to seek honourable and well-rewarded positions (ibid., p. 13).

Quiescence, therefore, had evil effects. It has been claimed that Machiavelli was the first to perceive the benefits of strife: his intellectual forebears had praised concord (Skinner, 1978, ii, 151–2). In fact he followed Bruni and Cicero. A qualified approval of discord was the conclusion of Bruni's disapproval of quiet. As indolence produced calm, activity bred discord. Thus civil dissension sprang up in Tuscany as its cities began to grow (p. 25). Bruni's approval of discord was a qualified one. He commonly observed that disputes arose in the wake of peace and he stopped short of Cicero's declaration that through civil division the Roman people had overthrown the kings and established their power against the nobles (*De Oratore*, II, xxviii, 124; cf. II, xlviii, 199). Nevertheless, if discord abroad was for Bruni to be preferred to strife at home, it is implied that both arose from a healthy community in which individual ambitions were vitally engaged. Equally, approval of the establishment of republican institutions against nobles and tyrants at home implied agreement with Cicero's sentiment.

This 'Bruni thesis' is an historical explanation. Florence expanded as its republican institutions were established and individual energies were mobilised. Values which placed war, poverty and glory higher than peace, wealth and personal gain made this possible. Bruni's narrative thus demonstrated how Florence was able to establish itself and overcome its enemies. Like Sallust's, the *History* of Bruni also furnished lessons. The Bruni thesis accounted for events and as such it provided morals: wisdom could be gained by reading of the reasons for Florentine success. It is important to stress the identity of causes and morals. It is not helpful to think of Bruni's *History* as a moralising work or as an explanatory one from which the emphasis upon lessons somewhat detracts. The causes *are* the lessons.

From where did Bruni derive the material for this contribution to historical method? As we have seen, the ancient rhetoricians, historians and biographers provided some of the elements. Sallust and Plutarch had a pyschological view of history whilst Bruni probably found his approval of civil discord in Cicero. The idea of the state being sustained by public virtue was more diffused in antiquity. Yet Bruni differed from his sources in writing a history in which the events were shown to have been determined by such moral conceptions.

The most significant reason for this departure was the situation in which the humanists found themselves. They perceived an historical process which called for an explanation. They saw themselves (and Italy) as the disinherited heirs of antiquity; they wished to explain how this had happened. Why had Rome's greatness passed away and their own successor-cities emerged? This preoccupation had first been clearly voiced by Petrarch and was reiterated by the humanists of the *Quattrocento*.

The concern was *itself* an historical perception of major importance. In expressing an idea of the Dark Ages, Petrarch forged the notion of the Middle Ages, a dark time when the greatness of Rome was submerged by barbarism. Petrarch and his successors also believed that Rome's greatness could be restored by a self-conscious rediscovery of its values. Thinking in this way, the humanists came to an idea of antiquity as a lost world and of modern history being separated from it by a middle age. This was the beginning of the idea of European history, though later intellectuals ceased to think of the Middle Ages as a time of barbarism, or of modern history beginning in the Renaissance. It is, however, not always appropriate to scoff at the humanists' talk of barbarians: the humanists were right to see that the medieval West was dominated by the non-Roman countries of northern Europe and their culture. In some ways scholars like Bruni and Valla were correct in thinking that their age was the start of something new or less 'barbarian'.

But their most important legacy here lay in general conceptions. The humanist idea of ancient, medieval and modern history has never been shed. It is doubtful whether we could forget it, so integral is it to our idea of European civilisation itself. The development of Europe *is* the slow emergence of a culture partly by reviving what had been lost of antiquity and in part by moving away from it. Quite apart from economic periodisations there are other ways of regarding Europe. The fact, however, that we do not customarily invoke them shows the power of humanist historical conceptions.

The key, then, to the historical achievement of the Italian historians of the *Quattrocento* lay in this new idea of their own past. It conjured up an historical problem as well as historical periods. Why was Italy disinherited? The question demanded an answer and explanations came to animate the new histories being written by the humanists. At least as much weight needs therefore to be given to the historical situation of the humanists as to their novel use of ancient sources.

This situation also provided Italians with a unique vantage-point. The humanists possessed a jaundiced view of the past which constituted their new historical vision. Because of this they were encouraged to 'bracket' their position in history by reference both to antiquity and to the European culture of recent centuries. This exercise finely tuned their minds. The new approach to the past invigorated Bruni's *History* as it did the *Decades* of Flavio Biondo. Bruni's achievement was to develop the procedure of historical explanation and he did this because he wished to account for Florence's rise to power and glory from its feeble state in Roman times. The problem induced the explanation.

In this sense Bruni's *History* is the first of a series of essays in medieval history. A greater contribution in the field was made by Flavio Biondo. Bruni had limited himself to Florence, whilst Biondo's *Decades* constituted a history of the Middle Ages (as argued by D. Hay, 1959). Biondo was concerned to understand the position of Italy as the heir of Rome in an altered world. His achievement partly lay, therefore, in his story of how the world had altered. Biondo recognised how the papacy had given Italy a renewed importance as the leader of a new civilisation. It was made evident from the *Decades* that through the Crusades it had continued to be an engine of this new Christian or 'medieval' world. Biondo also gave much weight to Italian events and successes in his own day. Therefore, whilst he did not furnish an explanation, his view of the Middle Ages was an important achievement.

At the heart of the humanists' historical work was a novel consciousness of historical development. As well as the consequences we have glimpsed it may have been the spur which encouraged them to unearth the psychological approach in Sallust or the classical biographers. Certainly this was why they perceived the usefulness of certain conceptions in later Roman historians. The humanists closely read Tacitus and Orosius who had pondered the great 'landslips' of Roman history: the revolution which had destroyed the Roman republic and the catastrophe which ended the Roman Empire. Each furnished a key element of the respective accounts by Bruni and Biondo of post-Roman Italy. Tacitus had observed that able writers capable of writing on the Roman state had disappeared since the rise of the Empire (*Histories*, 1, i). Hans Baron has suggested that the observation was the source of Bruni's conception that the ending of liberty had injured the commonwealth by limiting the motivation of citizens to pursue public careers (H. Baron, 1966, pp. 58–60). Orosius supplied Biondo with an idea of Christian Rome replacing the Roman

Empire. This furnished a method by which he could show that Italy and Rome continued to guide the world though its Empire had gone, even though Biondo failed to apply the idea consistently (D. Hay, 1959).

The historical approach of Bruni and Biondo continued down to the early sixteenth century. Machiavelli's *Florentine Histories* were one of the last important as well as most brilliant examples of it. Machiavelli's work demonstrates more clearly than its forebears the approach and achievements of the genre. It is customary to discount Machiavelli as an historian: did he not employ a literary and 'moral' approach and even expand its rhetorical component? It was observed in assessing the works of Sallust and Bruni that what we are inclined to call moralising is also explanation. Should our estimate of Machiavelli's *Histories* be similarly revised? Machiavelli was concerned to draw certain morals from his history of Florence, for example, that the city's difficulties arose from the prevalence of faction and civil discord. To judge whether this is 'moralising' or explanation it is necessary to consider the scope of the *Florentine Histories* and the role which the idea of faction plays in them.

Machiavelli's work extends from the incursion of the barbarians of the fifth century to the year 1494. He seems to have intended to continue it down to the 1520s, the time at which he was writing. Only fragmentary drafts survive of what would have been an additional book. The author's purpose was to write, within an Italian framework, a history of Florence from the arrival of the ancient barbarians to the coming of new French 'barbarians' in 1494. The advent of the French in Italy in that year marked the beginning of a series of foreign invasions of Italy, as Machiavelli in the 1520s was well positioned to judge. In the work, as we have it, he alluded to this significance of 1494 (esp. the closing passage of Bk VIII, ch. 7; in *Opere*, eds Mazzoni and Casella, p. 621). The emphasis upon these dates reveals that Machiavelli wished to dwell upon the role of the barbarians in dividing Italy in ancient and modern times. The terminal dates seem to reveal a sense of modern Italian history similar to Bruni's. It is tempting to think that if Machiavelli had continued his history he might have emphasised the hopes of an Italian resurgence as he had already done in the last chapter of *The Prince*.

However this may be, Machiavelli's prevailing assumption must have remained the divisions and weaknesses of Italy. In this his starting-point was quite different to Bruni's. The latter had begun with the premise that Florence was strong and achieving greatness; writing in the 1520s, Machiavelli was preoccupied with the frailty of both Florence and Italy. How had this come about? In Book I Machiavelli was concerned to answer this question. He told how modern Italian cities, regions and the despotic families of his own day had sprung up. Throughout the succeeding books he demonstrated how Florence had come to its present form. The *Histories* recounted the weakness as well as the making of Florence and Italy. In drawing out this story Machiavelli focussed on two contrasting institutions, the development of warfare and of papal power. Besides dwelling on these matters there is much about morality. To judge Machiavelli's intentions it is necessary to understand how all these topics are related.

In the first two chapters several instances are given of the dramatic public consequences of personal morals. A sack of Rome followed when Maximus, a pretender to the Imperial throne, invited the widow of the Emperor Valentinian to be his bride; insulted, she asked the Vandal king to attack Italy. A century later the Ostrogothic kingdom was ruined when Theodatus seized the throne; this alienated support and raised hopes amongst the Byzantines of a successful conquest. In its turn the triumph of the Lombard invasion was accounted for by insult and treason. Narses, the Byzantine general, was offended by the Greek empress; in revenge he incited the Lombards to enter Italy.

Thus ambition, greed, and private honour injured the state. The power of virtue is also occasionally acknowledged. Theodoric, for example, restored order to Italy. However, through most of the subsequent books Machiavelli makes few references to individual vice and virtue, and is more ambiguous in his treatment of it. This is true of his guarded and ironical depiction of Lorenzo de' Medici in Book VIII. Here Machiavelli was dissimulating because the *Histories* had been commissioned by the Medici. For long stretches of the work Machiavelli was more concerned with the generality of citizens and the clash of factions. Is this concentration upon individual and collective behaviour given a moral colour?

In Book VII, Chapter 1, the author's view is set forth:

> In a city reputation is acquired by citizens in two ways: either by public methods or by private means. Publicly one acquires it by winning a day's battle, gaining a territory, conducting a diplomatic embassy with care and prudence, counselling the republic wisely and judiciously. Privately one acquires reputation through benefiting this or that individual, defending them against the magistrates, subventing them with money, drawing them up to unmerited honours and gratifying the common people with public games and gifts. This method of proceeding gives birth to factions and partisans and just as reputation gained in this way injures, so is the other of service.

> (In *Opere*, eds Mazzoni and Casella, p. 563)

Faction, therefore, was caused by the same moral failings that beset individuals. Machiavelli seems to have felt that this same fault rendered the Medici unsuitable as leaders of Florence: the passage above is immediately followed by a reference to the coming to power of the party of Cosimo de' Medici. In later chapters, where Machiavelli pretends to praise Lorenzo de' Medici, he reiterates the latter's pursuit of private pleasures.

Why are private amusements bad and public virtues so much to be admired? Machiavelli believed in a constant relationship between individual and public morality which his accounts of faction or of individual vice do not reveal. In Book V (eds Mazzoni and Casella, pp. 498–9) there is an arresting passage in which he spells out his view that virtue influences the destiny of states.

> Prowess (*virtù*) has issue in peace (*quiese*); peace in cultured leisure (*ozio*); leisure in disorder; disorder in ruin; and similarly from ruin is born order; from order, prowess (*virtù*); from this, glory and good fortune. Whence it is observed by the prescient (*prudenti*) that letters follow arms and that in provinces and city-states captains precede philosophers. This is because strong and well-established military institutions (*armi*) having given birth to victories, and victory peace, the strength of martial spirits cannot be corrupted with a more honest idleness (*ozio*) than that of letters; nor can idleness enter a well-founded city with a greater or more dangerous deceit than by this one.

He went on to say that peace, leisure and letters had brought the ruin of ancient Tuscany, the Roman Empire and the modern Italian city-states. He admitted that no modern state in Italy deserved to be compared to Rome in its great days, but he insisted that they were living in freedom and with dignity. It was his theme, however, from Book VI to Book VIII, that the arts of peace in the *Quattrocento* had weakened the peninsula and left it unprepared to beat off the barbarians in 1494.

Individual vice led to treachery, division and faction; virtue stimulated public success through arms. Machiavelli was quite clear how this personal valour could be encouraged and exploited. In Book I he declared: 'with these leisured princes (*oziosi principi*) and such rabble armies (*vilissime armi*) my History will therefore be full' (eds Mazzoni and Casella, p. 407). 'Leisured' princes were those who occupied their time improving their minds whilst they employed soldiers of fortune to fight their battles. What was needed was soldier–princes and citizen armies. The evils of idle rulers and their *condottieri* were explored in the last three books of Machiavelli's *Histories*. How could private virtue and public good be achieved? The answer lay in 'good laws and institutions' which could be established by a strong and enlightened leader. He alone could restrain private appetites.

Wise leaders could re-establish good laws and institutions or, to some extent, sustain the state in their absence (p. 158). Rulers of this kind checked licence and ambition, led the soldiery, established colonies (Bk II, ch. 1) and occupied their capital where they could best oversee the welfare and security of their peoples. It was the failure of the Roman emperors to maintain their seat at Rome which had allowed the barbarians to control Italy (Bk I, ch. 1). Theodoric's determination to base his government at Ravenna had given to the papacy the opportunity to establish its dominion. This is why the papacy occupies an important place in the pages of Machiavelli's *Histories*. It was an example of the consequences of bad laws and institutions; it also produced them, as Machiavelli explained in Book I (eds Mazzoni and Casella, p. 388).

> All the wars which from this time were waged by barbarians in Italy, were in greater part caused by the pontiffs, and all the barbarians who inundated it were most often summoned by them. The same way of proceeding which has kept and keeps Italy disunited and weak, still persists in our times . . . And it will be seen how the popes, first with censures and afterwards with these and arms mixed together with indulgences, became terrible and venerable; and how from having abused the one and the other they have wholly lost the one; they are, for the other, at the discretion of others.

The popes were therefore supreme examples of 'idle' princes who employed mercenaries to do their soldiering. They were also instances of how Christian virtues were inappropriately combined with political and military power. This was only hinted at in the early part of the work when Machiavelli remarked that the early popes were less noted for their power than for their sanctity and the miracles they performed. Machiavelli had written more plainly of Christianity at the very start of the *Histories*. Christian faith had made the Roman world pitiable, fomented strife through its own divisions and rendered men doubtful of the very nature of God. The reader was to understand that states should not be regulated according to Christian principles.

Do these themes constitute a form of 'moralising' history? Machiavelli began with an historical question: Why had Florence and Italy become divided? His answer was the failure of laws, institutions or leaders to foster or preserve public virtues. Consequently, private vice and licence were allowed to flourish and generate factions and military weakness. In this way a good deal of blame is apportioned to the popes as leaders guided by inappropriate values.

This surely is an explanation and an impressive one. Machiavelli's moral scheme is drawn from Sallust and Cicero but he used it more effectively than they had done. Cicero had not written a history and Sallust's moral views were set forth in preambles to the *Catiline Conspiracy* and the *Jugurthine War*; they do not inform those works. Bruni employed the same ethical viewpoint to help interpret his narrative, but Machiavelli used it to forge a more effective and explicit explanation. His nostrums are not perfectly integrated with the narrative. All the content is nevertheless consistent with the general interpretation. Machiavelli also expected lessons to be drawn from his *Histories*, but once again the 'morals' *were* the explanation. Moreover, contemporaries believed that men were responsible for their actions. Historical events had been brought about by men; readers could learn from them how to govern their own behaviour and hence events as well.

Machiavelli therefore reminds us that the humanist historians discovered creative elements in familiar texts. Petrarch had achieved this with Cicero; Bruni and Machiavelli did so with Sallust and Suetonius, aided a little by what was for them the newly found *Lives* of Plutarch. They had the vision to see there a psychological view of history. It is doubtful if Italian scholars could have done this had they not possessed the sense of an historical problem which the ancients had not known. Classical histories were informed by the feeling of a gulf between 'barbarism' and civilisation, with the culture of Greece and Rome near the light and the inferior peoples outside the Pale. The Romans had an idea of decadence, of a golden age in the past from which they had declined. The idea, however, was lacking to them of ancient and modern history, as well as the problem it pushed to the fore of explaining how modern times had come to pass.

The humanists, therefore, had a novel historical perspective; equally they could learn from the ancient approach which divided the world into Romans and barbarians. From the start they employed the dichotomy to account for modern history. From Petrarch onwards the dark ages were seen as the time when Rome had been submerged by barbarians. When Tacitus began to be read once more, the classical idea of 'barbarism' was turned to a new purpose.

Mention of Tacitus's name raises the question of how far historical writing was influenced in the fifteenth century by the discovery of new historical texts. The first unknown histories to circulate were Greek ones in translation, especially Thucydides, Herodotus and Polybius. Their works had been preserved in Byzantium, but had not been available in the West since ancient times. Their impact is sometimes held to have been considerable, but justifiable admiration for them has perhaps made scholars wish to exaggerate their importance in the Renaissance. There were two reasons why it was limited at that time. The early translations, though undertaken by famous men of letters, were often faulty or inelegant. Furthermore, Herodotus and Thucydides dealt with the history of Greece, a subject which seemed remote from the concerns of Italian historians. Polybius enjoyed a wider readership because he did write about Rome, but he suffered in translation and his influence has also been overstated.

The impact of Tacitus outstripped that of the Greek historians, although it was a century after the first discovery of the *Histories, Annals, Germania* and *Agricola* before it was felt strongly. Tacitus wrote about Roman history and in a wonderful style. His works also possessed unique qualities. Of the other pagan historians who were to hand, Caesar's bent was military, Justinus was an epitome, mainly of the earlier historian Pompeius Trogus, while the enormous length of Livy made him difficult to use. Tacitus offered something which even Sallust lacked. In the *Germania* he gave a thoroughgoing description of a barbarian society and in his *Histories* he narrated Roman politics from the senatorial viewpoint (see esp. R. Syme (Paris, 1958)).

Tacitus's *Histories* are accounts of the author's own times, and represent the personal view of someone who was an actor in the events. Their stance is distinctive and so is the cynical attitude they contain. Tacitus was describing the antics of emperors who had displaced his own class. The cynicism owed something also to the horrors he claimed to have seen. We are given an almost Thucydidean picture of slaughter and death, in which grim events are observed with a jaundiced eye. To understand this disdain we need to appreciate how the senatorial class saw itself as the guardian of Roman morals and traditions. His high estate gave Tacitus perspective. Knowledge combined with jaundice and the psychological approach he had inherited from earlier historians and biographers. All this enabled him to show how human character drove the wheel of fortune at the highest level of the Roman world.

The Emperor Galba failed through integrity, bravery, old age, complacency and meanness (cf. esp. I, xlix). The contrasting facets of character are justly and proportionately observed. There is a similar sense of proportion in the depiction of the *dramatis personae*. The imperial court, the Praetorian Guard, senators and the generals of provincial armies are graded according to their weight. The analogy of linear perspective describes this skill. Persons nearer to the viewer are drawn larger; those more remote or less important are on a smaller scale. Equally, the ability to regulate the size of persons and objects according to their distance allowed Tacitus to demonstrate the relations not merely of the viewer and the viewed but *between* things within the whole field of vision.

The *Histories* therefore had several unique properties to offer European historiography. No less important was the *Germania*. The author's purpose there was to describe German life, tribes, religious practices, attitudes to war, buildings, dress, marriage and domestic manners. The most characteristic and memorable element was Tacitus's concentration on the simplicity and artlessness of German *mores*. He was impressed by the beneficial absence of money and commended the plain life-style of the Germans.

Mothers suckled their own babies, children were brought up simply and no outward distinction was admitted between master and slave (ch. 20). Tacitus judged that the austerity and faithfulness of German marriage deserved the highest praise. He concluded his observations on this topic with the remark that 'good customs are worth more to them than good laws are to others'. These good customs had produced a morally vigorous community which was strong in war and peace. Good customs promoted war-like as well as peaceable virtues: princes (*principes*) and retinues strove to outmatch each other in *virtus* so that idleness (*quies*) was suppressed and society prepared for war (ch. 14). The favourable effects generated by the German struggle through the ages to defend their homeland against Roman aggression are also noted (ch. 37).

No other text presented so clear a picture of the noble savage who was uncorrupted by money, licence and repose. At the same time the *Germania* offered an arresting picture of a society. It sketched in three dimensions social facets of landscape, buildings and tribes which were related to the more hidden morals and domestic manners.

The impact of Tacitus can be sensed in the writings of Machiavelli and Guicciardini, although the main impact came later. The former shows influence of the *Germania*, the latter of the *Histories*. Via their writings, the reverberations reached the north of Europe. There are signs of this influence in *The Florentine Histories* and *The Prince*. *The Florentine Histories* begins with a striking account of the social practices of the Germans. Machiavelli drew attention to their habit of dividing their peoples into three groups, containing equal parts of the different social classes. One third was then required to leave the territory and establish itself abroad so as to avoid the perils of over-population. Machiavelli reported this to explain the barbarian invasions of the Roman Empire.

Had Machiavelli continued the *Histories* beyond 1494 it is likely that he would have dwelt upon the disposition and strength of the French who had invaded Italy. He gave hints enough earlier in the work that he wished to focus upon the recrudescence of the old barbarian threat. In *The Prince* and the *Ritratto di cose di Francia*, Machiavelli analysed the social composition of the French nation and claimed that the existence of a baronial class dedicated to arms explained the military strength demonstrated in the Italian expedition of Charles VIII. In chapter 3 of *The Prince* the government of conquered lands is related to language and customs. In this and the following chapter Machiavelli took examples from France. In chapter 3 we are told that Brittany, Burgundy, Gascony and Normandy (unlike the duchy of Milan) were easily governed by French kings because of the similarity of their *mores* to those of the rest of the French kingdom. France is cited in chapter 4 as a state governed by king and barons. Such a realm could be invaded easily but governed with difficulty. Turkey or Alexander the Great's empire, on the other hand, were entities to which the reverse conditions applied: they were states governed by royal officials. The reason why this difference made France hard to hold but easy to conquer lay in the 'ancient multitude of lords recognised by their own inferiors and loved by them'. This multitude surrounded the king (ed. Burd, p. 201).

These ideas were explored by Machiavelli in two remarkable tracts. In his 'Portrait of French affairs' (*Ritratto di cose di Francia*) he outlined what he took to be the cardinal features of the French state. In his discussion a large place is occupied by what we would call the social structure of France. He commented on the integration of the old ducal provinces into the French kingdom. This enriched French kings and impeded invading armies.

The strong points of France in regard to its neighbours are discussed. Geographical factors are used to explain the country's advantages *vis à vis* Spain and Italy. The chief strength of the French kingdom lay in its domination by a rural aristocracy. Its wealth was agricultural and this passed via taxes into the hands of lords. Primogeniture ensured that these riches remained confined whilst younger sons were forced to undertake a martial career to win lands of their own. The social system therefore made France a formidable military power (*Ritratto*, eds Mazzoni and Casella, pp. 731–9).

In the *Ritratto delle cose della Magna* Machiavelli explained German affairs by the country's disunity. The *Ritratto di cose di Francia* had claimed that the French cavalry had become formidable but its infantry weak through baronial might. Here the different social structure of Germany was made to account for its strong infantry. In the Empire nobles enjoyed a less favoured position and in Switzerland there was no distinction of gentleman and commoner (eds Mazzoni and Casella, pp. 740–3).

Machiavelli was perhaps extending to Switzerland Tacitus's judgement that the ancient Germans had allowed no public distinction between master and slave. Elsewhere, however, the source was Machiavelli's own observations aided by the humanist analysis of ancient society. But the *idea* of composing portraits of France and Germany was surely suggested by a reading of Tacitus as well as the practice of diplomatic reporting. Machiavelli also improved upon his model. Where Tacitus had drawn a 'perspectival' picture of Germany, Machiavelli sought to explain French success and German weakness. His *Ritratto di cose di Francia* is cast as a series of reasons to account for the power and wealth of the French king. Once again the historical situation in which the Italian humanists found themselves enabled them to use an ancient source to a novel purpose.

In Machiavelli, Tacitean influence was blended with a Renaissance zeal for understanding antiquity which modern scholars often deride as 'antiquarian'. However, when the humanists collected and catalogued manuscripts, coins, medals, inscriptions, statuary and other 'antiques' they were seeking to gather material for an analysis of ancient civilisation. The first modern study of society was the humanist study of the Roman world. The perception that the ancient world had been lost led them both to analyse and explain. Asking why antiquity had gone also involved examining the origins and institutions of their own world. When Machiavelli questioned the state of France, he was repeating a question asked by the humanists of antiquity and of modern Italy. Tacitus's *Germania* and the Renaissance analysis of antiquity formed the distant roots of modern social science.

Guicciardini also betrays the influence of Tacitus in his *History of Italy* (the *Storia d'Italia*). His great *History* is usually seen as expressing the 'modern' side of the Italian achievement. On this view it was the outcome of the author's personal experiences in the Italian Wars. Classical models were so assimilated by him that they frequently escape notice. The situation which commanded the author's attention was the series of foreign invasions of Italy after 1494. Guicciardini wished to shed light on conflicts in which he had played a conspicuous role in the 1520s. He was addressing the governing classes of Italy, especially his fellow Florentines, to justify his part in the Italian Wars and answer the charge that his own activities had been guided by personal ambition.

Guicciardini's model was Tacitus. Features of Guicciardini's great work show the marks of his reading. In choosing to write of his own times, Guicciardini was entering terrain not occupied by surviving Roman historians other than Tacitus. The only exception to this had been histories of military campaigns. Like Tacitus's *Histories* too, the *Storia d'Italia* focussed upon leaders and the moral choices of individuals. Princes like Lodovico *il Moro* of Milan, the civic leaders of Florence or Venice and the Popes Alexander VI, Julius II, Leo X and Clement VII threw everything into the hands of Fortune by overestimating their own power, through irrational ambition or lack of prudence. Guicciardini's *History* is a drama in which events were determined as much by a fearsome necessity as by the agency of individuals. For this reason there is a gloomy colouring to the narrative which resembles that of Tacitus's *Histories*. Whilst it lacks Tacitean horror, Guicciardini's narrative does have its grim hue. It characterised Italian history of his age as a series of invasions by barbarians which culminated in the sack of Rome in 1527 and the siege of Florence in 1529–30.

Whilst Guicciardini was writing, humanist influence had long since begun to filter beyond the Alps. A hot stream of prejudice against northern 'barbarians' had run from the pens of Petrarch, Valla, Pope

Pius II and many other humanists, firing northerners to cultural rivalry with Italians. The sentiment was felt in all fields of learning, but it affected historical writing in a particular fashion. The new Italian histories were of a markedly patriotic stamp and the humanist periodisation of history had a consciously Italian significance. The Dark Ages were when Rome had been submerged by barbarism – in other words, the culture of northern Europe. The implied ending of darkness was the revival of Roman culture in Italy. Here was something to rebut.

Northern historians also had to hand the *Germania* of Tacitus. A portrait of barbarian society was provided by one of the most prized writers of ancient Rome. It contained, moreover, the flattering notion that barbarians were nobler than corrupted Romans.

These were the spurs which goaded the ultramontanes of early modern times. In the works they had composed on Italian history, the Italian humanists had left models to emulate. What had been done for Italy could be re-done for other lands. Each European country had a history and antiquities deserving to stand alongside the Italian ones. Northern scholars also wished to demonstrate that the Middle Ages was an era when native customs and institutions had been developed which were worthy of interest. Here the authority of Tacitus was enormously important, for his name was enough to prove the respectability of recording the customs of a barbarian people.

This is the springing of the arch that carried historiography from Italy beyond the Alps. It is, however, obscured by the adjoining scenery of Italian and transalpine historical scholarship. Early modern historians are widely acknowledged as having imitated the antiquarianism of fifteenth-century Italy and the glitter of the humanist style. Northern writers learnt at first hand from those Italians who worked abroad. Scholars like Polydore Vergil in England introduced certain classical literary practices to ultramontane scholarship: a more concise and speedy narrative style, correct latinity and, where they impinged upon ancient history, a critical attitude to legends. Beyond this, humanist influence is hidden by the different subject-matter of the historians of Italy and the later ones of the North.

The Italians furnished models and methods, but since northern scholars were inspired to emulate as well as copy, they came to produce work of a markedly different stamp. In order to 'validate' their barbarian past, German, French and British historians commemorated their medieval antiquities and institutions. The Italian humanists had created a sense of medieval history, by way of identifying and in large measure disparaging the non-Roman element in contemporary and recent culture. Although an historian like Biondo wished to convey an understanding of how Italy had assumed its contemporary form, it was not his purpose to celebrate the Middle Ages. If anything, the implication of the *Quattrocento* histories was that Italians were only now beginning to revive antiquity or to achieve something worthy of it. The northern historians attached a quite new importance to the medieval period by praising it at a time when non-Roman customs and institutions had been born.

This is surely the reason why the Italian contribution to the historiography of the early modern age has been undervalued. The chief inspiration of the greatest historians after 1500 lay in the work of the Italian humanists and the ancient sources they had unearthed. But their work looks dissimilar because much of it was seeking to overturn assumptions made by the Italians. It was also touched by classical influences which had been released by the Italians and yet had made little impact upon the historical writing of the peninsula.

The historical achievement of northern Europe lay in telling the story of northern nations and in exploiting Tacitus for the purpose of writing contemporary political history. Both these things were much more important than this description makes them sound. The histories of nations were not merely narrations of affairs, but social histories. The customs and institutions of peoples were examined and used to organise their history and to elevate the medieval period or barbarian *mores*. The 'Tacitism' also represented the complete assimilation of an ancient model for a new purpose and here the work of Guicciardini had been no more than a pre-figuring.

The example of Conrad Celtis (1459–1508) shows how important a part was played in the progress of these new interests by a patriotic re-assessment of Italian work under the inspiration of Tacitus. He returned from Italy in 1487 determined to promote German rivalry with proud Italian scholars. The names of his historical writings are sufficient to show the source of their inspiration. In 1500 Celtis published an edition of Tacitus's *Germania*. A year later he turned his hand to the publication of medieval German sources, which included the plays of the medieval German dramatist, Hroswitha. His great project, which he left unfinished, was a *Germania Illustrata*, modelled upon Biondo's similarly entitled work on Italy. Like the latter, it was intended to be a history organised around antiquities. The discovery of German medieval history and the interest of German customs happened under the influence of Tacitus and Biondo.

Conrad Celtis publicised a programme which others were left to accomplish. Before passing to consider them, Celtis's career draws our attention to how writers of history were influenced by the political climate. This, of course, is true of historical writing in all periods, but there was a novel dimension to this in the early modern period. Ultramontane historians were anxious to hold aloft a patriotic standard and advertise the grievances of parties or apologise for their own careers. This was combined with traditional motives like glorifying dynasties.

Celtis was one of a group of scholars at the court of the Emperor Maximilian. The two other leading historians of Germany at that time, Albert Krantz (1450–1517) and Jacob Wimpheling (1450–1528) also belonged to it. Through Maximilian's patronage Celtis became Professor of Rhetoric at the University of Vienna and the others were advanced in their careers. The remarkable historians of the French Civil War period such as Pasquier (1529–1615), de la Popelinière (1540–1608), de Thou (1553–1617), Hotman (1524–90) and Davila (1576–1630) were royal councillors, lawyers, officials or the protagonists of the civil war parties. Other countries furnish equivalent examples.

History became a learned expression of lay society. Before the fifteenth century it was rare for laymen to write history and unknown for them to be steeped in classical culture. Few of the sixteenth-century historians were clerics. Most used their mastery of ancient literature to express the claims of princes, parties or their personal needs. The causes were the religious and political conflicts of the time and the expansion of Europe. In all this the pattern had been set in Italy.

Celtis's idea of documenting the customs of Germany was realised abroad. Albert Krantz had written histories of Saxony and of the Wends and he had German successors. None of them, however, equalled the ground-breaking work of William Camden, the English antiquary whose *Britannia* (1586) was a monument equal to Biondo's *Italia Illustrata*. It recorded the landscape, produce, language, names, towns, roads, manners and institutions of Britain in a Latin worthy of the Italian humanists. The greatest Spanish and French writers managed something still more remarkable in that they combined Camden's record of customs and institutions with a philosophical idea of how nations had been formed by them.

This happened earliest in Spain. There the contemporary experience of the Discoveries united with humanist tradition. The first scholar to work in this field was Peter Martyr (or Pietro Martire) (1500–62), a pupil of Pope Pius II. In 1520 Martyr became secretary to the Council of the Indies and in instalments down to 1530 he issued his *Decades of the New World*, which formed effectively a history of the Indian people. This was the first of a line of histories of the New World. Their genealogy ran from the mainstream of Italian humanism via Peter Martyr and a Spaniard who worked in the Indies to a native of the New World. Martyr's successor was Hernandez de Oviedo y Valdes (1475–1557), a Spanish governor of Darien; it was probably under the inspiration of Peter Martyr that he wrote his *General and Natural History of the New World* in 1535.

At the end of this road lay the remarkable *History of Peru* by Garcilasso de la Vega (published 1609–17). The author had been born in Peru, the son of a conquistador and the grandson of the last Inca ruler. The work treats of the Inca people, their kings, laws and religious practices and of their conquest. The idea of writing the social history of a native people thus developed as it passed from Italian to Spanish and native hands and took root amongst the Spanish *noblesse de robe* and the governing classes of Spanish America.

More notable still for the future development of European historical writing was Hotman's *Franco-Gallia* and Étienne Pasquier's *Recherches de la France* (1611). These French scholars strove amidst the conflicts of the Wars of Religion to reach an understanding of the lineaments of French history and the monarchy. They tried to explain how the rights and institutions of the French kingdom were products of history. This was a direction signposted by the humanists. One of the novelties about this French group was that they wrote histories or studies of France: Pasquier wrote *Recherches de la France* and de la Popelinière an *Histoire de France*. These were not chronicles or histories written in France nor accounts of dynasties or events, but histories *of* France. There was a conceptual innovation here: these were attempts to *conceive* of what a country was through understanding how it had come to be. Their imagination had been fired by the example of Biondo writing about Italy.

The institutional and social orientation of these works and of German and Spanish historical writing came partly from Biondo. But they derived in a larger measure from the study of ancient literature and history. As we have seen, the interest in social history was encouraged by the new knowledge of the *Germania* of Tacitus. Of importance also was the influence of Cicero. His rhetorical writings elaborated the point that truth should be discovered in what people did and had believed. The *De Legibus* was an effort to demonstrate that scholars should look at how the law of Rome had actually emerged if they wished to know what law was best. Historical writing after 1500 was also moved by the Italian antiquarians such as Biondo and Pomponio Leto. They had tried to study and recover Roman society as a whole: its language, names, customs and institutions by means of its monuments, manuscripts and coins.

In order to combat the arrogance of the Italian humanists ultramontane scholars applied the method to their own lands. This was not a great mental leap, because in studying the ancient world the Italian humanists felt they were approaching merely an earlier stage of their own history. In investigating the institutions and customs of their various lands the northern humanists were imitating the method and reacting to the prejudices of the Italians: the history of their own countries was as worthy of study as that of Italy.

Inevitably, however, this led them to recover a past that was less classical and was even 'medieval' – in part this was a deliberate effort to 'vindicate' the Middle Ages against the scoffs of Italian humanists. This 'social' approach to history advanced the cause of historical explanation because this sort of history was an approach to explanation. A country could be understood by regarding its customs and institutions.

At the same time this progress of historical method was being helped further by the influence of what can be called the 'rhetorical' approach to history. This had been represented in its most brilliant form in Italy by the work of Bruni and Machiavelli. Their bent was psychological: the character and values of men determined the outcome of events. However, Machiavelli had given this a Tacitean colour by arguing that the strength of France lay in the values of its baronage.

The most remarkable historians of this type in the non–Italian world were Juan de Mariana (1535–1624) in Spain and George Buchanan (1506–82) in Scotland. Today their style of history is out of fashion and it is often misunderstood. However, such scholars contributed to historical explanation in taking up the idea that values determined the course of individual lives and the fate of societies. Moreover, without them the great historical enterprises of the eighteenth century cannot be understood. The *History of England* by Hume and Gibbon's *Decline and Fall of the Roman Empire* were the last and perhaps the most important works in a tradition which sought to account for the progress of states according to the values espoused by their rulers and their societies at large.

Meantime this tradition had been strengthened and a part of its current deflected by the impact of the *Histories* of Tacitus, which were felt strongly for the first time in the later sixteenth century. The imprint of Tacitus is to be seen on many of the great historians of the period. It was particularly strong on Jacques August de Thou's *Historia sui temporis*, Henrico Davila's *Istoria delle guerre civile de Francia*, Peter Cornelius Hooft's *Nederlandsche Historien* (published 1642–56) and Clarendon's *History of the Rebellion* (1702–04). The 'Tacitism' of these works is shown in their conceptions, style and stance.

Like Tacitus these works were histories of their authors' own times. They recorded actions which the historian had observed and in which he had frequently participated. This is true of Davila, de Hooft and Clarendon. Their theme was strife or civil war and the events were narrated with a Tacitean irony appropriate to their subject. The standpoint was detached: they purported to describe parties and conflicts with an objective eye. These works are some of the greatest historical works of the early modern age. Tacitus not merely served them as a model, he provided the essential vehicle for their success.

Tacitus taught these authors how to portray and explain events in which an author had taken part. Tacitus's style and approach were fit for describing dissension, crisis and disaster. His ironic detachment was appropriate to the layman's view of conflict and to an aristocratic point of view. All the imitators of this age were courtiers or state servants and the Tacitean detachment allowed them to express opinions of their rulers' deeds and merits. Tacitus had a yet more important service to render in refining the psychological viewpoint. The *Histories* had examples to offer and the possibilities were developed in Tacitus's *Agricola*. Psychological depth was deepened further by an increased knowledge of Plutarch's *Lives*, translations of which were contemporaneous with the great histories of the sixteenth century (French translation by Jacques Amyot, 1559; English rendering from Amyot's by Sir Thomas North, 1579).

The concern of these writers with the individual is the very thing which has caused them now to be neglected. Today there is just sufficient belief in free will for us to allow that the great historians of this age could have been right in believing that values determined the great events about which they wrote. They were ahead of their successors in recognising that human beings and classes do not contend with, and are even less willing to die, from appetite, circumstances or oppression. Rather it is because they possess arguments and morals that justify possessing those appetites, or provide the grounds for altering circumstances and remedying oppression. The Greeks had perceived that it is not desire but the system of ethical values operating *upon* it that determines human action. This is the truth breathing life into the historical writing of Sallust, Tacitus, Bruni, Machiavelli, Clarendon, Hume and Gibbon. Instead of advancing beyond it, we have retreated into a clumsy materialism ill supported by common sense.

Turning aside from creative ideas to those which continue to influence present thinking, the most permanent historical legacy of the Italian humanists lay in what was most original to them. Their concept of historical change gave birth to an idea of antiquity as well as the periodisation of European history. A sense of dislocation from the classical world enabled them to study both antiquity and their own world as *societies*. Here was the source of subsequent achievements in advancing historical explanation. It was also the beginning of social history.

Chapter Fifteen

Renaissance and Reformation

I n discussing artistic ideals the names were mentioned of patrons who
sought to gain public esteem by commissioning works of art which
would advertise their moral and intellectual worth. This had been first
done by Florentine citizens in the early *Quattrocento*, greatest amongst
whom was Cosimo de' Medici. In the middle and later part of the
century the ideal passed to such patrons as Lionello d'Este of Ferrara,
Federigo da Montefeltro of Urbino, the Sforza dukes of Milan and the
Gonzaga family of Mantua. These cultivated princes were the first of
a type which was to feature in the history of the Reformation. What
they represented can be glimpsed most clearly at Urbino, from where
some monuments to Federigo's ambitions still survive.

Federigo was interested in history, philosophy and theology, and
appointed a lecturer who would teach him the principles of Aristotle's
Ethics. There exists at Windsor a Flemish painting, executed for the palace
at Urbino, depicting Federigo and his son listening to a lecture. This is a
telling image for it records a moment when rulers gained access to the
book-learning of the Church. Besides this painting there is a record of
an inscription which Federigo erected in his palace, which shows how
much this ideal of cultivation was an ancient one.

In the inner sanctum of Federigo's great library within the palace lay
a room which housed his archive, known as the Cancelleria. Along with
representations of the arts and sciences Federigo had placed here these
words:

In this house you have wealth, golden bowls, abundance of money,
crowds of servants, sparkling gems, rich jewels, precious chains and

girdles. But here is a treasure that far outshines all these splendours. In these halls you have pillars of snowy marble and gold, painted figures set in deep recesses; within, the walls are hung with the tale of Troy, without, are gardens fragrant with bright flowers and green foliage. Both within and without the house is glorious. But all these things are dumb; only the library is eloquent. Whether they speak or hold silence, books have power to profit and charm the reader. They teach the story of the past, and unfold the meaning of the future. They explain the labours of earth and impart the knowledge of heaven.

> (J. Denistoun, *Memoirs of the Dukes of Urbino, 1851*, p. 162; tr. in J. Cartwright, *Baldassare Castiglione* (1908), i, p. 61)

Here the glory of the Montefeltro Palace is held to lie not in its visible splendours, but in its books. At the invisible heart of the library, moreover, was a philosophical notion, originally Socratic, that wisdom imparted a knowledge of human and divine affairs. The glory of a princely palace lying in its library is only a comprehensible idea when we realise that Plato's philosopher–ruler, grafted onto Roman notions of the cultivated man, had been reborn in *Quattrocento* Italy.

The philosopher–prince (and the ideal of virtue as knowledge inbuilt behind it) was a specific example of the ancient notion of virtue which the humanists had revived. Its general principle was the possibility of attaining the good life by reason. This was a commonplace assumption of ancient ethics and its implication was that human life was controlled neither by God (or Destiny) nor chaos. Instead, man possessed sufficient free-will and the rational faculty to guide him towards it. These ideas had a decisive effect upon sixteenth-century thought. The notion of the philosopher–prince, learned in theological questions, helped to fashion the 'virtuous' prince of the Reformation era. The beliefs that man could aspire to virtue by reason, and that life was governed equally by seemingly contradictory principles of virtue and fortune, helped to form the theology, respectively, of Luther and Calvin. It is necessary to examine the nature of the intellectual and religious changes effected by those Reformers in order to see how this was so.

1. Attitudes to the prince and the beginnings of the Reformation in Germany and England

1.1 The problem: Luther's doctrines and their origins

In the nineteenth century, it was held that the individualism, scepticism and secularism of the Renaissance animated the religious revolt. This assumed a certain view at once of Humanism and of Reform. It was convincing as long as the Reformation was thought to be a rational and individual rebellion against an obscurantist Church, sustained in darkness by the misuse of literary and scriptural authority. Nowadays scholars are inclined to be less kind both to the Renaissance and the Reformation.

The Reformation is seen today not as the revolt of the enlightened individual, but as the establishment of orthodoxy, under the aegis of state power. One coercive institution, supported by intellectual partisans, was replaced by another. Equally, the Renaissance is thought to have been little enlightened. Historians no longer maintain that it was a secular affair in the sense that it was characterised by paganism or hostility to Christianity. Nor is it generally accepted today that the Renaissance brought to light a new conception of the individual or of man. The humanists did revive an antique idea of humanity, but it was of limited application and circulation. The notion was ethical in character, conformable to Christianity and played a small part even in the writings of the humanists.

This redefinition of Renaissance and Reformation does raise the possibility, however, of a different relationship between them: if neither was enlightened, both were possibly religious. The Renaissance (and especially its northern component) has indeed come to be seen almost as an 'evangelical preparation' for the Reformers. The adage of the sixteenth century is now repeated: 'Erasmus laid the egg which Luther hatched.' Common Christian threads led from Petrarch and Valla via Erasmus to the Protestant Reformers. The latter inherited from the humanists a suspicion of the old scholasticism, a preference for ethics and a concern to find a reliable text of the scriptures on which ecclesiastical authority could be firmly based. In the Low Countries, Germany, England and Scandinavia, Erasmus, Ulrich von Hutten (1488–1523), Melanchthon (1497–1560), Thomas More, Thomas Starkey (*c.* 1499–1538), Paulus Helie (*c.* 1485–*c.* 1535), Christian Peterson, Lars Andersson (d. 1552) and Peter Starkilaks betray the influence of these ideas. Some of the other reformers, particularly in Switzerland and Scotland, reveal a robust loyalty to the old scholasticism.

These thinkers had been brought up in the new learning and they used its skills to restore theology and reform the Church. In particular, Erasmus took up a distinctive position. It was evangelical and defined by emphasis rather than by dogmatic statement. He tried to construct a better text of the New Testament, and find a Christian life properly based upon it. Christ as the teacher, and a stress upon the desirability of a simpler form of worship and doctrine were prominent notes of his piety. Another was his preference for the relative virtues of lay devotion and state power.

These ideas influenced many individuals in the early sixteenth century. Some of these, like the scholars at Wittenberg (chiefly Melanchthon) were to take a leading part in the Reformation. Many who did not wish to break with Rome welcomed the beginnings of the Lutheran reform and only later drew back. It is accepted, then, that Erasmian ideas were a preparation for the Reformation. Does the work of these thinkers explain the later events in the sense that without them they would not have happened? Or did they only hasten along a predetermined course, or guarantee victory? Moreover, by 'preparation' do we mean a preparation of the minds that conceived the ideas, or of those that received them? Historians are by no means unanimous in answering these central questions.

Some have suggested that Humanism and Reform were two independent and widely differing movements which, at most, were brought into a relationship. They had different and even opposed ends, and pursued contrary methods. Other historians have suggested that the ideas of the humanists played a more active part. For them humanist learning made new ideas acceptable and also was responsible for their appearance. The weakening of the old theology on the Continent and the *via media* of the Anglican Church have alike been attributed to this cause. Such a view is difficult to sustain. It is one thing to describe certain individuals (like Thomas Starkey) as Erasmians; it is harder to demonstrate that their ideas were indeed the cause of the changes that took place.

Therefore, only a limited version would seem to be true of the modest modern view that the Renaissance contributed to the Reformation. The new learning and new religious reform were separate movements although they shared some principles and personnel.

If we examine the ideas voiced by the chief protagonists are we led to the same conclusions? One possibility is that they were traditional theological propositions or demands for reform; if so, the only problem is to explain their acceptance. If, however, they themselves were new there will be two aspects to understand. Either way, do any humanist conceptions lie behind the events of the sixteenth century? Naturally this raises great difficulties: problems are never harder to define than in the history of ideas where the frontiers are so vague. Nevertheless, it is safe to say that virtually all the Reformers' ideas had been espoused before.

Indulgences had been attacked before and so had the authority of the papacy, as well as the doctrine of transubstantiation and the validity of the other sacraments. Equally, many earlier critics of the Church had rejected ecclesiastical wealth. The simplification of liturgy, the use of the vernacular, a reliance upon preaching, the call to the secular power to reform the Church and remove its landed property and the appeal to the authority of the scriptures, had all been demanded before 1500.

The fact, however, that the protests had been made earlier does not prove that they, or the objects they were seeking to remedy, were not the causes. Old ideas may have new consequences when advanced more emphatically. Well-rehearsed arguments may be put forward for new reasons, and a virtual identity of claims may mask a decisive divergence.

The first of these possibilities is the easiest to determine. The consequences which followed the claims of Luther and the other early Reformers were too novel and dramatic to be explained merely as reactions to more forceful enumeration of traditional complaints. Either there must have been important novelties in the reforming ideas themselves, or the effects must be accounted for by a new acceptance or encouragement of old ideas. There is a case for saying that the effects which came after should be attributed to the circumstances in which they were expressed. Several considerations support this point, of which one is what may be called the general disproportion of cause and effect.

The clamour which greeted Luther's proclamations seems out of proportion to the novelty of his words, unless it was their emphatic tone which explains the effect. However, it is doubtful whether Luther was so much more emphatic than earlier heretics and reformers. He can be most closely compared to John Hus (1369–1415), the progenitor of the Hussite movement in early fifteenth-century Bohemia. Luther was more outspoken and impassioned than the English heresiarch John Wycliffe (1330–84), but Hus exhorted huge congregations from the pulpit of Bethlehem Chapel in Prague. Luther, however, probably did speak with fewer qualifications than Hus had done.

Above all Luther acted with more despatch. Hus had developed his ideas over more than ten years, from 1400 to 1412, whereas Luther evolved his own with dramatic speed. The Ninety-Five theses of 1517 were little more than a criticism of the use of indulgences by the papacy. But the manifestos issued by Luther in 1520 showed a nearly full development of his ideas. There is doubt about the date at which he evolved the doctrine of salvation, but even if we accept the suggestion that it was well before 1519, it is still to be doubted whether his ideas would have been recorded by history, were it not for the events which followed them. Did they have consequences because they were vehement, or did they become vehement in train with their having effects? It seems possible that Luther was pushed along by the reactions which he evoked.

The criticisms of the early Reformers, then, did not make an impact because they were expressed dramatically. Did they do so because they were made for different reasons? This possibility is harder to decide: the reasons why earlier critics had pressed their arguments are not always known. In other cases the formal reason for which a certain position had been taken up may be known but not the subtler processes of thought behind it. However, the grounds employed by the early reformers for their advocacy of change were conventional. Luther, Melanchthon, Bucer and many others criticised what they saw in the Church, and suggested remedies either because of the authority (or lack of it) in Scripture, or on the ground of reason.

All the same there were three novel grounds on which Luther attacked the Church. First, he criticised it as an 'Aristotelian' institution. There had been criticisms before of the scholastic methods and of its Aristotelian foundations, but before *c.* 1350 no one would have rejected the Church as an 'Aristotelian' body, because they would not have conceived of an alternative. The Italian humanists passed on to Luther, via Erasmus, a hostility to the logical and scientific writings of Aristotle, and the doctrines and institutions based upon them, rather than upon the ancient moralists. This was a handy instrument with which to beat the Church. There was also an historical justification for Luther's attacks. This he would also not have chosen, but for the work of the humanists. Luther examined the Church from the historical angle, and rejected the papacy (for example, in the Leipzig Disputation) as an institution whose powers and principles had grown up in the previous thousand years.

In addition, Luther propounded a doctrine of his own, of Justification by Faith. It is sometimes claimed that this notion was not new, but this is a half-truth. It had always been accepted that faith was required for salvation, but the grace of God and the good works practised by the individual had been also necessary. Luther firmly rejected the necessity of good works and, whilst he continued to stress that salvation was the free and unknowable gift of God, the sure promise of salvation offered by faith was emphasised.

Why was Luther so anxious to assert the sureness of salvation by faith? It is said that he derived his notion from a reading of the Epistles of St Paul, or that he was influenced by the dilemmas of late medieval scholasticism and by the German mysticism of Eckhart (1260–1327) and Tauler (1300–61). But these claims beg questions. It is true that Luther himself recorded in his autobiographical note of 1545 that it was in reading the Pauline epistles that he grasped what he took to be the true meaning of the Gospel promise of salvation. This raises the further question, however, of why he was so preoccupied with the certainty of salvation. The derivation of it from his mystical or scholastic studies is a paradox. The immediate accessibility of God to man, so that human beings might be united with God (forestalling any need for salvation) had been taught by Eckhart. Conversely, Luther himself broke down those bridges left by the scholastics by which man might reach God. The schoolmen had emphasised the hard justice of God, but they had not presented this as a problem to their audiences in the way in which Luther did.

It helps to quote the passage in which Luther recorded his discovery of Justification by Faith, for it reveals starkly his extraordinary anger at divine justice. He wrote:

I hated the words 'righteousness of God', which by the customary use of all the doctors I had been taught to understand philosophically as what they call the *formal* or *active righteousness*, whereby God is just and punishes unjust sinners.

For my case was this: however irreproachable my life as a monk, I felt myself in the presence of God to be a sinner with a most unquiet conscience, nor could I believe him to be appeased by the satisfaction I could offer. I did not love, – nay, I hated this just God who punishes sinners, and if not with silent blasphemy, at least with huge murmurings. I was indignant against God . . . And so I raged with a savage and confounded conscience.[1]

This passage creates some wonder at how Luther justified his righteous indignation. Being conscious of sin and threatened with punishment, it is hardly surprising that he should have felt fearful or discouraged, but why did he feel it legitimate to rail against God? Luther's personality or emotions may explain why it was he and not another man who spoke out, but even he needed *justification* for his wrath. This carries us from psycho-history to the realm of ideas.

It is only possible to speculate on the intellectual origins of this indignation. Luther was seeking to balance the poles of divine righteousness and human virtue. There was an intellectual tradition which could have brought this consciousness to him. It was enshrined in the writings of Erasmus, which reveal a tension deriving from the two main sources of the latter's piety. From his acquaintance with Italian humanists, Erasmus drew a belief in man's capacity to attain virtue by reason. He combined this with the Dutch lay piety of his youth at Deventer. He had met there an austere imitation of a Christ whom man could only obey, and await uncertainly for his verdict on Judgement Day. Had Luther exploited one part of the Erasmian legacy to destroy another? Perhaps he justified his indignation against a righteous God on account of a recognition of man's ability to attain virtue by reason, which he also inherited from Erasmus.

Certainly Luther's attitude towards religion and the miraculous seems to have derived from Erasmus. The latter's preference for private piety and holiness instead of the cult of saints reached Luther in the *Enchiridion Militis Christiani* and the *Praise of Folly*. In these writings Erasmus had attacked the practice of seeking miraculous help through divine images and hoping for succour from the relics of saints' bodies rather than from imitating their virtue. This was the source of Luther's attack on relics and the worship of saints in his early sermons from 1516 to 1518

1. *Dokumente zu Luthers Entwicklung (bis 1519)*, ed. J.O.Scheel (Tübingen, 1929), pp. 191ff; tr. of E.G.Rupp, B.Drewery, *Martin Luther* (London, 1970), p.6.

(*Werke*, Weimar edn, i, 62, 130, 420; iv, 411, 639). Erasmus's attitude derived probably in equal measure from the piety of the New Devotion in which he had been brought up and the ancient ideas sponsored by the humanists.

Here and in his attack on an 'Aristotelianised' Church, and advocacy of an historical assessment of it, Luther and his followers were following the humanists. The historical critique of the Church played a larger part in his thinking than immediately appears, because it was important to his attack on the papacy, which in turn was central to his early proposals for reform. Still more important was Justification by Faith. It implied a sense of moral responsibility so strong that it could allow Luther to reject a universally held idea of God as well as the authority of the Church. Moreover, what had moved him might equally spur others. Nevertheless, it is doubtful whether what happened can be explained by this or by Luther's attack on the Aristotelian Church.

The reaction which greeted them was too immediate. This suggests that Luther's ideas alone cannot explain events. We must look rather to the inspiration of the support his doctrines received. It may be that a belief in a more rational system of personal ethics had acquired sufficient currency for some to accept Luther's tenets, for the same reason that he felt justified in rejecting a too-righteous God. The support, however, which counted was that of certain princes and specific ideas determined their conduct.

1.2 Luther's support

The effects of Luther's blasts upon his trumpet between 1517 and 1521 were greater than they would have been in earlier times because of their support. The encouragement which mattered was from princes. Earlier heretics had received popular support. When they had demanded religious reforms Hus and his immediate heirs in Bohemia had been welcomed by a whole society, excepting only its ruler and a party of opponents. Such reform, however, had never before enjoyed the endorsement of princes.

The support of Luther's lord, Frederick the Wise of Saxony, was decisive: Luther's success is attributable chiefly to him. Frederick dissimulated and hid his own views. Down to 1522 he avoided formal contacts with Luther, but from the autumn of 1517 to that of 1521 his tacit support was a protective shield behind which Luther and his friends at Wittenberg asserted and developed their ideas.

Frederick claimed that his concern was limited to ensuring that Luther was given a lawful trial. His actions belie this. Some historians maintain that Frederick was a 'good Catholic' who defended Luther only as a matter of aristocratic honour. Certainly he added to a huge collection of relics which he had inherited at the castle church at Wittenburg, but any notion that Frederick was always faithful to traditional ideas is contradicted by his own words.

He could have suppressed Luther had he chosen to do so, as Cardinal Riario complained to him. From the start Frederick refused to accede to requests from Rome for Luther to be sent there for trial: he pursued instead suggestions that he should be tried in Germany. As early as 1518 Pope Leo X observed to him in a letter that public rumour reported that Frederick was supporting Luther (C. Guasti, 1876).

It is not true that Frederick's only motive was to secure a lawful hearing in Germany, because when Luther was examined at Worms and condemned Frederick did not abide by the decision (from which he himself had abstained) and instead moved to 'kidnap' Luther and hide him at the castle of the Wartburg. The idea is unconvincing that in this Frederick was guided by honour. He himself did not refer to this, and he did allude to religious principles. Indeed, nothing but such motives could explain why he tolerated the consequences of his protection of Luther.

What is remarkable is Frederick's readiness to assume responsibility. He refused to allow the case to pass to Rome. He sought the opinion of Erasmus. The latter's declaration that Luther had only sinned against the privileges of the papacy and of monks must have strengthened his resolve. Later, Frederick attacked the burning of Luther's books and remarked that Luther himself had protested that he would do everything 'consistent with the name of Christian'. Frederick was determined to be the judge of this.

In a letter to the papal legate Cajetan, Frederick observed that if he believed Luther's doctrine to be impious or untenable he would not defend it. 'Our whole purpose', he declared, 'is to fulfil the office of a Christian prince' (Breifwechsel in *Weimar Ausgabe*, i, 250). Later, at Worms, Frederick suggested the criterion by which Luther should be judged: conformity to the Gospel. In short, Frederick chose to judge what was true or false in matters of doctrine. Later he was happy to propose the standard by which others should judge. He called this the office of a Christian prince.

In that harmless sounding phrase we catch hold of the ideas that were dictating this prince's actions. It had always been the office of a Christian prince to protect the faith. What was new about Frederick was that for him the prince rather than the ecclesiastic was to determine what to protect, even in the face of the Church's opposition. Ideas were abroad convincing rulers that it was rightly their duty to define doctrine and reform the Church. As we shall see, precisely the same belief was shared by Henry VIII of England. Fortunately for the historian he was much less reticent than Frederick the Wise in voicing it.

1.3   The attitude of King Henry VIII

Henry's decisive role in the English Reformation is unmistakeable. When scholars have peered beyond the Divorce issue to explain the religious changes of the 1530s, they have usually dwelt on Henry's enlarged vanity or appetite for power. Humanist influences upon the English Reformation will not be proven by showing that Erasmian ideas were current in England, unless they can be shown to have motivated Henry himself. The king did suffer from vanity and greed, but he was not alone in his readiness to take charge of the Church. In the 1520s this became common with the princes of Germany and Scandinavia. Henry, however, had shown signs of such an attitude as early as 1518.

Just as Frederick felt obliged to support the actions of Luther, Henry opposed them in his tract the *Defence of the Seven Sacraments* (or *Assertio Septem Sacramentorum*), written in 1521. This is a remarkable work, and far more so than is sometimes allowed: the very fact of it is notable. Too often its composition is attributed to Henry's grandiose illusions. Did he not wish to cast an enlarged shadow over English history and foreign affairs? As the author of the *Assertio* he could claim to be the first English king since Alfred to have written a book. He may have hoped the book would equip him to play a part in European religious politics. He correctly believed it would earn him his papal title of 'Defender of the Faith'. To this end the book was dedicated to Pope Leo X and thirty copies despatched to Rome. Leo X read and admired the work. This was true also of a wide European audience which purchased the twenty editions and translations in which it was issued before 1600.

Several hands seem to have been engaged in the preparation of the *Assertio* (perhaps Thomas More's amongst them). Henry, however, composed the book, which is a competent and effective if uninspired reply to Luther. What is remarkable about it is the fact that it was written. Since the sixth century there had been few kings who could read and write, and there were fewer still who knew Latin. Of the learned kings of the Middle Ages none composed a work of theology. Alfred was a translator, the Emperor Frederick II wrote about falconry, Alfonso the Wise of Castile was a patron of legists and illuminators and James I of Aragon wrote an autobiography. At the Council of Constance (1414–17), when the clergy engaged in theological debate, the princes went out to hunt. This had been the order of things for a thousand years.

For all its orthodoxy the *Assertio* announced Henry's determination to have his views heard on matters of faith. Subsequently, Henry refused to allow the issue of a bull against Luther until he had read it. By 1529 Henry was distinguishing between Luther's propositions: he told the imperial ambassador that Luther was right to the extent that he demanded that the Pope and Sacred College must revert to apostolic purity. On this occasion he also expressed views of the proper power of lay rulers over the clergy. If Wolsey is to be believed, Henry had already voiced doubts about the legitimacy of his marriage to Catherine of Aragon on the grounds of consanguinity (she having been married previously to his brother Arthur). It is said that Henry experienced these doubts as a result of what he had read in the book of Leviticus.

At a later conference of bishops and theologians, which he had summoned, Henry claimed, on the authority of St Paul, that it was a king's duty to punish those who refused to surrender forbidden books. The implication was that he knew best what was desirable for the moral welfare of his subjects, announcing that he was intending to have the New Testament translated into English for his subjects' benefit. Henry's voice was loud in the subsequent religious controversies. He himself pursued the supreme Headship of the Church, correcting with his own hand the great religious documents of the next decade. These included the Bishop's Book of 1537, the Six Articles of 1539 and the King's Book of 1543.

Henry VIII's impact –

Henry's theological prognostications have been belittled as a pedantic amateur's amusements after Jane Seymour's death or in the interval before Catherine Howard hoved into sight (Scarisbrick). Whatever the quality of his theological views, the *fact* of them is remarkable and must be taken on board if the causes of what was happening are to be understood. The Reformation in England must be attributed to Henry's feeling that he should express views about matters of faith, and enshrine this resolve in a royal control over the Church.

The sixteenth-century writer Thomas Starkey alleged that a sound commonwealth could only be established if the right policy was formed at the top and the ruler was virtuous and wise (*Dialogue*, ed. Buston, p. 59). Starkey was prescribing what we would call state action. Whence had come this attitude which so closely described Henry VIII's (and Frederick of Saxony's) own policies? In the public field a great extension of the power of the state was the most important consequence of the Reformation. The way in which secular governments now came to regulate matters of doctrine and faith perhaps represented the most unfettered expansion of governmental power since northern kings had been encouraged by missionaries in the Dark Ages to exert their authority so as to proscribe paganism. The earlier episode was brought about by Roman ideas of government mediated by the Church. This time the state's authority was being extended into an area traditionally regulated by the Church.

The lay power had been asked before to reform the Church. Calls for this had been heard in England since the fourteenth century. Agitators like the heretical theologian John Wycliffe and a line of friars had defended the right of kings to tax the Church and discipline sinful clergy (A. G. Little, 1917, pp. 53–4). When princes like Frederick the Wise and Henry VIII did so after 1517, it was not because they were suddenly inspired by ancient appeals. Now the call came mostly from laymen and was made upon different grounds. The process can be discerned most easily in England where men like Thomas Starkey and Thomas More looked to royal authority because of its superior capacity to judge the issues. This was far more deadly than Wycliffe's call of old.

Thomas More believed that kings should be guided by philosophers, but this could only happen if the philosophers were kings. These ideas sprang directly from what has been called the 'good absolutism' of Erasmus (Renaudet, 1939). In his *Education of a Christian Prince* Erasmus had alleged that no prince deserved the name unless he was a philosopher. Without philosophy the ruler was a tyrant (ed. Born, p. 150). Royal authority was made the judgement-seat of worldly action because of the king's superior capacity to judge. Thus, for Erasmus the beneficent prince was the living likeness of God (Born, pp. 157, 191). Here was the 'office of the Christian prince' which Frederick the Wise sought to fulfil. Such a prince, as a philosopher, was to determine what was morally right (Born, pp. 174, 186).

The Erasmian office of the Christian prince was a bridge between Italian humanists and the Reformation. Erasmus quoted Plato: behind his prince lay Plato's philosopher–king and the Guardians of his Republic who were guided by philosophy. There was also the more general influence here of the humanist idea that wisdom was the property of every cultivated individual. Ahead were the virtuous princes of sixteenth-century Europe. Erasmus had corresponded with Frederick the Wise and he had met Henry VIII in 1499. As an adult Henry had only to consult Thomas More or William Tyndale's *Obedience of the Christian Man* to be reminded of his godly rule and rights. Certainly Erasmus was careful to emphasise that kings must be upright in their conduct: it was nevertheless left to the prince's discretion. Wisdom conferred new rights upon the ruler, whilst duty was left to his conscience. Besides, who could gainsay a prince who was at once a philosopher and a king?

Frederick the Wise and Henry VIII's new readiness to be the sufficient judges of theological questions, and even to take the Church under their governance, is the key to the early Reformation. Without their connivance or encouragement those reforms in Germany and England would not have happened. The prince's new willingness to settle moral and theological questions was also, in the political field, the chief consequence of the Reformation because it led to a dramatic advance in what we would call the 'interference' of the state – an increase of its scope. There is a road from the Neo-Platonists of Florence to Erasmus, and from him to the Reformation. Erasmus's role in preparing the ground for the Reformation lay not in his critique of the Church but his endorsement of the god-like ruler.

The new philosopher–kings therefore took charge of the Church. In practice this meant examining and sometimes enforcing the criticisms of

213

the Church which had been voiced by Erasmus, and previously by many other reformers since the fourteenth century. There followed a myriad of doctrinal, liturgical and institutional changes in Protestant countries. These flowed from ancient discontents and the new sense that it was the ruler's office to remedy them. However, the Reformation also ushered in (or reflected) a profound alteration in what may be called God's role in the world. Was this the consequence of old complaints or novel circumstances or could it have been owing to the impact of Italian ideas?

The general change in its turn affected the idea of the Church, and of its priests, sacraments, ritual as well as of ordinary piety. The phenomenon represents what has been called the 'decline of magic' – the decline, that is, of a belief in miracles, relics and the supernatural. This decline calls for explanation. A challenging hypothesis has been advanced by Keith Thomas: it was produced by the society of early modern Europe. There is, however, an alternative: that new attitudes towards God (chiefly discernible in Calvinism) were as much the product of new ideas as were those princely actions which determined the Lutheran and Henrician reforms.

2. Calvinism and the 'decline of magic'

2.1 The thesis of Keith Thomas

Keith Thomas has plausibly suggested that technological progress undermined the belief that supernatural power intervened in the world.[2] Beliefs in magic were strong when the technology to control human misfortunes was weak. The Middle Ages are for Keith Thomas a primitive society whose under-development occasioned the supernatural beliefs of the medieval Church. Thomas has recognised that churchmen and theologians sought to limit popular credulity, but the persistent legacy of conversion and clerical propaganda itself combined to make the Church 'a repository of supernatural forces'.

On the eve of the Reformation, a strong superstition remained, and ritual and sacraments continued to be seen as instruments of divine power. The 'essential background' to these beliefs was the feeling that man was the helpless subject of natural forces he could not control – plague, poverty, fire and general misfortune. Primitive technology had produced helplessness and in its train a hope in the efficacy of 'magic'.

All this was changed by the Protestant Reformers, who largely eliminated the old 'instruments' of Heaven. The sacraments were reduced in number and given a ceremonial meaning; relics were generally destroyed, and God came to be conceived largely as a judge in time to come. The

---

2. *Religion and the decline of magic* (Harmondsworth, 1973).

emphasis now was upon self-help in this life and consolation in that to come. Some of this was foreshadowed in the tenets of the Lollard heretics of fifteenth-century England, but the decisive change came in the sixteenth and seventeenth centuries.

Were the less 'magical' beliefs of this period produced by advancing technology? Thomas is too good an historian to assert easy connections where they cannot safely be made. Indeed, it is his acceptance of the paradox that there was no decisive technological change in the 1500s that enables him to develop the most subtle part of his thesis. In the sixteenth century humanity continued to be confronted by uncontrolled misfortune. This conflict forced it to create a new magic: this was the astrology, prophesying and witchcraft of early modern times.

This solves one problem and creates another. If the want of technology produced early modern magic, where was the advance of technology that should have led the Reformers to curtail its proper bounds? Thomas faces this difficulty squarely, and has suggested ways of overcoming it: technology was not the whole answer; there were supplementary social and intellectual causes. Technology was not transformed until after 1700, but the sixteenth century had already had in view its later triumphs (Thomas, p. 788). The seventeenth century witnessed 'the emergence of a new faith in the potentialities of human institutions' (pp. 791–2). There was urban development and intellectual advance. The growth of towns created an outlook unconducive to the supernatural, whilst the Scientific Revolution brought into being a rational account of natural phenomena.

These attempts to supply the failings of the technological theory are not quite convincing: aspiration is not the same as achievement, rationalist views had existed before the Scientific Revolution and religious beliefs persisted after it (p. 774). Moreover, there had been commercial towns for centuries. Thomas finally admits some puzzlement (p. 797):

> It is therefore possible to connect the decline of the old magical beliefs with the growth of urban living, the rise of science, and the spread of an ideology of self-help. But the connection is only approximate and a more precise sociological genealogy cannot at present be constructed.

Thomas's unease springs from his conviction that magic declined in the sixteenth century, but is this belief correct? He himself has drawn attention to the Lollard rejection of the supernatural. Similarly, there was conspicuous faith in human institutions before 1600, of which there is no better sign than the Lutheran Reformation, whose cardinal principle was faith in the capacity of princes and monarchs to reform the Church.

The example of the Lollards is significant, because it raises the possibility that a belief in the supernatural was disappearing before the Reformation. Were the doubters therefore isolated schismatics or harbingers of change? If they mark the beginning of a less 'magical' devotion, this can certainly not be accounted for by technological progress, of which there was even less sign in 1400 than 1500. But to weigh the significance of Wycliffe and the Lollards it is necessary to consider whether they were isolated schismatics or forerunners of the Reformation in the sense that they were few and excluded from the medieval Church.

The Lollard attack on relics, images and the supernatural character of the sacraments was continued by the Taborites in fifteenth-century Bohemia. Nor was the idea of religion as self-help the property of heretics. Thomas à Kempis's *Imitation of Christ* – the greatest literary work produced by the school of lay piety in the Low Countries, known as the New Devotion (*Devotio Moderna*) – was guided by a spirituality in many ways akin to that associated with Calvin. The emphasis in Thomas à Kempis was upon right thinking and righteous living in imitation of Christ: the only hope was in the world to come. Man was weak, sinful and remote from God, and despite his best efforts must await uncertainly for Christ's verdict on Judgement Day.

Similarly, the orthodox Italian faithful in the fourteenth and fifteenth centuries 'helped' themselves. Relics and sacred images continued to be favoured, but alongside them devout laymen dispensed with what anthropologists would call the magical agencies of Church life – with priests, sacraments and ritual. Italians instead fended for themselves in confraternities and family chapels. They prayed and read sacred poetry and plays. They listened to sermons; they did penance and good works. They conducted their own devotions; praying before private images which were no longer hieratic but the humanised Madonnas of Renaissance art. This devotion, indeed, goes a long way in explaining why Italy experienced no Reform, corrupt though its Church had been.

From where did these new attitudes originate? Italian devotional practices had been established by the friars. The Christocentrism of Thomas à Kempis also displays a Franciscan character. But what of the Lollards and the Hussites? The Hussites derived most of their views from Lollard and Wycliffite teachings. With Lollardy the trail goes dead in the late fourteenth century.

The earliest known group of Lollards, associated with William Smith and William Swinderby, provides clues. Smith and a chaplain called Waytestathe established a Lollard school in a disused chapel by a leper hospital outside the walls of Leicester in the early 1380s. Smith went barefoot, ate no meat and lived a chaste life. With Waytestathe he held conventicles for disaffected townsmen and taught their sons. They were joined by William Swinderby, who had already gained a local notoriety. He had lived as a hermit in a cell of St Mary's Abbey on the nearby

religion as self-help –

15 thc. Italian devotion –

Italian devotional practices –

estates of John of Gaunt. Episcopal wrath had been directed at him for conducting preaching tours, in which he had attacked the vainglory of women and the wealth of the Church. He had demanded that defaulting debtors should go unpunished, and that tithes should not be paid to sinful priests. At Leicester Swinderby was protected by the townspeople from the attentions of the bishop, but soon he had to move to Coventry where again he enjoyed the favours of citizens, before passing on again, last to be heard of in the Welsh Marches.

In this story the townsfolk are to the fore, and distinguished individuals play a role. Swinderby was associated with great men, such as John of Gaunt and Sir John Oldcastle. Gaunt was the most powerful layman of the day, and from one source we know that while he was living on the Welsh Borders, Swinderby converted Oldcastle, a celebrated adherent of the sect. Nothing, by contrast, is heard of John Wycliffe, whom many historians consider the founder of Lollardy, although he was living only fifteen miles away from Leicester at this time.

Most interesting here are echoes of the mendicants. Smith's vegetarianism, his bare feet and abode by a leper hospital, together with Swinderby's eremitical life, his preaching tours and the themes of his sermons recall St Francis. An idea begins to form that the origin of Lollardy lay not in Wycliffe, but in an urban puritanism and anti-clericalism called into being by the friars. This was given sectarian shape by the political crisis of the late fourteenth century in which John of Gaunt, Wycliffe and knights like Oldcastle were directly involved.

The influence of St Francis upon later spirituality can hardly be exaggerated. His work invoked the lay piety which is so marked a feature of the religious scene down to 1700. Mendicancy placed lay folk in a flattering and god-like position as the ones who gave the friars their daily bread. In the fourteenth century the friars who were alienated by the Church's abandonment of their founder's insistence on absolute poverty looked to lay rulers for support, and this new attitude combined with the old to forge the idea that the state was the proper agency for the reform of the Church.

The friars tried to reform morals, encourage good works and an imaginative identification with the Gospel. Rather than focus on relics or miracles, the members of the congregation were asked to imagine how things would have been if they had been present at the Gospel scenes. The Franciscans gave lay people a notion of what a later age would have called godly living. They brought a literal and historical idea of Christ into vogue, and they began to take magic out of it. The decline of 'magic' therefore began in the thirteenth century; it was carried much further in the Reformation.

The problem remains of explaining this further development. Since the idea of the supernatural had already been curtailed and self-help recommended before 1500, was the effect of the Reformation merely to enforce or extend what had been established? Thomas is surely right to see the Protestant view of the supernatural as a very general change of perception. It is one that cannot easily be accounted for by compulsion. Attention should be paid to religion itself in relation to the assumptions which have been brought to it.

Materialist and secular preconceptions lie behind most social interpretations of history like Thomas's. His instincts are those of a materialist, but they are displayed more in relation to religious than secular ideas. There are, for him, material causes for religious ideas but when they fail, secular ideas are introduced to supplement them. Secular ideas like the Scientific Revolution can therefore sometimes claim a place in explaining religious beliefs, while the latter are evidence of changing material conditions (or responses to them) and have an 'ideological' character.

The contrasting role which Thomas assigns to secular and religious ideas, raises the question whether he has been unfair to the latter. Might the decline in the magical character of religion not have been due to changing religious notions themselves? If we accept as an important insight that religion does closely depend on the human condition, we do not have to agree with the further assumption that it is only to be considered in material terms: our perception of the matter must be given independent weight. It may be that the latter will have changed and not the former. Supernatural 'magic' might be one way of looking at a world we do not control and a religion shorn of magic, perhaps another. According to this hypothesis, the variable would have been not material conditions or technology but our outlook on the world.

2.2 The Calvinist conception of God

The decline of magic which Thomas has described began in the later Middle Ages. The Reformation did, nevertheless, represent a new stage in its advance. Suspicion of miracles, relics and the sacraments by reformed churches replaced that by a few sects. The theology of Calvin was the most influential and clearest source for the 'unmagical' piety, which characterised the Protestant churches on the Continent, as well as those of Scotland and the English Puritans analysed by Thomas.

In examining the possibility that the decline of magic happened by an alteration in religious sentiment there is an elementary question to be asked: did the religion of the Reformers represent a decline of 'magic' at all? Certainly Calvin (like Luther before him and the Hussites and Lollards still earlier) rejected relics and diminished the number and significance of the sacraments. They discarded what were taken to be superstitious practices. However, if we mean by magic the alteration of events by some control over nature effected by secret knowledge, the issue is less clear. According to Calvin, events were constantly brought about by God. For

Calvin (and for other Reformers) supernatural power daily intervened in the world, for reasons and by means which human beings could not conceive. Thus the world was altered by a divine power over nature. The only difference to magic was that this control was not 'orchestrated' by man but by God's free agency. This is an important distinction, but equal weight must be given to the fact that a world animated by supernatural power was not being replaced by one released from it.

Moreover, the Calvinist view of divinity was offered as a consolation for misfortune. Calvin himself deliberately presented Providence as answering this need. The general character of the world and the promises God made to the faithful were both consoling. They derived from the nature of God who had not abandoned the world: if He had He could not have been all-powerful (*Institutes*, I, iv, 2). He was the original creator and also the governor and provider (I, xvi, 1) whereby all events happened by His 'specific appointment' (I, xvi, 2; III, xxiii, 6; cf. III, xxiii, 8).

God governed even those events which were customarily attributable to Fortune (I, v, 11; I, xvi, 2). Alike, those affairs ascribed to ill and good fortune, and contrasts of wealth and poverty usually credited to the fickleness of fortune, were God's work (I, xvi, 6). It was therefore true that 'if all success is blessing from God, and calamity and adversity are His curse, there is no place left in human affairs for fortune and chance' (I, xvi, 8).

Calvin conceded that the actions of God *seem* fortuitous because of human stupidity (I, xvi, 9). We should therefore accept all adversity patiently (I, xvii, 7–8). An adjacent passage (I, xvii, 10) reveals the relevance of this argument to the problem of declining 'magic' and advancing human competence. For Calvin, human lives were encompassed by danger and death, by accident, fire, disease and famine, and if these ills were brought about by chance we would be miserable, but as it is we are 'reminded of the inestimable felicity of a pious mind'.

Such thoughts would have failed to console was humanity not confident that God had a beneficent policy which could be comprehended in general terms. He aided the righteous and punished the wicked (I, v, 7), caring for His good sons and sending His angels to watch over them (I, xiv, 6; cf. I, xiv, 10). Moreover, communion with Christ furnished 'strong and sure proofs' that a Christian was one of the elect (III, xxiv, 5). In this happy state he could expect to enjoy prosperity or, conversely, await the righting of the scales on the Day of Judgement (I, xvi, 11). God lent support in the form of friends and frustrated the malice of enemies, for even the Devil could not act except by His command (I, xvii, 7–8).

The natural reading of this religious evidence is that 'magic' declined not because of technology or any enhanced confidence in human capacity, but because one supernatural view of the world had been replaced by another.

Thomas recognises that Protestant theologians maintained that nothing happened without God's permission. Puritans looked about them for evidence of this in the accidents of daily life. He feels, however, that these notions contradicted the un-magical premises of Protestantism (cf. p. 89) and in any case offered poor solace. Calvinism did not explain how God's judgements were enacted through the processes of nature, or else they were self-confirming. They gave gloomy comfort, offering at best rewards in the life to come. Consequently, the doctrine was attractive only when vulgarly interpreted (some followers claimed immediate rewards and punishments) or only to the rich or self-advancing (pp. 92, 93–4, 95, 122, 131–2).

These doubts do not do justice to Calvin who gave this theology currency. He did not betray his premises and was ahead of the crowd: the 'vulgarisation' is already present in his writings. Nor were his consolations self-evidently weak: he offered blessings, rewards and consolations in this world. The gloom sprang from his insistence that man was sinful and without worth. There was here no cause for bourgeois complacency and no especial grounds for complaint amongst the poor. Calvin never equated prosperity with wealth. Moreover, since the poor survived the rise of science, why should poor men have been any less disenchanted with technology than with the providential tenets of the Reformers? Finally, Calvin cannot be criticised for failing to stipulate which events were directed by man, God or nature. For him all affairs were wholly controlled by God.

It is a matter of opinion whether Protestantism is less consoling than notions that we do control the world, whether by a magical use of relics and broomsticks, or by the operations of science. A conviction that humanity lacks such control liberates us from the complacency of those who allege that they can do so. It may be good to deny ourselves a claim which is controverted by facts. The control of nature by magicians is against all the facts; the boast of science and technology to control it is also a pretence. Science has reduced the unpredictability of misfortune and the frequency of fire and infectious disease. It has not prevented their occurrence nor (surprising to have to say it) can it avail against death. In a sense the claim to control misfortune is less consoling than the more honest recognition of Calvin (and the Stoics) that we do not.

The hypothesis can indeed be advanced that magic declined precisely because man recognised the limits of his ability to control nature. A first push had been given to this by the mendicant-inspired spirituality, which encouraged the exercise of a practical Christian life and an attention to the Gospel, rather than the observance of rituals and ceremonies. At the same time this was not any theoretical rejection of supernatural intervention. These tendencies were buttressed by Luther's success. The desire to advance the layman against the cleric, and paradoxically insist that the ability to reach God was itself a gift of God, became evident. Both had already been manifest in the later Middle Ages but they were reinforced by the doctrine of Justification by Faith. Yet this notion would not have driven magic so successfully forth from official religion in the Protestant churches without Calvin's doctrine of Providence. It is therefore important to understand the character and origin of his idea of God's standing in the world.

Calvin combined the paradoxes that God was all-powerful and responsible, and that human beings were powerless and responsible for their conduct. This surprising teaching alerts us to its origin in Stoicism. Calvin's insistence on the omnipotence of God led him to reject both Fortune and free-will (I, xvi, 4). To believe in either would have detracted from the power of God. In passing, it is worth noticing that Calvin did not, as is sometimes said, so much abandon or replace the idea of Fortune by God as assert that fortune *was* God. The equation was clearly made afterwards by Knox:

> Fortune and adventure are the words of Paynims, the signification whereof ought in no wise to enter into the heart of the faithful . . . . That which ye scoffingly call Destiny and Stoical necessity . . . we call God's eternal election and purpose immutable.
>
> (*Works*, ed. D. Laing (Edinburgh, 1846–64), v, pp. 32, 119, quoted by Thomas, p. 91)

The identification of Fortune with God had been implied by Calvin: to human beings happenings are fortuitous when in fact they are His, and God's will is as compelling a force as Stoic necessity. God freely predestinates whom He chooses (III, xxii, 1). The instrument is the will of God rather than an infinite series of causes, but this difference fades when we remember that the will of God is unknowable. Instead of replacing Fortune by God, Calvin equated them. The importance of this distinction will become clear later.

God's will was all-powerful and free; equally it was not exercised irresponsibly: God did not toss men up and down willy-nilly (I, xvi, 1). Calvin's God operates on righteous principles: He is absolute righteousness and power (I, i, 2) and He rewards the righteous Christian who is 'justified by faith' (III, x, 2). Indeed, the will of God *is* righteousness (III, xviii, 2). The logical conclusion of these statements is that God could not act against righteousness, but to have admitted this would have contradicted Calvin's tenet that God had free will. He therefore retreated to the assertion that God was unknowable (III, xxiii, 2). This same difficulty emerges from the problem of Damnation. God had fore-ordained humanity to be damned or saved, but does not a predestined damnation excuse the sinner and condemn God? Calvin was led to remark that since God was equity, inequity must be equity. The only excuse for this casuistry is that divine justice is an 'equity unknown to us' (III, xxiii, 9). Calvin was surely attempting here to marry two warring conceptions: that God was Fortune and that He was equity.

At this point we have in sight Calvin's second paradox. Man was fore-ordained but must act as if this was not so: he must pursue the religious life prescribed by Scripture (I, xvii, 3). The feeble justification for this is that God had entrusted humanity with the care of human life and the means of avoiding danger (I, xvii, 4), but how could human efforts avail and what purpose was there in them when all was predestined? Calvin returned to this problem in Book III of the *Institutes*. God, he said, had not made us for unclean purposes: for we are His handiwork, created unto good works (III, xxiii, 13). Thereby it is implied that regeneration, which was the end of election, was something that human beings could rationally perceive and pursue. God was righteousness and all must make themselves conformable to Him.

Surely this contradicts Calvin's propositions elsewhere that human reason could not penetrate the greater reason of God; that there was no good in man until cleansed by God and that everything was governed by His necessary will? The latter tenet, moreover, does not fit easily with Calvin's argument that the unregenerate must do good works in order to manifest their obedience to God (III, xi, 20). Moral obligation did not avail Calvin in his former argument; here the force is wanting that could compel obedience. For if good works are compelled, why trouble to lay an obligation upon human beings to perform them?

Related Calvinist propositions reinforce the impression that man was powerless, predestined and corrupt, but was nonetheless responsible for his actions. Calvin repeatedly insisted that man was worthless in his fallen state and yet recognition of his unworthiness was itself the means of achieving reward (III, xii, 7). Accordingly, even a saint was not wholly pure (III, xiv, 9), but the saints who were elected by God had 'intimations' of their purity, such that they perceived their calling (III, xiv, 19–20; III, xxiv, 1; III, xxiv, 5). Therefore man was weak, sinful, remote from God and uncomprehending of His reason and equity. Yet he knew the righteous paths, understood his own progress along them and could earn reward for his efforts.

Finally, there is something similarly problematical, but intellectually consistent, in Calvin's notion that unmeritorious good works were rewarded by God. Calvin reiterated the argument that no man could attain salvation by good works (III, xi, 2, 13–19; III, xiv, 12, 19). The latter were themselves the gifts of God and believers recognised in them not their own merit but signs of calling (III, xiv, 20). Although they were God's gifts, He still chose to reward them as if they were man's own

(III, xv, 3). The position is therefore reached that while Justification was not by works it was never without them (III, xvi, 1). In this state God did reward the cultivation of righteousness (III, xvii, 2) for man having been sanctified by Christ was acting by free will (III, xix, 5).

In these passages virtue seems to be imputed to the righteous, whilst even the saints are impure. At the same time God chooses to reward as virtue what He himself has freely bestowed as a gift. Another curiosity is that, in his treatment of good works, Calvin declares that God counts them as the righteous acts of true believers, and elsewhere man is assumed to be rational and virtuous enough to perceive the paths of righteousness and his progress along them.

Calvin had inherited an idea that God was omnipotent and merciful whilst fallen man was corrupt until redeemed by Christ. Onto this he grafted a notion that God was Fortune and that He was also reason and equity. Accordingly, God (at least as far as human beings could perceive) was arbitrary and inscrutable, and He was also righteous and equitable. For his part man was both the hapless victim of predestined law and capable of aspiring to equity and righteousness. Whence did Calvin draw these assumptions which lie partly buried at the base of his theology?

Calvin identified God both with Fortune and with reason. The first equation had been familiar to the scholastics; the association of Fortune and reason derived ultimately from the Stoics. Only in the writings of the humanists or ancient moralists could Calvin have discovered this surprising combination. Alberti, more than a century before Calvin, had written of God as if He was at once Fortune and equity (see above, esp. p. 48). This was an assumption shared by a number of Italian humanists and which they had taken from the Latin moralists. Cicero's writings show that the ancients had already grasped this as a contradiction springing from Stoic sources (see above, p. 32). Calvin's main source for this idea, however, is more likely to have been Seneca. The latter was consistent in his advocacy of Stoic ideas; his writings give testimony to an idea of God as a provider for mankind, whose just principles could be gauged by reason, and who was the inescapable force of necessity. Furthermore, Calvin in his early career had worked as a translator of Seneca. The likely conclusion follows that Calvin's idea of God was rooted in a Stoic contradiction.

As the ideas of Calvin illustrate, the Reformers transformed conceptions of the supernatural by introducing into theology Renaissance notions of virtue and fortune. This change did not reflect a partial alteration in material conditions, the incompleteness of which was remedied by the unofficial magic of the witch. It was brought about by the impact of ideas: one attitude to God was replaced by another. A God who consoled human beings in their misfortunes by magic was not superseded by a distant creator who punished and rewarded in the world to come. Instead, the consolations of providence displaced those offered by the miraculous.

The notion of a supreme being operating through miraculous agents was alien to the major ancient thinkers – even to Plato, corrupted forms of whose teachings had influenced deeply the scholastic theologians. For such Greek philosophers God was an original creator and provider whose principles could be discovered by reason. Plato is often said to have been a 'supernatural' thinker but his other-worldliness consisted in intellectual generalities or the general form of things. Therefore, in antiquity, when material conditions were less advanced than in the sixteenth century, Greek and Roman philosophers offered still less consolation to those who despaired of their misfortunes. Instead, they taught the hard lesson that we must simply accept bad luck. In an age of misfortune the ancient philosophers had done without magic. What better proof is there that material conditions did not cause its later decline?

The Greek thinkers taught hard truths which can be more consoling than soft illusions. This was part of the attractive power of ancient attitudes towards God in the fourth century B.C. as well as in the sixteenth century A.D. Divinity could be understood by reason; reason aided mankind even in showing that there were things that could not be comprehended or controlled. This qualified endorsement of the power of the mind lay behind that contradiction amongst Stoic thinkers to which Cicero drew attention. These attitudes and contradictions equally affected the humanists and the Reformers.

Here was philosophy open to the intelligent by means of almost casual inspection. The mundane was not buried beneath metaphysics, nor was it the property of theologians or priests. The divine and the human alike could be measured by reason, a measurement enshrined in that vocabulary of fortune and virtue beloved of the humanists. As well as appealing to lay opinion this also attracted the theologians. It afforded an opportunity to consider traditional questions from a novel angle that placed emphasis upon God's role and man's. Mediated by Erasmus and Melanchthon, it influenced Luther. The twin cries of Luther's theology, 'Let God be God', and the individual's justification by faith, seem like an answering echo to the humanist stress upon virtue and fortune, as well as to the mendicant-inspired spirituality of the later Middle Ages.

Ancient moral ideas are nevertheless more clearly to be seen in Calvin's thought. Calvin's *Institutes* cannot be understood without positing the existence of contradictory ideas of Stoicism lying at their heart. Renaissance and Reformation, therefore, were not separated by theology, or joined by a critical or secular spirit. These great movements were connected by an idea of man's moral and intellectual capacity and a certain attitude towards God.

Future Prospects

Outside the domain of classical scholarship the phrase 'man and society' defines the achievements of the Italian Renaissance. Yet this raises a problem. If the Renaissance contributed so much in this direction, why is it so faintly praised? As an intellectual group the humanists of Italy and the north failed to break the Aristotelianism of the universities. In fact, they were content with the Socratic and Ciceronian approach of avoiding abstraction for the actual ways of men. The frailty of this position is illustrated by Petrarch's riposte to certain Aristotelian critics in *On His Own Ignorance*. He made some telling points in his rejection of speculative knowledge (see above, pp.35–9), but for the most part he was forced to retreat into the tenet of St Paul that the wisdom of this world is 'foolishness with God'. This was only an effective defence of his intellectual stand and use of classical morals if the latter were held to possess no value independent of Christian ethics.

Having failed to dislodge Aristotelianism, the humanists strengthened it by their improved knowledge of ancient texts. The best example of this carries us to the world of natural science. The arrival of classical texts from Byzantium included those of the Greek mathematicians. Their influence, combined with the new concepts of the universe offered by Plato's cosmology and the old Aristotelian science of the universities became causes of the Scientific Revolution. Thus, by an irony Italian studies contributed to one of the most important of modern movements and undermined humanist ethics.

Another reason for the allegedly small impact of Renaissance ideas was that they ran by a concealed conduit into a strange land. The humanists exerted a huge influence on art, moral philosophy, classical scholarship, historiography and political theory. Nevertheless, their chief effect was religious. Their moral notions helped to fill a vacuum in Italy where the Church was weak and pastoral self-help the order of the day. They were almost always assumed by the Italian humanists to be in conformity with Christian doctrines; all the more easily could they be absorbed into the mainstream of religious thinking, and this happened after 1500.

The humanists provided a critical spirit with which the Reformers belaboured orthodoxy. Italian influence upon the moral outlook of the individual mattered still more. Were personal actions governed by free will and did they need the guidance of priests to reach ethical or religious truth? The Renaissance changed much in answering these questions. In introducing the notion that human affairs were controlled by one's own moral preferences and by necessity (by 'virtue' or 'fortune'), the humanists effectively enlarged the area of personal choice. Necessity did not govern all; there was a zone subject to human power. It was possible to choose to be happy, but not to have material prosperity.

This rooting of ethics in the human condition nevertheless did admit an ambiguity. In the Reformation the dichotomy between fortune and a rational virtue was drawn by Calvin into the heart of his theology. For all the awesome stress which he laid upon a necessitous Providence, Calvin also insisted on an enhanced moral responsibility. This was required by his belief in an equitable reward for virtue grounded in reason (cf. Chapter 15, Section 2). This enlargement of personal responsibility in the field of ethics, so characteristic of the reformed churches, assumed the principle of rational expectation of a reasonable God. For all the studious good behaviour of late medieval sects and Franciscan tertiaries, the Stoic rooting of virtue in the 'right reason' of God was a necessary preparation for the 'right' thinking of the Puritans and their fellow-travellers.

The Renaissance dispensed the layman from clerical guidance. This revolution 'sanctified' the world. In achieving this it undid the effects of the Investiture Contest. That great movement of the eleventh and twelfth centuries had freed the Church from lay control by denying the sacred character of secular authority. This was made possible by the superior intellectual resources of the Church. Its special weapon was the ancient principle of equity long since carried into canon law and deadly against the claim of rulers to govern by law or custom. Rulers of the central Middle Ages, like Henry IV of Germany and Henry II of England, could not gainsay the papacy when it raised debate from the level of customary prerogative to one of philosophical principle. They were literally lost for argument. Owing to the work of the *Quattrocento*, the princes and educated laymen of the sixteenth century had broken into the armoury of the Church and were able to fight it with its own arms.

Because of the work of the humanists, the Church was losing its advantage. Educated laymen (even laywomen) now possessed the Latin culture which the Church had formerly monopolised. Indeed, clerical intellectuals had now a lesser mastery of Greek and Latin culture than some laymen. The educated prince was also a new type. This had been foreshadowed in the accomplishments of such individuals as Lorenzo de' Medici and Federigo da Montefeltro in fifteenth-century Italy. Its devastating consequences were seen in the 'virtuous' princes of the following century, notably Henry VIII of England and Frederick the Wise of Saxony. These rulers were sufficiently versed in clerical culture for them to feel able to determine issues of theology without reference to ecclesiastical authority (see Chapter 15).

The governing classes were now on a level footing with the clergy in that they enjoyed a general access to its culture. The Italian humanists handed down an effective weapon against equity. Ancient rhetoric furnished the principle that right was to be established according to what men had done and believed. The shout of *mos* could be loudly made once more against the cries of *ius*. For these reasons the Renaissance can be said to have cancelled the Investiture Contest and sanctified the world anew. The good and evil consequences of this were to be seen in the reforming zeal and authoritarianism of early modern states.

There is a sense in which the Renaissance failed because it succeeded. It ran into channels where we no longer recognise it – in the Reformation as in the rise of science. Even traditional moral philosophers, historians and political thinkers assimilated the humanists' method and approach. At the same time the failure (so to call it) of the humanists to free their ideas from Christianity left them vulnerable to a Christian reaction.

The claim of the Renaissance to be more than a narrowly critical, aesthetic or aristocratic movement rests on its ethical legacy. The inability of the humanists to re-establish an idea of ethics grounded in the human condition was ensured when the Reformation reinvigorated theology and an ideal of equality based not upon human knowledge or consciousness but on divine vision. In the seventeenth and eighteenth centuries the moral outlook of the humanists began to look like self-indulgence for the few. Stoic universalism was mistaken for complacency and the Renaissance found its most welcoming home in an aristocratic world. The humanists did, therefore, succeed because they failed. A double failure and success was to allow the Reformers to absorb their teachings and to prepare the way for the detachment of rationality from ethics. This had in fact been foreshadowed in the fifteenth century by the development of the inductive method. As well as preparing the way for the Reformation, this allowed another failure and success. Induction, freed from ancient in addition to Christian ethics, was to produce deformed descendants in those observations of what human beings think and feel and do, which today are called the social sciences (see further, above pp.130–1). They were to be the final legatees of the Renaissance, once the wisdom had been left behind and when, from the nineteenth century, liberal education and aristocratic manners began, in unison, to fade.

Bibliography

General Works on Humanism

General Works

G. Voigt, *Die Wiederbelebung des classischen Altertums* (Berlin, 1893), French tr. Paris, 1894; E. Garin, *Der italienische Humanismus* (Bern, 1947), Engl. tr. P. Munz, *Italian Humanism* (Oxford, 1965); P. O. Kristeller, *Renaissance Thought*, vol. i (New York, 1961); idem, *Eight Philosophers of the Italian Renaissance* (Stanford, 1964); E. F. Rice, *The Renaissance Idea of Wisdom* (Cambridge, Mass., 1958); C. E. Trinkaus, *Adversity's Noblemen, the Italian Humanists on Happiness* (New York, 1940); idem, *In our Image and Likeness* (London, 1970); idem, *The Scope of Renaissance Humanism* (Ann Arbor, 1983); J. E. Seigel, *Rhetoric and Philosophy in Renaissance Humanism* (Princeton, 1968); H. H. Gray, 'Renaissance Humanism: the pursuit of eloquence', *J. History Ideas* **xxiv** (1963), 497–514; C. Dionisotti, 'Discorso su l'Umanesimo' in his *Geografia e storia della letteratura italiana* (Turin, 1967).

The Humanists

Biographies

M. E. Cosenza, *Biographical and Bibliographical Dictionary of the Italian Humanists 1300–1800* (Boston, 1962–7); L. Martines, *The Social World of the Florentine Humanists 1390–1460* (London, 1963); V. Rossi, *Il Quattrocento*, 6th edn, ed. A. Vallone (Milan, 1956).

The Humanist

P. O. Kristeller, 'Humanism and Scholasticism in the Italian Renaissance', *Byzantion* **xvii** (1944–5), 346–74; A. Campana, 'The origin of the word Humanist', *J. Warburg and Courtauld Institutes* **9** (1946), 60–73; G. Billanovich, 'Auctorista, humanista, orator', *Rivista di cultura classica e medioevale* **vii** (1965),

229

143–63; V. R. Giustiniani, 'Homo, humanus and the meanings of "Humanism"', *J. History Ideas* **xlvi** (1955), 167–95.

Ancient Ethics

General Studies

W. K. C. Guthrie, *A History of Greek Philosophy* (Cambridge, 1962–81); W. W. Jaeger, *Paideia*, tr. G. Highet (Oxford, 1939); A. W. H. Adkins, *Merit and Responsibility* (Oxford, 1960); D. L. Clark, *Rhetoric in Graeco-Roman Education* (New York, 1957); J. Ferguson, *Moral Values in the Ancient World* (London, 1958); J. M. Rist, *Human Value* (Leiden, 1982); F. Überweg and K. Praechter, *Die Philosophie des Altertums* (Basle, 1953).

Humanitas

Thesarus linguae latinae, s.v. Humanitas; F. Klingner, 'Humanität und Humanitas' in *Römische Geisteswelt* 5, Aufl. (1965); W. Schadewaldt, 'Humanitas Romana' in H. Temporini (ed.), *Aufstieg und Niedergang der Römischen Welt*, vol. I, 4 (Berlin, 1973), pp. 43–62; L. A. Moritz, *Humanitas* (Cardiff, 1962).

Roman culture and the Greek World

M. L. Clarke, *The Roman Mind* (New York, 1968); A. E. Astin, *Scipio Aemilianus* (Oxford, 1967); M. T. Griffin, *Seneca : A Philosopher in Politics* (Oxford, 1976); C. W. Macleod, 'The Poetry of ethics', *J. Roman Studies* **lxix** (1979), 16–27.

Cicero

Biography

M. Gelzer, *Cicero, ein Biographischer Versuch* (Wiesbaden, 1969).

Philosophical ideas

W. Süss, *Cicero: eine Einführung in seine philosophischen Schriften* (Wiesbaden, 1966); W. Rüegg, *Cicero und der Humanismus* (Zurich, 1946); R. Poncelet, *Cicéron, traducteur de Platon* (Paris, 1957); A. Michel, *Rhétorique et philosophie chez Cicéron* (Paris, 1960); H. A. K. Hunt, *The Humanism of Cicero* (Melbourne, 1954); H. Guite, 'Cicero's attitude to the Greeks' in *Greece and Rome*, 2nd ser., **ix** (1962), 142–159; P. Boyancé, 'Les Méthodes de l'histoire littéraire : Cicéron et son oeuvre philosophique', *Revue des études latines* **xiv** (1936), 288–309.

Petrarch and Successors

Petrarch

Primary sources to which reference is made: De sui ipsius et multorum ignorantia, ed. L. M. Capelli (Paris, 1906), tr. in *The Renaissance Philosophy of Man*, eds E. Cassirer, P. O. Kristeller and J. H. Randall (Chicago, 1948), pp. 47–133; *Lettere di Francesco Petrarca* ed. and Ital. tr. by G. Fracassetti (Florence, 1863–7); *Le familiari* ed. V. Rossi (Florence, 1933–42); Some of these letters are translated into English in M. Bishop, *Letters from Petrarch* (Bloomington, 1966); *F. Petrarcae Virgilianus Codex* ed. G. Galbiati (Milan, 1930). Selections from other works in F. Petrarca, *Prose*, eds G. Martellotti, P. G. Ricci and others (Milan–Naples, 1955).

Secondary sources : General works: E. H. R. Tatham, *Francesco Petrarca* (London, 1925–6); J. H. Whitfield, *Petrarch and the Renaissance* (Oxford, 1943); E. H. Wilkins, *Studies in the Life and Works of Petrarch* (Cambridge, Mass., 1955); idem, *The Making of the 'Canzoniere' and other Petrarchan Studies* (Rome, 1951); idem, *Life of Petrarch* (Chicago, 1961); C. N. J. Mann, *Petrarch* (Oxford, 1984); T. E. Mommsen, *'Petrarch's conception of the "Dark Ages"'* in his *Medieval and Renaissance Studies* (New York, 1959).

(For Petrarch's classical scholarship see the bibliography on that subject below.)

B. L. Ullman, 'Petrarch's Favorite Books' in his *Studies in the Italian Renaissance* (Rome, 1955), pp. 117–37; V. Bosco, *Francesco Petrarca* (Bari, 1961); P. de Nolhac, *Pétrarque et l'humanisme* (Paris, 1907); G. Billanovich, 'Petrarca e Cicerone' in *Miscellanea in onore di Giovanni Mercati* (Vatican City, 1946), iv, pp. 88–106; H. Baron, 'The evolution of Petrarch's thought : reflections on the state of Petrarch studies', *Bibliothèque d'Humanisme et Renaissance* **xxiv** (1962), 7–41.

Secondary sources : Petrarch's views on art
Prince d'Essling and E. Müntz, *Pétrarque, ses études d'art* (Paris, 1902); L. Venturi, 'La critica d'arte e F. Petrarca', *L'Arte* **xxv** (1922), 238–44; T. E. Mommsen, 'Petrarch and the decoration of the Sala Virorum Illustrium in Padua', *Art Bulletin* **xxxiv** (1952), 95–116, reprinted in T. E. Mommsen, *Medieval and Renaissance Studies* (Ithaca, 1959); E. H. Wilkins, 'On Petrarch's appreciation of art', *Speculum* **36** (1961), 299–301; M. Baxandall, *Giotto and the Orators* (Oxford, 1971).

The Fifteenth Century

Transitions
B. L. Ullman, *The Humanism of Coluccio Salutati* (Padua, 1963); R. G. Witt, *Hercules at the Crossroads* (Durham, N. C., 1983); G. Billanovich, 'Giovanni del Virgilio, Pietro da Moglio, Francesco da Fiano', *Italia medioevalia e umanistica* **vi** (1963), 203–234 and **vii** (1964), 279–324; J. E. Seigel, *Rhetoric and Philosophy* (see above).

Civic Humanism
Primary sources: L. Bruni, *Historiarum Florentini Populi Libri XII*, eds E. Santini and C. di Pierro in Muratori, *Rerum Italicarum Scriptores*, n.s., **xix**, 3 (Città di Castello, 1914–26); idem, *Ad Petrum Paulum Histrum Dialogus* in E. Garin (ed.), *Prosatori Latini del Quattrocento* (Milan, 1952), pp. 44–99; L. B. Alberti, *I Primi tre libri Della Famiglia*, eds F. C. Pellegrini and R. Spongano (Florence, 1946); idem, *Opere Volgari*, vol. i, ed. C. Grayson (Bari, 1960); C. Landino, *Disputationes Camaldulenses*, ed. P. Lohe (Florence, 1980); M. Palmieri, *Della Vita Civile*, ed. F. Battaglia (Bologna, 1944).

Secondary sources: H. Baron, *The Crisis of the Early Italian Renaissance* (Princeton, 1966); J. E. Seigel, '"Civic Humanism" or Ciceronian Rhetoric?', *Past and Present*

34 (1966), 3–48; idem, *Rhetoric and Philosophy* (see above); L. B. Alberti, 'Intercoenales' ed. E. Garin in *Prosatori latini del Quattrocento*, pp. 636–56; E. Garin, *Italian Humanism*, tr. P. Munz; G. A. Holmes, *The Florentine Enlightenment* (London, 1969); J. R. Gadol, *Leon Battista Alberti* (Chicago, 1969); C. Grayson, 'Alberti' in *Dizionario biografico degli Italiani*, vol. i, (Numo, 1960) pp. 702–9.

Lorenzo Valla

Primary sources: *Opera Omnia*, ed. E. Garin (Turin, 1962); idem, *De libero arbitrio*, ed. M. Anfossi (Florence, 1934), Engl. tr. in *The Renaissance Philosophy of Man*, eds E. Cassirer, etc., pp. 155–82; Italian translations of various works in L. Valla, *Scritti filosofici e religiosi*, ed. G. Radetti (Florence, 1953) and in *Prosatori latini del Quattrocento*, ed. E. Garin.

Secondary sources: L. Barozzi and R. Sabbadini, *Studi sul Panormita e sul Valla* (Florence, 1891); F. Gaeta, *Lorenzo Valla* (Naples, 1955); H. H. Gray, 'Valla's Encomium of St Thomas Aquinas and the humanist conception of Christian antiquity' in *Essays in History and Literature Presented to Stanley Pargellis*, ed. H. Bluhm (Chicago, 1965), pp. 37–51; S. I. Camporeale, *Lorenzo Valla : umanesimo e teologia* (Florence, 1972).

Neo-Platonism

Primary sources: M. Ficino, *Opera Omnia* (Basle, 1576 and Turin, 1959); idem, *Supplementum Ficinianum*, ed. P. O. Kristeller (Florence, 1937); G. Pico della Mirandola, *Opera* (Basle, 1572); idem, *De hominis dignitate, Heptaplus, De ente et uno e Scritti vari*, ed. E. Garin (Florence, 1942), Engl. tr. of *De hominis dignitate* in *The Renaissance Philosophy of Man*, pp. 223–54.

Secondary sources: N. A. Robb, *Neoplatonism of the Italian Renaissance* (London, 1935); G. Saitta, *Marsilio Ficino e la filosofia dell'umanesimo*, 3rd edn (Bologna, 1954); P. O. Kristeller, *Il pensiero filosofico di Marsilio Ficino* (Florence, 1953); E. Garin, *Giovanni Pico della Mirandola* (Florence, 1937); idem, *Giovanni Pico della Mirandola* (Parma, 1963); E. Cassirer, 'Giovanni Pico della Mirandola', *J. History Ideas* **iii** (1942), 123–44, 319–46; C. Bec. 'Recherches sur la culture à Florence au XVe siècle', *Revue des études Italiennes* **xiv** (1968), 211–45.

Renaissance Art

Primary sources: G. Vasari, *Le vite de' più eccellenti pittori, scultori e architettori* in Vasari's *Opere*, vols 1–7, ed. G. Milanesi (Florence, 1878–85), Engl. tr. J. Foster and J. P. Richter, besides various later translations and selections; C. Cennini, *Il libro dell'arte*, ed. D. V. Thompson (New Haven, 1932); L. B. Alberti, *Della Pittura*, ed. L. Mallè (Florence, 1950), Engl. tr. J. R. Spencer, *On Painting* (London, 1956); idem, *De re aedificatoria*, eds G. Orlandi and P. Portoghesi (Milan, 1966), tr. J. Leoni, *Ten Books on Architecture* (London, 1955); F. Filarete, *Trattato d'architettura*, ed. J. R. Spencer (New Haven, 1965); L. Ghiberti, *I Commentari*, ed. O. Morisani (Naples, 1947); Leonardo da Vinci,

The Literary Works, ed. J. P. Richter (Oxford, 1939, 1970); C. Pedretti, *Leonardo da Vinci on Painting. A Lost Book, Libro A* (London, 1965).

General

General Histories
F. Hartt, *A History of Italian Renaissance Art* (London, 1970); P. and L. Murray, *The Art of the Renaissance* (London, 1963).

Background, problems and reference
P. Toesca (ed.), *Storia dell' arte italiana* (Turin, 1927), vols 1–4; J. E. White, *Art and Architecture in Italy, 1250–1400* (Harmondsworth, 1966); R. Oertel, *Die Frühzeit der italienischen Malerei* (Stuttgart, 1966), Engl. tr. L. Cooper, *Early Italian Painting* (London 1968); E. Borsook, *The Mural Painters of Tuscany, from Cimabue to Andrea del Sarto*, 2nd edn (Oxford, 1980).

Sources for Chapter 6
The San Damiano Crucifix: E. Sandberg-Vavalà, *La croce dipinta italiana* (Verona, 1929), p. 123; E. B. Garrison, *Italian Romanesque Panel Painting* (Florence, 1949), p. 183. For the episode in St Francis's life to which this relates cf. K. Esser in *Franziskanische Studien* **xxxiv** (1952), 1–11.

Leonoardo's Virgin and the Rocks: K. Clark, *Leonardo da Vinci* (Harmondsworth, 1939 and 1967), pp. 49–53, 128–9; M. Kemp, *Leonardo da Vinci, the Marvellous Works of Nature and of Man* (London, 1989) pp. 94–9.

Statistics on Giotto, Leonardo and Botticelli: *The Complete Paintings of Leonardo da Vinci*, ed. A. O. della Chiesa, tr. L. D. Ettlinger (London, 1969); *The Complete Paintings of Botticelli*, ed. G. Mandel, tr. M. Levey (London, 1970); *The Complete Paintings of Giotto*, ed. E. Baccheschi, tr. A. Martindale (London, 1969).

Patronage

General Works
F. Antal, *Florentine Painting and its Social Background* (London, 1947); E. H. Gombrich, *Meditations on a Hobby Horse* (London 1963); M. Baxandall, *Painting and Experience in Fifteenth-Century Italy* (Oxford, 1972) esp. ch. 1; H. Glasser, *Artists' Contracts of the Early Renaissance* (New York, 1977); C. Hope, 'Artists, patrons and advisers in the Italian Renaissance' in *Patronage in the Renaissance*, eds G. F. Lytle and S. Orgel (Princeton, 1981); *Patronage, Art and Soceity in Renaissance Italy*, eds F. W. Kent and P. Simons (Oxford, 1987). For patronage in relation to iconology, cf. E. Panofsky, *Studies in Iconology* (New York, 1939); idem, *Meaning in the Visual Arts* (New York, 1955); E. H. Gombrich, *Symbolic Images* (London, 1972).

Documents on Isabella d'Este and Perugino's 'Battle of Chastity and Lasciviousness'
The original documents are in J. Gaye, *Carteggio inedito d'artisti dei secoli*, xiv, xv, xvi (Florence, 1839–40); F. Canuti, *Il Perugino* (Siena, 1931), ii, pp. 209–35; translations in J. Cartwright, *Isabella d'Este* (London, 1903), i, pp. 329–40;

D. S. Chambers, *Patrons and artists in the Italian Renaissance* (London, 1970), pp. 134–42.

Discussion: E. Verheyen, *The Paintings in the Studiolo of Isabella d'Este at Mantua* (New York, 1971); C. Hope, 'Artists, patrons and advisers in the Italian Renaissance' in *Patronage in the Renaissance.*

Wackernagel and Florence's artistic role

General works: M. Wackernagel, *Der Lebensraum des Künstlers in der Florentinischen Renaissance* (Leipzig, 1938), Engl. tr. A. Luchs, *The World of the Florentine Renaissance Artist* (Princeton, 1981); H. Lerner-Lehmkuhl, *Zur Struktur und Geschichte des Florentinischen Kunstmarktes im 15. Jahrhundert* (Wattenscheid, 1936); D. E. Colnaghi, *A Dictionary of Florentine Painters from the 13th to the 17th Centuries*, eds P. G. Konody and S. Brinton (London, 1928); E. H. Gombrich, 'The leaven of criticism in Renaissance art' in *Art, Science and History in the Renaissance*, ed. C. S. Singleton (Baltimore, 1967), pp. 3–42.

Civic and collaborative patronage of great buildings: W. and E. Paatz, *Die Kirchen von Florenz* (Frankfurt am Main, 1952–55); G. Poggi, *Or San Michele* (Florence, 1885); H. Saalman, *The Church of Santa Trinità in Florence* (New York, 1966); M. B. Hall, *Renovation and Counter-Reformation, Vasari and Duke Cosimo in Santa Maria Novella and Santa Croce, 1565–77* (Oxford, 1979).

Effects of political turmoil: H. Gregory, 'Palla Strozzi's patronage and pre-Medician Florence' in *Patronage, Art and Society in Renaissance Italy*, eds F. W. Kent and P. Simons, pp. 201–20; E. Müntz, *Les Collections des Médicis au xve siècle* (Paris, 1888); A. Chastel, 'Le "Bûcher des Vanités"', *Cahiers du Sud* **xliv** (1956), 63–70; C. Roth, *The Last Florentine Republic* (London, 1925).

Innovation

Primary sources (In addition to those listed at the beginning (notably Vasari's *Lives*) the following are quoted in the text in relation to this topic): A. Manetti, *The Life of Brunelleschi*, ed. H. Saalman, tr. C. Enggass (University Park, Pennsylvania, 1970); F. Saccheti, *Delle Novelle* (Florence 1724); F. Petrarch, *Testament*, ed. T. E. Mommsen (Ithaca, 1957); *Angelo Polizianos Tagebuch 1477–1479*, ed. A. Wesselsky (Jena, 1929); L. Ghiberti, *I Commentari*, ed. O. Morisani (Naples, 1947).

Brunelleschi, Donatello and Masaccio

B. Cole, *Masaccio and the Art of Early Renaissance Florence* (Bloomington, 1980); H. Saalman, *Filippo Brunelleschi : the Cupola of Santa Maria del Fiore* (London, 1980); H. W. Janson, *The Sculpture of Donatello* (Princeton, 1957); S. Y. Edgerton, *The Renaissance Rediscovery of Linear Perspective* (New York, 1976); L. Berti, *Masaccio*, Engl. tr. (University Park, Pennsylvania, 1967); J. H. Beck (ed.), *Masaccio, the Documents* (New York, 1978).

Conceptions of the artist

J. von Schlosser, *Beiträge zur Kunstgeschichte aus den Schriftquellen des frühen*

Mittelalters (Vienna, 1891), Ital. tr., *La Letteratura artistica*, ed. F. Rossi (Florence, 1967); J. Larner, 'The artist and the intellectuals in fourteenth-century Italy', *History* **liv** (1969), 13–30; E. H. Wilkins, 'On Petrarch's appreciation of Art', *Speculum* **36** (1961) 299–301; L. Venturi, 'La critica d'arte e F. Petrarca', *L'arte* **xxv** (1922), 238–44; idem, 'La critica d'arte alla fine del *Trencento*', *L'arte* **xxviii** (1925), 233–44; E. H. Gombrich, 'From the revival of Letters to the reform of the Arts : Niccolò Niccoli and Filippo Brunelleschi' in his *The Heritage of Apelles* (Oxford, 1976) pp. 93–110; R. and M. Wittkower, *Born under Saturn* (London, 1963).

The Influence of Ideas
Religious ideas: H. Thode, *Franz von Assisi und die Anfänge der Kunst der Renaissance in Italien* (Berlin, 1885) with French tr., 1909; P. Francastel, 'L'Art Italien et le rôle personnel de Saint François', *Annales* **xi** (1956), 481–9; S. Settis, 'L'iconografia dell'arte italiana 1100–1500 : una linea' in *Storia dell'arte italiana*, vol. 3, eds G. Previtale and F. Zeri (Turin, 1979), pp. 175–270; R. C. Trexler, 'Florentine religious experience : The Sacred Image', *Studies in the Renaissance* **xix** (1972), 7–41.

Classical ideas: A. Blunt, *Artistic Theory in Italy* (Oxford, 1940); M. Baxandall, *Giotto and the Orators* (Oxford, 1971); G. Becatti, *Arte e gusto negli scrittori latini* (Florence, 1951); *The Elder Pliny's Chapters on the History of Art*, tr. K. Jex-Blake (London, 1896); R. W. Lee, '*Ut pictura poesis*: The humanistic theory of painting', *Art Bulletin* **22** (1940), 197–269; M. Kemp, '*Ogni dipintore dipinge sè* : a neo-platonist echo in Leonardo's art theory' in *Cultural Aspects of the Italian Renaissance : essays in honour of P. O. Kristeller*, ed. C. H. Clough (Manchester, 1976), pp. 311–33; idem, 'From "*Mimesis*" to "*Fantasia*" : the *Quattrocento* vocabulary of creation, inspiration and genius in the Visual Arts', *Viator* **8** (1977), 347–98; J. R. Spencer, 'Ut Rhetorica Pictura', *J. Warburg and Courtauld Institutes*, **xx** (1957), 26–44; A. Chastel, *Marsile Ficin et l'art* (Geneva, 1954); A. D. Fraser Jenkins, 'Cosimo de' Medici's Patronage of Architecture and the Theory of Magnificence', *J. Warburg and Courtauld Institutes* **xxxiii** (1970) 162–70; J. P. Larner, *Culture and Society in Italy 1290–1420* (London, 1971); M. Baxandall, 'Guarino, Pisanello and Manuel Chrysoloras', *J. Warburg and Courtauld Institutes* **xxviii** (1965), 183–204; A. A. Chastel, *Art et humanisme à Florence au temps de Laurent le magnifique* (Paris, 1959).

Man and Society

The achievements of the Italian Renaissance
On ancient and Renaissance activities, see also the bibliography above on Humanism

H. Baron, 'Cicero and the Roman civic spirit in the Middle Ages and the early Renaissance', *Bulletin of the John Rylands Library* **22** (1938), 73–97, reprinted in his *In Search of Florentine Civic Humanism* (Princeton, 1988), i, pp. 94–133; J. G. A. Pocock, *The Machiavellian Moment* (Princeton, 1975). J. Hexter, 'Republic, Virtue, Liberty and the Political Universe of J. G. A. Pocock', in his *On Historians* (London, 1979) ch. 4.

The Individual

J. Burckhardt, *The Civilisation of the Renaissance in Italy*, tr. S. G. C. Middlemore (London, 1965) and many earlier editions; N. Nelson, 'Individualism as a criterion of the Renaissance', *J. English and Germanic Philology* **32** (1933), 316–34; C. Morris, *The Discovery of the Individual* (London, 1972); C. Trinkaus, 'Petrarch's views of the individual and his society', *Osiris* **xi** (1954), 168–98; R. Wittkower 'Individualism in art and artists : A Renaissance problem', *Jl History Ideas* **xxii** (1961), 291–302; E. Panofsky, 'Artist, scientist, genius: notes on the "Renaissance-Dämmerung"' in *The Renaissance, six essays* (New York, 1962), pp. 121–82; S. L. Alpers, '*Ekphrasis* and aesthetic attitudes in Vasari's *Lives*', *J. Warburg and Courtauld Institutes*, **xxiii** (1960), 190–215.

Machiavelli

Primary sources: N. Machiavelli, *Il Principe*, ed. G. Lisio (Florence, 1899); reference here, however, is made to the more commonly available edition of L. A. Burd (Oxford, 1891), Engl. tr. G. Bull (Harmondsworth, 1975); N. Machiavelli, *Tutte le Opere*, eds G. Mazzoni and M. Casella (Florence, 1929).

Secondary sources: J. H. Whitfield, *Machiavelli* (Oxford, 1947); idem, *Discourses on Machiavelli* (Cambridge, 1969); G. Sasso, *Niccolò Machiavelli, storia del suo pensiero politico* (Naples, 1958); L. Russo, *Machiavelli* (Bari, 1949); C. Bec, 'Machiavelli tra Firenze, Italia e Francia' in his *Cultura e Società a Firenze nell' età della Rinascenza* (Rome, 1981); C. Dionisotti, 'Machiavelli letterato' in *Studies on Machiavelli*, ed. M. P. Gilmore (Florence, 1972), pp. 101–43; I. Berlin, 'The Originality of Machiavelli' in ibid., pp. 147–206; Q. Skinner, *Machiavelli* (Oxford, 1981); J. N. Stephens, 'Ciceronian rhetoric and the immorality of Machiavelli's *Prince*', *Renaissance Studies* **ii** (1988), 258–67, idem, 'Machiavelli's *Prince* and the Florentine Revolution of 1512', *Italian Studies* XLI (1986), pp. 45–61; F. Gilbert, 'The Humanist concept of the prince and *The Prince* of Machiavelli', *J. Modern History* **ll** (1939), 449–83; T. Flanagan, 'The concept of *Fortuna* in Machiavelli' in *The Political Calculus*, ed. A. Parel (Toronto, 1972), pp. 127–56; J. Plamenatz, 'In Search of Machiavellian *Virtù*', in ibid., pp. 157–78; idem, *Man and Society* (London, 1963), vol. i, ch. 1.

Castiglione

Text: Il Cortegiano, ed. V. Cian (Florence, 1910); Engl. tr. G. Bull (Harmondsworth, 1967).

Secondary sources: J. Woodhouse, *Baldesar Castiglione* (Edinburgh, 1978); G. Bonadeo, 'The Function and purpose of *The Courtier*', *Philological Quarterly* **50** (1971), 36–46; P. Floriani 'La Genesi del *Cortegiano*', *Belfagor* **24** (1969), 373–85; idem, 'Esperienza e cultura nella genesi del *Cortegiano*', *Giornale storico della letterature italiana* **166** (1969), 497–529; L. V. Ryan, 'Book Four of Castiglione's *Courtier* : climax or afterthought ?' *Studies in the Renaissance* **19** (1972), 156–79.

The Intellectual
Changing attitudes to literacy and the intellectual

J. W. Thompson, *The Literacy of the Laity in the Middle Ages* (Berkeley, 1939);

J. le Goff, *Les Intellectuels au Moyen Age* (Paris, 1957); L. Martines, *The Social World of the Florentine Humanists* (London, 1963); J. E. Seigel, *Rhetoric and Philosophy in Renaissance Humanism* (Princeton, 1968); A. Scaglione, 'The Humanist as scholar and Politian's conception of the *Grammaticus*', *Studies in the Renaissance* **8** (1961), 49–70.

Niccolò Niccoli and his generation
Vespasiano's life of Niccoli: Vespasiano da Bisticci, *Le vite*, ed. A. Greco (Florence, 1976), ii, pp. 225–42. On Vespasiano: G. M. Cagni, *Vespasiano da Bisticci e il suo epistolario* (Rome, 1969); A. Greco, *La Memoria delle lettere* (Rome, 1985).

Niccolò Niccoli: R. P. Robinson, 'The Inventory of Niccolò Niccoli', *Classical Philology* **xvi** (1921), 251–5; H. Baron, *The Crisis of the Early Italian Renaissance* (Princeton, 1966); B. L. Ullman, *The Origin and Development of Humanistic Script* (Rome, 1960), ch.3; B. L. Ullman and P. A. Stadter, *The Public Library of Renaissance Florence* (Padua, 1972); E. H. Gombrich, 'From the Revival of Letters to the Reform of the Arts: Niccolò Niccoli and Filippo Brunelleschi' in his *The Heritage of Apelles*.

Erasmus
Primary sources: F. N. Nichols, *The Epistles of Erasmus* (London, 1901–18); Erasmus, *Education of a Christian Prince*, tr. L. K. Born (New York, 1936); Erasmus, *The Anti-Barbari*, tr. M. M. Phillipps in *The Collected works of Erasmus*, ed. C. R. Thompson (Toronto, 1978); Erasmus, *Epistles*, ed. P. S. Allen (Oxford, 1954); Erasmus, *Collected Works* (Toronto, 1974–□).

Secondary sources: P. Smith, *Erasmus* (New York, 1923); R. H. Bainton, *Erasmus of Christendom* (London, 1970); A. Renaudet, *Érasme et l'Italie* (Geneva, 1954); idem, *Érasme, sa pensée religieuse et son action d'après sa correspondance (1518–1521)* (Paris, 1926); idem, *Études Érasmiennes, 1521–1529* (Paris, 1939); idem, *Préréforme et Humanisme à Paris (1494–1517)* (Paris, 1953); M. Mann, *Érasme et les débuts de la Réforme Française 1517–36* (Paris, 1934); P. Mestwerdt, *Die Anfänge des Erasmus; Humanismus und 'Devotio Moderna'* (Leipzig, 1917); R. Pfeiffer, *Humanitas Erasmiana* (Berlin, 1931); C. R. Thompson, 'Erasmus as internationalist and cosmopolitan', *Archiv für Reformationsgeschichte* **46** (1955), 167–95; W. K. Ferguson, 'Renaissance tendencies in the religious thought of Erasmus', *J. History Ideas* **xv** (1954), 499–508.

Classical Scholarship
General
R. R. Bolgar, *The Classical Heritage and its Beneficiaries* (Cambridge, 1954); R. Pfeiffer, *A History of Classical Scholarship, Vol. 2, 1300–1850* (Oxford, 1976); L. D. Reynolds and N. G. Wilson, *Scribes and Scholars* (Oxford, 1974); R. Sabbadini, *Le scoperte dei codici latini e greci ne' secoli xiv e xv* (Florence, 1914: reprinted 1967); idem, *Storia e critica di testi latini*, 2nd edn (Padua, 1971).
MSS formerly in Petrarch's possession (sources of Figure 12 on page 158 above : these are listed by order of publication. I am grateful for advice to Prof. A. de la Mare).

P. de Nolhac, *Pétrarque et l'humanisme* (Paris, 1907), esp. ii, 113–14; *Catalogus Codicum manuscriptorum Bibl. Regiae* (Paris, 1744); *Catalogue général des manuscrits latins de la Bibliothèque Nationale*, ed. P. Lauer (Paris, 1937–□); L. Minio-Paluello, 'Il "Fedone" latino con note autografe del Petrarca', *Atti dell' Accad. Naz. dei Lincei*, ser. viii, **4** (1949), 107–13; E. Pellegrin, 'Nouveaux manuscrits annotés par Pétrarque à la Bibliothèque Nationale de Paris', *Scriptorium* **5** (1951), 265–78; G. Billanovich, 'Petrarch and the textual tradition of Livy', *J. Warburg and Courtauld Institutes* **xiv** (1951), 137–208; idem, 'Un nuovo codice della biblioteca del Petrarca: il San Paolo', *Rendiconti dell' Accad. di archeologia, lettere e belle arti di Napoli* **26–7** (1951), 253–6; idem, 'Uno Suetonio della biblioteca del Petrarca', *Studi Petrarceschi* **6** (1954), 23–33; idem, (and E. Pellegrin), 'Un manuscrit de Cicéron annoté par Pétrarque au British Museum', *Scriptorium* **8** (1954), 115–7; R. W. Hunt, 'A manuscript from the library of Petrarch', *Times Literary Supplement*, 23 Sept. 1964, p. 619; G. Billanovich, 'Nella biblioteca del Petrarca', *Italia medioevale e unmanistica* **3** (1960) 28–58; A. Petrucci, *La Scrittura del Petrarca* (Milan, 1973); A. de la Mare, *The Handwriting of the Italian Humanists* (Oxford, 1973); A. de la Mare and R. Rouse, 'New light on the circulation of the "A" text of Sceneca's *Tragedies*', *J. Warburg and Courtauld Institutes* **40** (1977), 283–290; B. Barker-Benfield and A. de la Mare, *Manuscripts at Oxford : An Exhibition in Honour of R. W. Hunt* (Oxford, 1980), xxii, pp. 93–101; A. de la Mare, *I Manoscritti Petrarceschi della Biblioteca civile di Trieste incontro di studio, Trieste 22 Nov. 1984* (Trieste, 1987).

The Transmission and Discovery of MSS
*General:*G. Pasquali, *Storia della tradizione e critica del testo* (Florence, 1952); L. D. Reynolds (ed.), *Texts and transmission* (Oxford, 1983); G. Billanovich, 'Dall' antica Ravenna alle biblioteche umanistiche', *Aevum* **30** (1956), 319–62.

The pre-humanists: G. Billanovich, *I Primi umanisti e le tradizioni dei classici latini* (Freiburg, 1953); R. Weiss, *Il primo secolo dell'umanesimo* (Rome, 1949).

Petrarch   (see also the bibliography on Petrarch's classical MSS above): P. de Nolhac, *Pétrarque et l'humanisme* (Paris, 1907); G. Billanovich, *Petrarca letterato* (Rome, 1947).

Salutati and Poggio: B. L. Ullman, *The Humanism of Coluccio Salutati*; A. C. Clark, *The Reappearance of the Texts of the Classics* (London, 1922); P. W. G. Gordan, *Two Renaissance Book-Hunters : the Letters of Poggio Bracciolini to Nicolaus de Nicoleis* (New York, 1974).

The mid and late Quattrocento: B. L. Ullman, *The Origin and Development of Humanistic Script* (Rome, 1960); A. C. de la Mare, *The Handwriting of the Italian Humanists*; L. Mohler, 'Kardinal Bessarion als Theologe, Humanist und Staatsmann', *Quellen und Forschungen aus dem Gebiete der Geschichte*, der Görres-Gesellschaft **24** (1942), 70–90 [reprinted in book form (Aalen, 1967)]; R. Weiss, *The Renaissance Discovery of Classical Antiquity* (Oxford, 1969); J. E. G. Zetsel, *Latin Textual Criticism in Antiquity* (New York, 1981); A. Mercati in *Mélanges* F. Graf (Paris, 1946) II, pp. 357–66; M. Ferrari, 'Le scoperte a Bobbio nel

1493', *Italia medioevalia e umanistica* **13** (1970), 139–80; idem, 'Spigolature Bobbiesi', ibid., **16** (1973), 1–41; A. T. Grafton, *Joseph Scaliger* (Oxford, 1983).

Historiography

Medieval Background

J. W. Thompson, *A History of Historical Writing*, vol. i (New York, 1942); C. A. Patrides, *The Phoenix and the Ladder* (Berkeley – Los Angeles, 1964); B. A. Smalley, 'Sallust in the Middle Ages' in *Classical Influences on European Culture A.D.500–1500*, ed. R. R. Bolgar (Cambrdige, 1971); idem, *Historians in the Middle Ages* (London, 1974); E. M. Sanford, 'The study of ancient history in the Middle Ages', *J. History Ideas* **v** (1944), 21–43; M. P. Gilmore, 'The Renaissance Conception of the lessons of History' in *Facets of the Renaissance*, ed. W. H. Werkmeister (N.Y. etc., 1963), pp. 73–101.

Orientation on classical influences

B. Lacroix, *L'histoire dans l'antiquité* (Montreal, 1951); M. L. W. Laistner, *The Greater Roman Historians* (Berkeley, 1947); E. Löfstedt, *Roman Literary Portraits* (Oxford, 1958); W. Kroll, 'Die Entwicklung der lateinischen schriftsprache', *Glotta* **22** (1933–4), 1–27; A. Momigliano, *The Development of Greek Biography* (Cambridge, Mass., 1971); P. G. Walsh, *Livy* (Cambridge, 1961); V. Paladini, *Sallustio* (Milan, 1948); W. Schur, *Sallust als Historiker* (Stuttgart, 1934); R. Syme, *Sallust* (Berkeley, 1964); idem, *Tacitus* (Oxford, 1958); idem, 'The Senator as historian' in *Histoire et historiens dans l'antiquité classique*, Fondation Hardt, Entretiens sur l'antiquité classique, iv, Geneva 2–8 Aug. 1956 (Paris, 1958), pp. 187–201.

Humanist historiography

*General:*M. P. Gilmore, 'Freedom and Determinism in Renaissance historians' *Studies in the Renaissance* **iii** (1956), 49–60; W. K. Ferguson, *The Renaissance in Historical Thought* (Cambridge, Mass., 1948); H. H. Gray, 'Renaissance Humanism : the pursuit of eloquence', *J. History Ideas* **xxiv** (1963), 497–514; F. Gilbert, *Machiavelli and Guicciardini* (Princeton, 1965); B. R. Reynolds, 'Latin historiography: a survey, 1400–1600', *Studies in the Renaissance* **2** (1955), 7–66; R. B. Black, 'Benedetto Accolti and the beginnings of humanist historiography', *Eng. Hist. Rev.* **xcvi** (1981), 36–58; idem, 'The new laws of history', *Renaissance Studies* **i** (1987), 126–56; D. Hay, 'Flavio Biondo and the Middle Ages', *Proceedings of the British Academy* **45** (1959), 97–128; H. Weisinger, 'Ideas of History during the Renaissance', *J. History Ideas* **vi** (1945), 415–35; T. E. Mommsen, 'Petrarch's conception of the Dark Ages' in his *Medieval and Renaissance studies*, pp. 106–29; G. Weise, *L'Italia e il mondo gotico* (Florence, 1956); G. B. Alberti, 'Tucidide nella traduzione latina di Lorenzo Valla', *Studi italiani di filologia classica* **29** (1957), 224–49; idem, 'Erodoto nella traduzione latina di Lorenzo Valla', *Bullettino del comitato per la preparazione della edizione nazionale dei classici greci e latini*, n.s., **7** (1959), 65–84; Q. Skinner, *The Foundations of Modern Political Thought* (Cambridge, 1978).

Bruni and Machiavelli: E. Santini, *Leonardo Bruni Aretino e i suoi 'Historiarum Florentini Populi Libri XII'* (Pisa, 1910); B. L. Ullman, 'Leonardo Bruni and humanistic historiography', *Medievalia et Humanistica* **4** (1946), 45–61 (reprinted in his *Studies in the Italian Renaissance* (Rome, 1955)); B. Reynolds, 'Bruni and Perotto present a Greek historian', *Bibliothèque d'Humanisme et Renaissance* **16** (1954), 108–18; H. Baron, *The Crisis of the Early Italian Renaissance* (Princeton, 1966); D. J. Wilcox, *The Development of Florentine Humanist Historiography in the Fifteenth Century* (Cambridge, Mass., 1969). On Machiavelli's *Florentine Histories* see the general works on him cited above and also F. Gilbert, 'Machiavelli's "Istoire Fiorentine" : an essay in interpretation' in *Studies on Machiavelli*, ed. M. P. Gilmore (Florence, 1972), pp. 73–99.

Later developments: D. R. Kelley, *Foundations of Modern Historical Scholarship: Language, Law and History in the French Renaissance* (New York, 1970); F. S. Fussner, *The Historical Revolution, English Historical Writing and Thought, 1580–1640* (London, 1962); M. T. Hodgen, *Early Anthropology in the Sixteenth and Seventeenth Centuries* (Phila., 1964); R. L. Meek, *Social Science and the Ignoble Savage* (Cambridge, 1976).

The Reformation
Humanism and the Reformation
R. H. Murray, *Erasmus and Luther* (London, 1920); L. K. Born, 'Erasmus on political ethics', *Pol. Sci. Qtly*, **43** (1928), 520–43; H. A. Enno van Gelder, *The Two Reformations in the 16th Century* (The Hague, 1961); H. Holborn, *Ulrich von Hutten and the German Reformation*, tr. R. H. Bainton (New Haven, 1937); R. Stupperich, *Melanchthon*, Engl. tr. R. H. Fischer (London, 1966).

Martin Luther
E. G. Rupp and B. Drewery (eds), *Martin Luther* (London, 1970); R. H. Fife, *The Revolt of Martin Luther* (New York, 1957); R. H. Bainton, *Here I Stand* (London, 1951); H. Boehmer, *Martin Luther: Road to Reformation*, tr. J. W. Doberstein and T. G. Tappert (New York, 1957); E. G. Rupp, *Luther's Progress to the Diet of Worms, 1521* (London, 1951); E. C. Kiessling, *The Early Sermons of Luther* (Grand Rapids, 1935); P. S. Watson, *Let God be God! An interpretation of the theology of Martin Luther* (London, 1947).

The Henrician Reformation
J. J. Scarisbrick, *Henry VIII* (London, 1968); F. L. Baumer, *The Early Tudor Theory of Kingship* (New Haven, 1940); J. K. McConica, *English Humanists and Reformation Politics* (Oxford, 1965); P. Janelle, *L'Angleterre Catholique à la veille du schisme* (Paris, 1935); A. G. Little, *Studies in English Franciscan History* (Manchester, 1917).

Calvin
Calvin, *The Institutes*, tr. H. Beveridge (Edinburgh, 1845); R. N. Carew Hunt, *Calvin* (London, 1933); W. Niesel, *The Theology of Calvin*, tr. H. Knight (London, 1956); F. Wendel, *Calvin, the Origins and Development of his Religious Thought*, tr. P. Mairet (London, 1963); A. M. Hugo, *Calvijn en Seneca. Een inleidende studie van Calvijns Commentaar op Seneca*, De Clementia etc. (Groningen, 1957).

Index